Angel of Mercy, Angel of Death

Early on a Sunday morning, the prisoner was led out of his cell and taken across the street to the Somerset County Prosecutor's Office for interrogation. The existence Cullen retraced for the detectives was composed of self-hatred, betrayal, and secrecy. His life and the murders he committed were described as his "dirty, dark secret."

Late in the evening, near the end of the arduous confession, he told the detectives: "I did not want [people] to see me as this, what I am."

"What are you, Charles?" Detective Sergeant Braun asked.

"A man, person, who was trusted and had responsibility for a lot of people dying," he replied. "And whether or not they had a couple of days, or weeks, or whether even they sometimes had months, whether that was with pain or without pain, I had no right to do this. I had no right! I just couldn't stop! I couldn't stop it!"

The response didn't seem to satisfy even the prisoner himself, and he struggled to provide a better explanation.

"I—I hate myself for it 'cause I don't believe I had the right, but I couldn't stop," he said of the murders. "I couldn't."

"If what Charles Cullen says is true, he is one of the most prolific serial killers in American criminal history."
—Harvey Schlossbergh, Ph.D., Associate Professor of criminal justice, St. John's University

DEATH ANGEL

**CLIFFORD L. LINEDECKER
AND
ZACH T. MARTIN**

PINNACLE BOOKS
Kensington Publishing Corp.

http://www.kensingtonbooks.com

PINNACLE BOOKS are published by

Kensington Publishing Corp.
850 Third Avenue
New York, NY 10022

All Kensington Titles, Imprints, and Distributed Lines are available at special quantity discounts for bulk purchases for sales promotions, premiums, fund-raising, and educational or institutional use. Special book excerpts or customized printings can also be created to fit specific needs. For details, write or phone the office of the Kensington special sales manager: Kensington Publishing Corp., 850 Third Avenue, New York, NY 10022, attn: Special Sales Department, Phone: 1-800-221-2647.

Pinnacle and P logo Reg. U.S. Pat. & TM Off.

First Printing: December 2005

10 9 8 7 6 5 4 3 2

Printed in the United States of America

Florence Nightingale Pledge

I solemnly pledge myself before God and in the presence of this assembly, to pass my life in purity and to practice my profession faithfully. I will abstain from whatever is deleterious and mischievous, and will not take or knowingly administer any harmful drug. I will do all in my power to maintain and elevate the standard of my profession, and will hold in confidence all personal matters committed to my keeping and all family affairs coming to my knowledge in the practice of my calling. With loyalty will I endeavor to aid the physician in his work, and devote myself to the welfare of those committed to my care.

—This modification of the Hippocratic Oath, sworn to by physicians, was arranged by Mrs. Lystra E. Gretter and a Committee for the Farrand Training School for Nurses in Detroit, Michigan. It was named for the founder of modern nursing as a token of esteem.

It's easy to remember the night a police officer comes to your door to tell you how someone you love was murdered by a serial killer. I know firsthand that as a person receiving the news, you drift into a moment when your body separates from your spirit and you are physically numbed by the news.

—Zach T. Martin

Preface

By Harvey Schlossbergh, Ph.D.,
Associate Professor of Criminal Justice,
St. John's University

When I began reading *Death Angel*, it almost immediately became clear that this was not just another study of a serial killer. Usually these studies are clinically depersonalized, dressed up, cleansed, and sanitized for the consumption of morbid curiosity. There is a need to make ourselves feel safe by finding reasons why serial killers cyclically enter our life, and understanding serial killers so that we are removed as possible victims. We like to believe that they prey on those that excite them psychologically or sexually and in some way are very special.

We do not like to believe that being helpless or ill would make us a victim, but rather we would hope for a source of help and support in our time of need. We find comfort in the fact that we believe that killers are extremely selective in choosing victims that are exciting and alive. Our vision is of the killer in a high state of excitement on the hunt for an opportunity to play a cat-and-mouse game with a powerful and elusive foe. The outcome unfortunately results in a power struggle in which the victim is humiliated and manipulated. In the end he will ultimately yield his life and soul to the killer. The conquest enriches the killer by his osmosis of the essence of life from the victim.

The story of *Death Angel*, however, sends chills up the reader's spine. The nature of the victims and circumstances of their deaths are mundane, and therefore unexpectedly vile. He stalks hospital halls and corridors, unobtrusively and silently, delivering death to patients and grief to families.

The book is an excellent source for understanding a killer, and therefore should be read by police, psychologists, and others that want and need to understand one of the most horrible crimes that a person can commit. The taking of human life without provocation or need seems to exist throughout the history of mankind with little tempering by social, religious, or economic forces. Senseless murder exists as an independent phenomenon as if it were in a vacuum defying our ability to control it.

The dramatic difference in the story *Death Angel* is that it is told from the perspective of a family member of one of the killer's victims. The author has a strong religious and moral sensitivity. It is clear he is struggling to understand why and how this has happened to someone he loved.

Although he makes a strong attempt to remain detached, he gives the book its true value and special quality when the reader delves between the lines and sees the struggle to comprehend what has happened. The author feels the character of the killer would want forgiveness and even friendship, especially when offered by the victim's family member. This is clearly seen in the letter he sends to the killer offering forgiveness and even friendship in exchange for help in understanding. He searches for goodness and humanity, but his search is never fulfilled. The killer fails to reach out to the request made by the author to somehow unburden his guilt and explain his actions from his perspective. The author is left to ponder true evil.

For the reader there is the realization that even though the story is a personal commentary, it also applies to him in that he will never feel safe or quite the same when he or a member of his family must go to the hospital.

I have spent over thirty years as a forensic psychologist searching for methods and ways to do criminal profiling and to predict human aggressive behavior. Just when I thought I had seen it all, along comes a killer that's different, requiring some new insights.

This killer is an inadequate personality to the point of being unable to take his own life, in spite of twenty such attempts. He satisfies and compensates for his failures by taking the lives of as many people as he can. As many as forty victims, by his own admission, were killed. These were helpless and infirm victims of all ages and both sexes. The only common denominators among all of these victims were their vulnerability and helplessness.

The crowning achievement for the killer is the ultimate successful deal with the prosecutor's office to exchange his confession for avoiding the death penalty. Once again our killer escapes suicide. He must still be relishing and contemptuously laughing at society, for again he has had the excitement of the ultimate thrill of getting as close to death as possible without actually dying, while involved in the same adventure, he was able to kill others.

Death Angel is a wonderful book, clinically presented with the emotional overtones that add to our understanding of the forces that shape evil in its purest form. I strongly recommend it as a source book, textbook, and adventure in reading.

Introduction

By Clifford L. Linedecker

If what Charles Cullen says and what survivors whose family members died in hospitals and nursing homes, where the critical-care nurse worked, believe, he is one of the most prolific serial killers in American criminal history.

There is no question that he is one of the world's most appalling examples of health-care professionals who turn on their patients when the victims are at their most vulnerable and forge reputations as an especially notorious type of serial killer widely known as "Death Angels." As Cullen's kind often do, the gaunt New Jersey misfit claimed he snuffed out the lives of patients because he felt sorry for them and wanted to end their suffering. He was an "Angel of Mercy."

That is debatable at best, although there is evidence that a certain number of critical-care nurses sometimes turn on their patients with that intention, according to an article in the May 23, 1996, issue of the *New England Journal of Medicine.* The magazine cited a disturbing survey of some 1,600 nurses in the United States that disclosed that of the 1,139 who responded to the anonymous questionnaires,

852 said they were asked by patients or family members to engage in euthanasia or assisted suicide.

One hundred sixty-four of the nurses admitted engaging in the practice at least once. Of those, 129 said they took an active role in bringing about the death. The other thirty-five said they hastened the death of a patient by pretending to provide treatment ordered by a physician to sustain the patient's life, but not actually doing so. The most frequent method used by those who actively brought about a death was administering a high dose of opiates to a terminally ill patient, according to the University of Pennsylvania survey.

Cullen wasn't asked by patients or by their families to hasten the deaths of the men and women he preyed on in the critical-care wards of hospitals in two states. He set himself up as judge, jury, and executioner, deciding exactly who should die, when and by what means. And he was no Angel of Mercy, as he described himself, because some of his patients were gaining strength and clearly recovering when they were murdered.

One of the most troubling aspects of the nightmare nurse's savage murder rampage, which may have claimed forty or more lives, is the knowledge that similar outrages have soiled the reputation of the health-care profession before. Nurses, doctors, and aides have turned on their patients in alarming numbers. They have picked and chosen among their patients and the patients of unsuspecting colleagues, while playing God and deciding in accordance with their own perverted sense of morality who is to live and who is to die.

Curiously, although males make up only about 7 percent of the nurses who care for patients in hospitals and nursing homes, an inordinate number of medical murderers are men.

If Cullen has a rival Death Angel for the title of most prolific American serial-killer nurse, it is Donald Harvey, a meek little man who may have claimed the lives of as many as fifty victims in hospitals and nursing homes in eastern Kentucky and southern Ohio during the 1970s and 1980s. Both Harvey and Cullen played out their deadly game in two states and each continued killing for sixteen years before they were stopped.

Former Boy Scout Richard Angelo selected victims from among sick and helpless at Good Samaritan Hospital in West Islip on Long Island, New York. Patients began dying with disturbing regularity while he was on duty in the waning months of 1987, until a fellow nurse figured out that something was seriously wrong and took her suspicions to authorities. More than thirty-five bodies of former patients were exhumed for autopsies and sophisticated laboratory tests before Angelo was put on trial and ultimately convicted in four slayings. The cold-blooded killer told police investigators he tested stolen hospital drugs on field mice he caught himself before using the deadly potions on patients.

Nurse Robert R. Diaz achieved notoriety for his dark achievements after he was convicted of multiple murders committed during the early 1980s while working in the coronary-care units of Los Angeles area hospitals. The bespectacled, soft-spoken serial killer, who liked to be called "Dr. Diaz," often showed off by predicting when elderly patients would die. So many patients died on his watch after experiencing the same symptoms that an investigation was launched, leading to his arrest. Authorities picked out the strongest cases and convicted him of twelve murders.

Orville Lynn Majors Jr. was one of the most popular nurses with patients at the Vermillion County Hospital in rural Clinton, Indiana. They liked him for his efficiency and caring bedside manner. That all changed when the licensed practical nurse was arrested on suspicion of murder after an alarming series of deaths while he was on duty. Majors was convicted of six murders during 1994 to

1995, and is serving six consecutive sixty-year terms at the maximum-security Indiana State Prison in Michigan City.

Medical murder is in no way a purely American phenomenon and the United States has no monopoly on nurses, doctors, and others in the health-care field who turn on patients with frightful efficiency and deadly expertise. Early in 2005, while Cullen was poring over medical records in his jail cell, trying to recall the identities of victims, thirty-six-year-old nurse Roger Andermatt was sentenced to life in prison after murdering twenty-two elderly residents of nursing homes, and attempting to kill five others. With the convictions Andermatt became Switzerland's most prolific, known serial killer.

In France a nurse was sent to prison for ten years for giving lethal injections of morphine or potassium to six patients in a suburban Paris hospital during 1997 and 1998. In Vienna, Austria, a nurse and three aides admitted killing sixty-nine patients during a six-year blood spree, and authorities said the toll was believed to be in the hundreds. A nurse in the Netherlands was convicted in March 2003 and sent to prison for life after conviction for killing four patients at three hospitals in the Hague. An appeals court then found her guilty of three additional murders and three attempted murders.

The medical supervisor of an old-folks home in Orkdal, Norway, made international headlines when it was learned that he killed 138 people during a ghastly five-year orgy of violence. He explained to police that he was merely "doing God's bidding." During the past decade other medical serial murders have been uncovered in Germany and Denmark.

But the most prolific medical murderer in recent history was a trusted, kind-looking family physician, Dr. Harold Shipman. Nicknamed "Dr. Death" by the British media, Shipman was convicted of killing fifteen people. But a public high-court inquiry blamed him in the deaths of 215 people, and found that he may have been involved in another forty-five suspicious deaths. Britain has no death penalty, and the lethal Dr. Shipman was serving a life sentence in the Wakefield Prison in northern England until January 13, 2004, when he committed suicide by hanging himself with his bedsheets. He was found dead by guards the day before his fifty-eighth birthday.

The horror stories are ubiquitous and—without a doubt, despite the outrage and the nightmare headlines generated by Cullen and his ghoulish predecessors—somewhere in the United States and elsewhere in the world today, Death Angels are going about their deadly work. They are snuffing out the lives of innocents, the very people who should be able to trust them most.

That's a dirty shame, because according to Gallup Poll surveys, nursing is the most respected profession in the United States. In 2004, nurses were named as the most ethical and honest of all professional workers in the country, the fifth time in the past six years they were so honored. The only year in the span they failed to capture first place was 2001, when the 9/11 terrorist attacks on the Twin Towers helped firefighters beat them out. Others in the health-care profession also did well in the 2004 poll, including pharmacists who drew 72 percent approval ratings, and doctors who were rated at 67 percent.

Nursing is the backbone of the health-care system, and every time a Death Angel is exposed, an honorable profession is unfairly soiled and cast under a black cloud of suspicion. It is time to learn from past mistakes and put a stop to the cancerous spread of a growing abuse.

A nurse who kills is guilty of abominable evil. The act is an unpardonable violation of trust—the ultimate betrayal.

another, to the sprawling medical center, about a fifteen-minute drive from her home in nearby Bedminster.

Her latest stay at the hospital had begun only three days earlier, on February 6, 2003, after she complained of breathing problems and was rushed to Somerset Medical by ambulance.

Mrs. Stoecker was a woman who was familiar with hospitals and the health-care profession, even before her own illness led to her frequent admissions to the medical center. Before she became ill, she worked as a medical assistant for a local doctor, managing the office, doing the billing, and prepping patients. She weighed them, took their blood pressure, and got them into gowns for examinations. She once studied to be a nurse, and the job was a natural calling.

After two decades as a full-time homemaker, raising three sons and a daughter, she had developed a near unflappable composure and sympathetic concern that helped put even the most troubled or nervous patients at ease. She was an experienced and compassionate listener and caregiver whose concern was real—and patients realized that.

Now that it was her turn to be a patient, she understood and commiserated with her own caregivers. She had been on both sides of the bed, and even when she was propped up on her back in a quiet, sterile room, where she was fussed over by doctors and nurses, or was rebuilding her strength after being poked with needles, plied with pills and potions, or submitted to energy-draining sessions of chemotherapy, she still managed to keep a positive attitude.

She was talking and joking with her nurses right up to the time three days after her admission to Somerset Medical when she apparently suffered a slight heart attack and was transferred to the coronary-care unit (CCU).

Martin was understandably concerned about his mother—but he wasn't panicked. She was a fighter, who had shown before that she was fully prepared and capable of putting up a plucky fight for her life. When his father assured him that she was doing well and suggested he arrange to visit her the next day, Zach continued on to Philadelphia, driving through the soot gray winter-afternoon gloom to do his show. He planned to visit his mother at the hospital the next morning.

He was a busy professional with a wife and two-year-old daughter, juggling family responsibilities with a challenging, rapidly expanding career that was currently focused on his high-profile role as DJ on leading rock-radio shows in two of the nation's most populous cities.

Zach T. Martin is a professional name that William and Eleanor's oldest child, Richard Stoecker, adopted a few years after he broke into the radio business. He launched his career when he walked into WVRM, a public-service station in Hazelet, New Jersey, and confidently announced that he wanted to work for them. He worked there without pay, learning the business from the ground up, until he heard that an older part-time employee had quit, asked for the job, and was put on the payroll. There were other stints at stations in New Jersey, Indiana, Colorado, Maryland, and Virginia before a slot opened up with WAXQ-FM (Q-104) in New York City in 1998.

He'd been there ever since, becoming one of the most listened-to radio personalities in Manhattan, while broadcasting a market-leading Saturday-night classic-rock show, and producing the popular and long-running "Scott Muni Show" at the same station. Interviewing celebrity rockers of the past and present and getting down in the "Big Apple" is a long way from toiling as an unpaid gofer for WVRM or broadcasting Top 40s and oldies at Station WZZQ in Terre Haute, Indiana.

But the hard-driving professional was still energetically building his career, doing the show in Philadelphia and laying the groundwork for going into national syndication when an unexpected tragedy linked to his mother's illness intruded in his life.

It was almost 10:00 P.M. when Zach drove the last few

miles to his home in the upscale commuter community of Oradell. The neighborhood was quiet and the few lights that were visible inside other homes on his street were the muted flickering of television sets, when he parked his car and walked wearily inside the house.

A quick telephone call to Somerset Medical brought the promising news that his mother was doing better. She was sitting up in bed, drinking a soda, and talking about leaving the hospital and going home soon. Zach figured that he could finally go to bed, secure in the knowledge that his mother merely had experienced another bump in the road in her continuing battle against her cancer. They could talk again the next morning and arrange for him to visit her at the hospital.

Zach was sleeping at five o'clock Wednesday morning, when his wife, Emily, telephoned the hospital to ask about her mother-in-law. The news wasn't good. Eleanor had taken a turn for the worse and was hooked up to a respirator. When Emily phoned the charge nurse only three hours earlier, Eleanor was resting comfortably and appeared to be doing just fine.

Zach roused himself out of bed, sipped some coffee, wolfed down a light breakfast, and headed for the hospital. He was worried, but there was still good reason to hope for the best. Eleanor had been on a respirator once before after a bad reaction from medication, but she had fought her way back from the crisis and eventually returned home.

The false optimism over the patient's condition the previous day evaporated after her son drove to the hospital through a fierce winter storm that had descended on northern New Jersey. He and other family members were soon gathered at the woman's bedside for a deathwatch. Paul, the second eldest of her four children, was in New Jersey and drove to the hospital. The sick woman's only daughter, Diane, lived in nearby Keansburg, and also hurried to her mother's bedside. William Jr. "Billy," the baby of the family, flew in from Wisconsin. William Stoekcer Sr., the critically ill woman's brother, Peter, and her best friend, Janet Sonic, also squeezed into the crowded room to keep the somber vigil. Over the years, Bill Sr. had worked as a mechanic, insurance salesman, and finally as a bus driver. When he arrived at the hospital, he was still wearing his drivers' uniform.

The desperately ill woman was waging a spirited fight for life. Repeatedly she forced her eyes open to peer at the family gathered around her and struggled to speak through the breathing tube inserted down her throat.

A few hours into the long, emotionally exhausting night, Zach's wife, Emily, stepped outside into the semidarkened hallway to pick up a soda from a vending machine and noticed a little man with short-cropped, graying hair and a peaked face. He stood near a medication-dispensing cart, watching her. Unlike most of the nurses, who wore blue or green, he was dressed in white hospital scrubs. His eyes were dark and angry-looking and his mouth was turned down in a scowl. Neither of them said a word to each other.

Emily wondered idly if he was resentful of her for invading his territory, or if he considered her to be a trouble-maker. A person who believed in getting involved, she asked the nurses bustling around the sick woman a lot of questions. She asked about the pain medication Eleanor was given: how often it was administered, how much was too much, and whether something else might be better? She didn't recall specific exchanges with the male nurse she saw in the hallway, but she realized that people talk and word gets around.

Family members were so absorbed in their worry and grief that they barely noticed the skinny little night nurse with the quiet manner and skin that was so pale and tightly drawn over his face that it looked like bleached leather. He was a gaunt, pasty-faced, almost cadaverous-appearing man dressed totally in white from his shirt to his shoes, who slipped silently in and out of the room, going about his work with all the grim detachment of a grave digger. The RN didn't chat with visitors, or with his fellow health-care professionals, while he fiddled around meticulously tending to IVs, passing out pills, and recording vital signs of patients on the ward.

Most of the time the nurse was so unobtrusive that he was almost like part of the spartan hospital furniture. He drifted quietly in and out of the room, barely noticed while he carried out whatever task he was faced with at the time, then vanished back into the hallways. Early in the evening, although he wasn't Eleanor's primary nurse, he gave her an intravenous injection.

The sixty-year-old woman's life was clearly slipping away, and a priest was summoned to administer the last rites. Her eldest son stepped outside the room for a few minutes to talk with one of his mother's doctors.

"Is she gone?" he asked.

"There's a little electricity there, but she's gone," the doctor replied.

The doctor explained as gently as she could that it seemed all the chemicals being used to fight the poisonous growth eating at Eleanor's vitals were taking a lethal toll on her organs. The plucky grandmother was gravely ill. Even if she was able somehow to rally briefly from the current crisis, it was clear that she didn't have much longer to live. Zach walked back into his mother's room and, in a voice that was muted and choked with emotion, told family members and friends what the doctor had said. As the oldest son, he felt that it was his responsibility.

Sitting at his mother's bedside while she struggled stubbornly for breath with such courage and grace, he stared into her eyes and was struck by how strikingly bright blue they were. He could recall seeing eyes that were so beatifically bright blue only once before in his life: when he managed to get close enough to peer into the careworn face of Pope John Paul II, during the pontiff's 1979 appearance in Philadelphia.

The former Eleanor Sova was a New Jersey girl in her early twenties when she first met her future husband during a traffic jam while driving to Palisades Park. Bill Stoecker was working at his first post-high school job, as a mechanic. And if it wasn't love at first sight for the young couple, it was close enough. They married in 1964 and were living in Clifton when Richard was born almost exactly nine months later. He was four, and already the big brother to two siblings, when his grandfather Peter Sova died of a heart attack and the family moved to East Keansburg before it became known simply as Middletown Township.

While the children were young, their mother was a full-time homemaker. She presided over a busy household filled with kids and pets. She tended solicitously to the children's physical and emotional bumps and bruises, volunteered at St. Catherine's School, where they attended classes, and helped with their homework. Even then, her firstborn was impressed by her beautiful, graceful handwriting. She was a loving, attentive mother. Raising their brood on a bus driver's salary, William and Eleanor Stoecker sacrificed to get their children the best possible education.

After St. Catherine's, Richard attended Divine Word High School Seminary in Bordentown, New Jersey, then decided that he wasn't cut out for a career as a priest. He had his eye on the U. S. Military Academy at West Point when he signed up for his final year of high school at the Marine Academy of Science and Technology in Sandy Hook, but by graduation time he had switched career plans once more and enrolled as a freshman at St. John's University in Queens, New York. He graduated with a Bachelor of Science in criminal justice. While Zach was attending St. John's and launching his radio career, his brother Paul was earning a Ph.D. in chemistry at Rutgers University.

Now Eleanor Stoecker's children were educated, married, and raising their own families, and the devoted grandmother was waging the fight of her life. She was flat on her back in bed, hooked up to an IV, a feeding tube and a breathing tube, while machines were monitoring her vital signs. Doctors and nurses were slipping in and out of the room, peering at her, checking the readings on the machines, and scribbling enigmatic entries onto charts.

Zach was touched, but chilled, when a blond nurse, who had chatted and joked with his mother only a night or two earlier, walked into the room, peered at the woman on the bed, listened a moment to the labored breathing—and burst into tears.

"Your mother's dying," she whispered. Then she turned, wiped at her eyes, and, with a rustle of crisply starched skirts, hurried from the room.

Mrs. Stoecker had always been the rock that held the clan together; the family diplomat who planned get-togethers and eased hurt feelings. It was she who helped find common ground when there were disagreements among the siblings. Her family was her life, and her love for them was unconditional. The love was reciprocated, and as the mournful vigil at her bedside neared its tragic end, the hushed talk turned to happier times. They reminisced about weddings, other family gatherings, and about beloved pets, including a favorite dog, Buster. They also prayed, sometimes joining hands, while they gathered around the bed chanting the "Hail Mary" and the "Our Father." At other times they sat or stood alone, eyes closed, praying silently.

The knowledge that the family matriarch was dying was an unexpected shock. Renal carcinoma is a brutally aggressive cancer, but in the months since the diagnosis she had been holding her own and apparently keeping the killer disease at bay. She crocheted, puttered around with ceramics, and lunched or shopped with her best friend, Janet, and other chums. She also busily monitored shopping channels and other TV shows, buying all kinds of things for her house and family. She was heavyset, and shortly before the latest emergency she sent away for a Weight Watchers kit.

The busy mother and grandmother wasn't planning on dying soon.

The last time Zach saw his mother alive was about 9:00 A.M. and the hospital was just picking up to the hustle and bustle of a new day while he and his baby brother sat at her bedside, watching life drain quietly away. Her eyes were at their most lustrous powder blue when she turned to peer at his face; then with a nod of gentle acceptance, she drew her last breath. Zach sat alone by her bedside for a long time after that, holding her hand and looking at the body of the graying woman who had given him life. At last his father walked back into the room, put a hand on his son's shoulder, and said it was time to go.

Zach would recall every night before he dropped off to sleep the final moments with his mother as she lost her doomed fight for life. It would be months before he learned that his mother's game struggle against death was a contest she never had a chance of winning. She was doomed to fail because of a puny little loser named Charles Cullen and his lethal obsession with playing God.

On the bleak, crisply cold February night of Eleanor Stoecker's wake at a Middletown mortuary, one of the worst blizzards of the decade swept over northern New Jersey, and her family canceled the funeral scheduled for the next day The call was made for safety's sake. The family didn't want anyone hurt trying to drive through the sweeping snow and ice storm. The snow and ice-covered ground was too hard to dig a grave, so the family matriarch was cremated for burial later.

It was May 20, before the Stoeckers, the Sovas, and their friends gathered again for a funeral mass at St. Catherine's Church in Middletown. That was her parish church when she was a young bride, and the mother of a growing family, but she hadn't been back there for years. Zach wanted the mass said there. He thought she would like that: it would be like returning to her roots.

Exactly one month later, on June 20, her sixty-first birthday, Eleanor Stoecker's ashes were carried to the old St. Peter's Church Cemetery in Lodi, where her father, Peter Sova, was already buried. The family matriarch's final remains were at last laid to rest. A headstone on the grave is inscribed with the words:

> *Eleanor Stoecker*
> *Our Beloved Angel*
> *Taken from us*
> *February 12, 2003*
> *Your Death is not in Vain*

Chapter 2

Charles

Eleanor Stoecker wasn't the first seriously ill patient to die on Charles Cullen's watch—and she wouldn't be the last.

Somehow, it seemed as if the pasty-faced critical-care nurse's whole life was jinxed, and the bad luck and hateful furies that stalked him from infancy were bound to infect just about everyone else who came in close contact with him.

Cullen was born on George Washington's birthday, February 22. But the squalling, undersize infant ushered into the world in 1960 at a West Orange, New Jersey, hospital would share none of the positive qualities of courage, loyalty, and trustworthiness exhibited by the man who became the nation's first president. The baby born into an intensely Catholic family was destined to be remembered for his betrayals, furtive thievery, and cowardly attacks on the elderly, frail, and helpless.

The year of his birth was an eventful year. While President Dwight Eisenhower was finishing up the final year of his second term, Massachusetts senator John F. Kennedy defeated Richard Nixon in a close race to succeed the former World War II general in the White House; young

Americans were caught up in a wild, new dance craze, the Twist; and the chilling scene in Alfred Hitchcock's classic movie thriller *Psycho* was leaving a generation of women terrified at the prospect of climbing into the shower.

In New Jersey, the star-crossed infant who was carried to his home in a working-class West Orange neighborhood, known as "Tory Corner," which was typically filled with parked cars and kids, was destined to leave his own blood-stained mark on history. But the horror of his crimes would exceed even the cinematic feats of Hitchcock's cross-dressing psychotic killer Norman Bates. The atrocities committed by Charles Cullen would be real.

The new baby was the last of eight children, including five girls, of Edmond and Florence Cullen, a former GI and the English war bride he fell in love with during World War II, and whom he brought home to New Jersey, where he went to work as a bus driver—the same profession later adopted by Eleanor Stoecker's husband, Bill. The Cullens lived on a one-block-long street, next door to a bakery. They resided in one of the big, old double-decker houses that marched in regimented rows along both sides of the noisy, narrow thoroughfares of the disorganized clutter of industrial and commuter communities west of the Hudson River and New York Bay.

The tragedy that would stalk Charles Cullen throughout his life first caught up with him before he was seven months old, when his father took sick and died. The hardworking, devoted husband and father was only fifty-six when his unexpected death left his widow with seven kids still living at home to care for and support. It seemed as if there was never enough money to go around even before he died, and after his death, family finances became even more meager.

Florence brought in a few dollars baby-sitting, and the older girls also baby-sat and did other odd jobs to augment the Social Security payments that became the distressed family's main source of support. A disabled aunt, who lived with the family, helped out as well, sewing for the Red Cross.

Populated largely by a mix of Irish and Italians, Tory Corner wasn't known for expensive cars, fine homes, and other ostentatious trappings of wealth, but neighbors helped out when they could. A plumber who lived nearby repaired the roof and did other fix-it jobs on the aging wood-frame house that the women couldn't do themselves. Another family passed down its used furniture to the Cullens, and other neighbors helped out with clothing that their own children had outgrown.

Survival for the Cullen brood was a continual struggle, and there was never enough money to go around for anything that wasn't absolutely essential—like haircuts. One day at Our Lady of Lourdes, a grade school, a furious nun grabbed one of the older Cullen boys by the hair and screeched at him in front of the other children, ordering him to get it cut. Episodes like that were humiliating, and deeply painful emotionally.

Charles grew up as a runty, skinny, awkward kid, who wore hand-me-downs and lived in a household dominated by women. Years later he would be remembered by neighbors as a quietly sober boy who had little to say and spent hours by himself. While other boys played stickball in the streets, shot marbles, roughhoused, and raced bicycles, young Charles was more likely to be holed up alone in some quiet corner of the house leafing through comic books or idly puttering around with a chemistry set.

One day when he was about nine years old, and busy heating test tubes and mixing compounds, he decided that his bleak, dreary existence just wasn't worth all the trouble, and he swallowed a witch's brew of chemicals. It was his first suicide attempt, and like others he would make throughout his life, it was unsuccessful. The chemicals tasted nasty and they made his stomach queasy, but they didn't kill him.

On December 6, 1977, Charles was a seventeen-year-old junior at West Orange High School when bad luck and tragedy caught up with him again. His mother was riding in a car, driven by a married daughter, a few miles north of West Orange in Verona when they crashed head-on with another vehicle. Florence was rushed by ambulance to a nearby hospital, but was dead on arrival.

The daughter was an epileptic, and when she was asked by a police investigator if she had taken her medicine that day, she said she hadn't, according to the accident report. She reportedly explained that she ran out of medicine the day before. The police report did not cite epilepsy as a factor in the crash.

Florence Cullen's estate was predictably modest. The house was valued at $15,000. Her personal effects were valued at less than $500. Five children were still living at home, but their mother left no will and there was no one in the household capable of taking the place of their lost parents. Charles and his brothers were free to come and go as they wished, and to make their own decisions.

As the baby of the family, Charles doted on his mother. Neighbors considered him to be a mama's boy, and he was crushed by her death. It was almost like the shy, gawky teenager was left adrift on a choppy sea without his navigator. But he didn't run wild, like he might have done. Instead, he withdrew further into himself, spent even more time alone, and a few weeks after the latest family calamity, he dropped out of West Orange High School and enlisted in the navy.

The military service couldn't replace his mother, or his father, but the U.S. Navy offered other practical benefits. The troubled teenager was provided with a roof over his head, good food, fine medical care, a regular paycheck, and discipline.

When he returned home for a two-week leave after boot camp, and walked around the neighborhood proudly showing off his starched, crisply pressed summer whites, people were impressed. They felt good for the skinny orphan, and it looked as if he had bounced back successfully from the family tragedies that blighted his early life.

and landed on his feet. He was even seen smiling a few times, some neighbors later recalled.

With boot camp behind him, and after his two-week leave, Cullen reported in June to the Basic Enlisted Submarine School at New London-Groton, Connecticut. The school for enlisted submariners was first organized in 1916 when it was converted from a navy yard, and by 1959 had become the largest sub base in the world. In 1969, eight years before Cullen joined the navy, the school assumed the task of providing training for sailors assigned to ballistic missile submarines.

At the school the neophyte sailor underwent rigorous psychological screening necessary to determine if he and his fellow students were ready and emotionally capable of handling the special stresses of being jammed in small spaces with more than one hundred other men while their boat prowled underwater in the world's oceans on lengthy patrols. In classrooms, and in the bowels of real submarines, he was also taught all about the sleek underwater craft he was preparing to serve on.

After completing the submarine school in August, the young sailor was ordered to attend Gunners Mate "A" School at Dam Neck, a navy training facility that is part of the Naval Air Station (NAS) at Oceana, Virginia. NAS Oceana is about five miles south of the popular Atlantic Ocean resort city of Virginia Beach, and Cullen spent eight months of intensive study at the training facility while preparing to qualify as a ballistic missiles technician.

The orphan boy from West Orange graduated from "A" school, as a newly promoted petty officer with a rating as a missile technician third class, and submarine qualification. His job specialty coupled with the submarine designation included a security clearance. After more than one year in the U.S. Navy, Cullen's schooling was completed. In June 1979 he was attached to Submarine Group Six, and on July 30, he was given his first fleet assignment aboard the nuclear submarine *Woodrow Wilson* (SSBN624).

By a curious twist of fate, the sleek killer ballistic-missile submarine was launched at the Mare Island Naval Shipyard in Vallejo, California, on February 22, 1963—the new crew member's third birthday.

The first navy warship named after the twenty-eighth president, who led the nation during World War I, the sleek 425-foot-long, 7,300-ton Lafayette class submarine was fitted with four forward torpedo tubes, and amidships was equipped with sixteen tubes designed to launch state-of-the-art nuclear-armed Polaris missiles. The missiles took up a big chunk of the meager space in the sub, and depending on the version, they could extend from 28.5 feet to 40.5 feet long, weigh 28,000 to 30,000 pounds, and fly 1,500 to 2,000 nautical miles.

Thirteen officers and 124 enlisted men lived on the boat, day and night, crammed together among torpedoes, missiles, and the sophisticated equipment needed to wage a modern war, along with bunks, mess, and everything else necessary to sustain them. Crewmen were assigned to separate port and starboard crews, one working while the other was off duty.

In one respect the newcomer fit in well among the crew. He was small, 135 or 140 pounds, about 5 feet 7 inches, give or take an inch, and didn't take up much space. That's important in the cramped quarters of a nuclear sub.

In many other respects Cullen's assignment was an unfortunate choice. About one month before he was assigned to the *Woodrow Wilson,* the boat ran aground in heavy fog while it was headed for a mooring at New London. Running aground was the nuclear submarine's first misfortune. Signing on the new crewman was the second.

All the schooling he had undergone and his acceptable performance mastering the new skills he was expected to acquire made little difference once he actually took his place in a submarine crew. He was a "newbie," a fresh fish, and that meant hazing. Every submarine sailor was submitted to the same test of abilities and pluck by their more experienced colleagues, and the crew of the *Woodrow Wilson* approached the task with relish. For most sailors the taunting and ridicule ended after they had proven themselves on their first patrol. It was like the sailor's initiation when crossing the international date line—you're only a shellback once. That didn't work for Cullen, and the heckling didn't end just because he completed his first patrol.

Every boat, ship, or shore-duty billet in the navy is inevitably shared with at least one sad sack who doesn't fit in. Cullen was the *Woodrow Wilson*'s misfit. Although he did well on navy-wide tests, and was promoted to second-class petty officer, he continued to be the butt of jokes and everyone's favorite whipping boy—even young sailors, whom he outranked, joined in the fun. The morose, misfit teenager was definitely not an alpha male.

His lubberly Ichabod Crane appearance, with a head that perched awkwardly on a skinny neck, and skin that was so pale it looked like fine rice paper drawn tightly over his cheekbones, may have been part of the problem. His skin was so sallow and chalk white that some sailors coined a crudely sadistic nickname for him—"Fish-belly."

The bony sailor with the perpetual hangdog look, who drifted silently through the hatches from one cramped compartment to the next, while barely speaking or acknowledging his shipmates, was strange; his behavior was weird. He didn't talk much, and when he did, he usually said something the other sailors could twist around and use to make fun of him. On a submarine there's no place to go to get away from people when they're picking on you.

Cullen wasn't a crybaby, and he didn't complain to officers or to senior enlisted men, but he made matters worse by withdrawing deeper into himself and responding to the cruel taunts of his shipmates with meekly accepting behavior. He hung his head, avoided looking his tormentors in the eyes, and muttered to himself under his breath.

Most of the time Cullen couldn't even climb into a liberty boat and head for shore for a few hours of play, like crewmen on many other submarines or navy ships. He was serving aboard the *Woodrow Wilson* during the last years of the Cold War, and as a missile-armed nuclear submarine the boat had a dangerous and critically important mission. It prowled silently, deep beneath the icy cold waters of the North Atlantic, sometimes for more than two months at a time before surfacing and putting in at some port. Serving aboard the nuclear sub was highly secret work for young men who were unable to keep many secrets of their own from crewmates because of the cramped quarters and long periods of time they were jammed into the sweaty compartments together. If you had a weakness in your personality or a behavioral glitch, it wasn't long before your shipmates knew all about it.

Cullen was timid, kept to himself most of the time, tended to avoid eye contact when talking, and didn't team up with a favorite buddy to check out the local eye-candy and chase girls during rare liberties ashore.

But he shared some good times with shipmates, and he would be remembered later for his generosity and willingness to help out when there was cleaning up to do or other chores. He especially enjoyed getting together with other members of the *Woodrow Wilson* crew for weekend oyster roasts on the beach, but even then he had to be careful not to get too much sun because of his sallow, cadaverous skin. He sunburned easily.

Michael L. Leinen, who served with him as a first-class petty officer, was quoted in a *Reader's Digest* article, years after both men left the navy, recalling the time when Cullen returned to the boat after liberty with the skin on his feet seared bright red from a fierce sunburn. Despite the torment from the painful burn, he refused to report to sick bay because he was afraid he would get into trouble. Leinen said he had to force him to get treatment.

It was true that navy regulations permit the punishment of sailors who through their own negligence are sunburned so severely they can't perform their duties, but there was no danger of that happening to Cullen. He could still do his job. And he already knew his way around sick bay. He was on good terms with medics and the ship's doctor. He liked hanging around sick bay, and volunteered to help out giving shots when the crew needed vaccinations or filled in performing other minor medical chores. He was much more at ease around the bandages, pills, and ailing sailors than the death-dealing missiles he was trained to work with. He confided to a bunkmate his desire one day to become a nurse. He said he liked to help people.

Cullen may have been thinking about the healing profession on the day Leinen discovered him bizarrely togged out in a green surgical gown, mask, and gloves, while sitting at the boat's missile-firing controls. The medical togs were filched from a medical cabinet. Leinen was in charge of the team of sailors that operated the boat's arsenal of nuclear-armed ballistic missiles, and finding the strangely garbed sad sack seated at the control panels was an unpleasant surprise. Nuclear-armed submarines have sufficient fail-safe mechanisms in force, and Cullen couldn't have fired a missile by himself. But he was out of uniform and clearly away from his duty station at that time.

Leinen reported the bizarre incident, and the errant sailor was disciplined, although the exact nature of the penalty and whether or not he was submitted to nonjudicial punishment, known in the navy as a "captain's mast," has not been publicly disclosed. Cullen never explained what he was doing, but the occurrence was among the most serious of various scrapes he got himself into while he was a submariner.

Ironically, almost two decades earlier, when the *Woodrow Wilson* was launched, the commissioning party had to drive into the Mare Island Shipyard past a motley gang of noisy picketers calling themselves the Committee for Nonviolent Action—West, and distributing leaflets describing the Polaris-armed submarine as "another finger on the nuclear trigger."

Cullen was found with his finger close to that trigger, and his bizarre behavior was alarming. The undersea superiority provided by the submarines, with their devastatingly lethal Polaris missiles, was an important element of America's Cold War strategy of deterring nuclear conflict with the Soviet Union by the threat of massive retaliation if the nation was attacked. The *Woodrow Wilson* and its sister submarines carried half of America's nuclear warheads while operating in the open oceans—even under the Arctic ice. The Soviets had their own nuclear-armed submarine fleet, and the accidental launching of a Polaris could have plunged the world into a mutually destructive Armageddon.

After more than two years aboard the *Woodrow Wilson,* Cullen was reassigned on October 30, 1981, to the USS *Canopus* (AS-34). Serving aboard the new ship carried none of the glamour or status that clung to submarine sailors, but the vessel was an important and necessary element of the Silent Service. The *Canopus* was a submarine tender, with responsibility for servicing and maintaining the underwater subs that were on the front line of America's offensive/defensive nuclear shield during the Cold War years.

Aboard the *Canopus* Cullen was still a square peg in a round hole, and he was apparently bothered by the fits of depression that had beset him since childhood. The navy doesn't share personal information about the physical and mental-health problems its servicemen and servicewomen or that its veterans may have experienced while on active duty, so there is much about Cullen's behavior aboard the submarine tender that is still shrouded in secrecy. But according to some reports, sometime after he left the *Woodrow Wilson,* he attempted to commit suicide, and was admitted to a psychiatric hospital for treatment of depression. Finally, on March 30, 1984, when he was almost exactly halfway into his second hitch, he was released from the navy and issued a discharge. Navy authorities have not made public whether or not the discharge was issued for medical or other reasons. Still in his early twenties when he returned to civilian life, Cullen was on his own again, footloose and fancy-free.

When the lost boy returned to his old haunts in North Jersey, his navy career was behind him for good, but he had a pretty good idea what he wanted to do. Cullen may have never in his life been truly happy, but he experienced a certain degree of comfort and pleasure when he was helping out in sick bay aboard the *Woodrow Wilson*. He liked the excitement, the authority, and the responsibility of caring for the sick and injured, and he had no difficulty in settling on a new career choice.

Early in 1984, he registered as a student at the Mountainside Hospital School of Nursing, a few minutes' drive from West Orange in Montclair, New Jersey. The former submariner had his heart set on becoming a registered nurse.

Chapter 3

Angel of Mercy/Angel of Death

At Mountainside, Cullen was once more surrounded by women. Most people who set their sights on nursing careers, especially a quarter of a century ago, were women. The word "nurse" first began to be used in the English language during the thirteenth century, and is derived from Latin terminology meaning "to nurture." Even today, only about six or seven percent of the approximate 2.7 million nurses in the United States are male.

The spindly, soft-spoken former sailor with the quiet ways was one of only two men in his class, and he bunked in a dormitory set aside for male students across from the hospital. He was older than most of his classmates, but he kept his head down, studied hard, and received A's and B's in most of his classes. The only times his grades dropped into the C's were when he was taking classes in maternal child nursing and a course in medical surgical nursing.

Mastering the scholastic and other requirements of nurses' training wasn't a job for slackers or weaklings. The study-intensive courses in the classroom and the practical hands-on training with real patients were tough and demanding. Cullen's academic achievements at Mountainside would be about the only accomplishment in his life he would ever be able to take pride in.

Even while he was studying and preparing to carve a career for himself in the health-care field, tragedy continued to intrude in his life. In March 1987, his brother James died in the family home from a drug overdose believed to have been a suicide.

But the baby of the Cullen family had his own life to live, and he was on a roll. Approximately two months after his brother's death, he completed the three-year study course. He graduated on schedule in May 1987, qualified to become a registered nurse. At commencement ceremonies he stood with other prospective RNs and proudly recited the "Florence Nightingale Pledge." Along with other graduates he was given a copy of the "Nurse Practice Act," which governs the professional behavior of nurses in each of the American states.

A week after that, on June 7, in a religious ceremony at the Atrium West in West Orange, he married Adrienne Taub. The June bride was a computer programmer.

The only thing the newly married man needed to achieve his dream of becoming a registered nurse was a New Jersey license. He took care of that in July by scoring high marks to pass a standardized test, the National Council Licensure Examination for Registered Nurses. Scores of 1,600 were considered passing. Cullen turned in a glowing mark of 2,437. He was all ready to begin earning a regular paycheck in his new profession.

The spanking-new RN began his first post-navy civilian job at the St. Barnabas Medical Center in Livingston, New Jersey. St. Barnabas was an impressive place to work, and not only was the medical center the largest nonprofit, nonsectarian hospital in the state, but it was the oldest—established in 1865, the year the American Civil War came to an end. More patients were treated annually at the prestigious medical center at 200 South Orange Avenue than at any other hospital in New Jersey. Cullen had landed a plum.

The slightly built newcomer was assigned to the burn unit, where he worked in the tank room and tended to patients whose bandages were being changed. Daily bathing and scrubbing in the tank room and having bandages changed were among the most painful hospital experiences for severely burned patients.

Even if Cullen hadn't started out in the tank room, an assignment to the burn unit would have been an emotionally taxing job for a newcomer just beginning a career in nursing. Burn patients, who have already lost skin and muscle, often face the loss of limbs to fierce infections, and pain and misery are constant companions. They can face repeated painful surgeries for skin grafts, amputations, and cleansings; the pain may be eased but never completely blotted out by powerful drugs. Right off the bat the new nurse found himself with an emotionally challenging job that called for a high level of education and training. It also traditionally called for as much patience and understanding as skill.

Jean T. Hackett, who was the chief burn technician at the time, and often worked with Cullen in the tank room, was impressed by how attuned Cullen was to pain. "One thing I remember clearly is that when a patient was in pain and needed medication, he was always right there with it," she was quoted years later in the Newark *Star-Ledger*. "He always had an interest in making sure the patient was comfortable. That is something that sticks out about him."

Cullen was efficient, but his bedside manner left much to be desired. It lacked the warmth and sympathetic concern shown by many of his female counterparts, who fit more easily into a comforting and caring mode. That wasn't especially unusual among male nurses, and keeping himself at emotional arm's length from the mind-numbing agony of terribly burned patients may have been an unconscious protective device that made his new job more bearable.

Hackett recalled her former colleague to a newspaper reporter years later as a man who was very private, but he could be funny and personable. He didn't encourage a lot of chitchat, and sometimes didn't even respond to a direct question with a direct answer, she said. The taciturn RN apparently impressed his supervisor with his approach to the emotionally demanding job. She remembered Cullen as a nurse who was "attuned to the needs of pain."

What he seemed to lack in compassion, he made up for with his industrious and efficient approach to the job. He was an industrious worker, who immersed himself in the tasks at hand, and even impressed some of his fellow nurses with what was later recalled as a dry sense of humor. He didn't waste much time chatting with other nurses, but when he did, he knew how to get a smile or a laugh. Much of the time he didn't even take a break for meals, but kept going by swilling down cup after cup of coffee. He seldom turned down overtime when he was offered extra hours.

If he was bothered by stress on the job, he apparently didn't complain about it, or blame it for troubles that began once more to emerge in his life. Stress was understandable, especially when working on the burn unit, where pain was an everyday occurrence—and the possibility of patients dying was ever present. Some of the deaths were more unexpected than others: like that of former Jersey City municipal judge John W. Yengo Sr.

Cullen had worked at St. Barnabas a little more than a year when the former jurist wound up in the burn unit after suffering a nasty reaction to a blood-thinning drug while vacationing over Memorial Day at the Jersey Shore. Yengo didn't realize that he was supposed to avoid the sun while taking the medicine and had become ill. When he was admitted to St. Barnabas, he looked as if he had suffered a fierce sunburn. The allergic skin reaction, known by its medical name as Stevens-Johnson syndrome, was as severe as it was rare.

The seventy-two-year-old patient was known among

friends and family as a tough, self-reliant man with a tremendous enthusiasm for life. A Jersey City native, he was outstanding in academics and athletics in high school. He obtained his higher education at Long Island University, then at the now-defunct John Marshall Law School. He even played a season of professional baseball in 1937 with the New York Cubans, and years later scouted for the St. Louis Cardinals and the Oakland Athletics. He was good with a baseball bat, and after he married and became the father of three girls and a boy, he once used a Louisville Slugger to chase a burglar out of the house.

During World War II he served his country in the navy, rising to the rank of captain, before returning to his hometown and opening a private law practice in his parents' house. Sometimes he was so moved by the financial predicament and other problems of clients that he worked for nothing, and he was even known to loan them money, daughter Suzy Rose Yengo later told the *Star-Ledger*.

Judge Yengo was best known in his hometown, however, for his abbreviated but colorful career on the municipal bench, which he was appointed to in 1974. Despite his sympathetic treatment of people he considered to be needy and deserving clients when he was in private practice, Yengo had no time for defendants who broke or flouted laws adopted to protect the public. He handed out so many maximum sentences that he acquired a colorful nickname that reflected his heavy hand. He became widely known in the press and in the local legal community as "Maximum John." Yengo wasn't the first law-and-order judge to be dubbed Maximum John, but he was the only one in Jersey City, and lawyers representing clients who were obviously guilty or likely to be convicted dreaded appearing before him to plead for lenient sentences.

Hard-boiled judges inevitably make political enemies and rub some fellow members of the bar the wrong way. Maximum John lasted two years before he was suspended from the bench, then permanently removed by the New Jersey

Supreme Court. Court documents show that the justices determined that Judge Yengo repeatedly failed to advise defendants of their constitutional rights, imprisoned defendants either without proper hearings or based on inadmissible evidence, and disregarded and mocked controlling legal precedents he disagreed with. The high court wrote in their decision to remove him that he was considered to be "totally unsuited" to the job because of "bizarre" behavior and repeated discourtesies to defendants and lawyers.

Supporters of the controversial judge were fed up with rampant crime, and slap-on-the-wrist punishment of criminals, and they were outraged over the treatment of Maximum John. They circulated petitions and staged protests calling for his reinstatement, but the suspension, then removal from the bench, was the beginning of the end of his public life. Yengo wasn't the kind of never-say-die political brawler simply to roll over and accept defeat, however, and the same year he was dumped from the bench, he ran for mayor of Jersey City as a law-and-order candidate. Yengo was an unforgettable, larger-than-life personality who approached politics the same way he played baseball when he was a star shortstop at Lincoln High School: he charged head-on into the center of the action and gave it his best.

His campaigns for mayor are best remembered in Jersey City for the electric chair he jury-rigged on the back of a flatbed truck and hauled around with him as a prop while shaking hands and giving speeches. The chair on the truck was safely inoperable, but Yengo promised voters that if they elected him, he would bring the real thing to Jersey City. He lost both mayoralty races, but he had a good time and went down fighting.

The scrappy political brawler knew how to take a punch, and he wasn't without admirers. In 1976, the year he lost his job as a judge, he was given an award as Jersey City's "Outstanding Citizen."

Yengo was still plucky and vigorous, definitely not the kind of fighter expected to give up easily—or to die of an allergic reaction to medication caused by too much sun, when he landed in the hospital years later.

When the former jurist died on June 11, 1988, less than two weeks after he was hospitalized, however, a deadly combination of too much sun and reaction from the medication was exactly what doctors who talked with his daughter Suzy—one of his four children—blamed as the cause of death. Looking back years later, she was quoted as saying she was suspicious because the death of the man she proudly called her "hero" occurred so quickly, but she had assumed it was God's will.

Cullen was one of the burn unit nurses who worked closely with Maximum John. He had witnessed death before, but that wasn't unusual for nurses. Among those who worked with critically ill patients, the very old, the very young, and the very frail in hospitals and nursing homes, it's only the rawest rookies who haven't lost patients. Every critical-care nurse knows her turn will come only too soon—that it is merely a matter of time. Cullen was no rookie. He was a seasoned professional, and during the periods when he worked in the burn unit, 150 patients died, including at least one whose death occurred at his hands.

It wasn't some onetime miscreant holding a longtime grudge against Maximum John for a stiff sentence, any more than it was a combination of sun and an allergic reaction to prescribed medication that killed the judge. It was his nurse. Cullen carried out the cowardly assassination while Yengo was flat on his back and alone in his room; he injected the judge's intravenous tube with the powerful heart drug lidocaine. The synthetic compound is used as a local anesthetic and to control irregular heartbeat. Like most medications it can be dangerous if it is given to the wrong patients or otherwise misused. In Cullen's hands it was lethal.

The experienced RN was an industrious and accommodating member of St. Barnabas's nursing staff, and he worked full-time on the burn unit for two years before

Livingston Services Corp. became his official employer. Livingston Services was a wholly owned subsidiary of the St. Barnabas Health Care System, which operated a nursing service at the hospital, but the change was more than merely a paperwork transfer. When Cullen's official employment was shifted to Livingston Services, he also became a part-time floater. In hospital parlance, at the time, that meant he no longer worked full-time in the burn unit, but "floated" among different units, including intensive care, cardiac care, and the ventilator and telemetry units, as well as the burn unit.

As a roving nurse he was called on to help care for patients with a broad range of serious injuries and illnesses, varying in scope from people dreadfully mangled in traffic accidents to heart attacks, strokes, cancer, and AIDS. Like most floaters, Cullen worked twelve-hour shifts. He especially liked the graveyard shift, when he reported for work before midnight and continued on duty until early morning.

The graveyard shift and critical-care wards are often favored by medical serial killers for the opportunities and camouflage they offer. Wards are empty of visitors at night, most nurses and other health-care professionals are off duty, and there is unlikely to be anyone around to question why any particular nurse may be in a patient's room or what he or she is doing there. One nurse is often responsible for several patients, including some who may be unconscious. Supervisors may be off duty, leaving the graveyard-shift nurse to work largely on his own, alone with the patients and the rhythmic beeping or softly flashing lights of devices monitoring vital signs. On critical-care wards the deaths of patients already known to be gravely ill are accepted as normal occurrences, and are unlikely to raise suspicions of anything underhanded going on.

A former supervisor later recalled that Cullen was willing to work any shift, anywhere in the hospital, and always was quick to volunteer to help whenever he was needed.

The supervisor also observed that although Cullen's nursing was only "mediocre," he never neglected his patients.

On at least one occasion he impressed another nurse with his compassion. Eileen Morrison didn't work with him, but she was one of his classmates at Mountainside, and three years after they graduated, her father landed in St. Barnabas with serious heart problems. When his daughter came to visit, she found Cullen taking care of him. The older man liked the male nurse, and seemed to be gaining strength when he unexpectedly died early one morning. When Morrison arrived at the hospital, she found her old classmate consoling the family. He was especially attentive to her mother. The older man's death was a shock, because he had seemed to be doing so well, and the night before he died, he was sitting up in bed, chatting with visitors, eating and watching TV.

While Cullen was coping with the oppressive day-and-night challenges of working with the critically ill and injured, and dealing with the constant fears and pain of patients, his life on the home front was deteriorating and his marriage was crumbling.

He was morose and depressed, and often when he wasn't working his regular shift or piling up overtime at St. Barnabas, he was home drinking. He was perfectly satisfied to settle down on a sofa by himself and polish off a six-pack of beer, or more. Adrienne quickly learned that he wasn't a very energetic communicator. When she tried to talk to him, he usually either threw a conniption fit or stared blankly and silently off into the distance, as if she weren't even there.

The star-crossed union produced two daughters, one born in 1988, the other four years later. But Cullen treated normal family life as a burden, and even the most inconsequential thing could cause him to lose his temper and explode in a rage. If he didn't fly off the handle over some imagined slight or perceived failure on his wife's part, he might react instead by going into a snit and withdrawing into himself. He was moody, sullen, and abrasive. At best, he was difficult to deal with; at worst, impossible and frightening.

The thrill and challenge of a new job in a new profession, plus a new wife and family of his own, had rapidly faded. Cullen sank deep into a troubling depression that made him behave as if he were mad at the world. He couldn't even drive on errands or back and forth to his job without getting into trouble. In 1989, he was stopped for speeding. The next year he blew a stop sign in Phillipsburg, New Jersey, and was blamed for causing a fender bender. A few months later he was caught breezing through another stop sign. Over the next few years he accumulated more black marks on his driving record for speeding tickets and accidents.

He repeatedly turned the heat off during the winters of 1990 and 1991, Adrienne later recalled in court documents. When he repeated the behavior two years later, she objected that it was too cold in the house, leading her huffy, irritable husband to retaliate by setting the thermostat on eighty. Then, while his wife and the girls sweltered in their bedrooms, he slept in the living room with the window open.

His atrocious behavior was especially humiliating to his wife when he showed off his insensitivity in front of her parents. She was seven months pregnant with her second daughter when they visited Disney World with her parents, and Cullen seemed to go out of his way to ignore and humiliate her. He didn't help her climb on or off buses or demonstrate any awareness that she was on her feet all day and that it was exhausting and difficult for her to get around.

One night, when they gathered to watch a Wild West show, he left the family group. When he returned, he showed more interest in chugging down beers than in the show. He did a lot of that at home, and boozing had become a serious problem for him and for his family. Adrienne eventually acquired some books about Al-Anon, a support group for the families of alcoholics. Cullen was boozing too much; he was profoundly depressed; his marriage and his personal life were in irreversible death spirals. Gravely serious troubles were also beginning to shape up on the job.

Despite Cullen's obvious skills and willingness to accept overtime, some of his colleagues and senior staff members were beginning to be pestered by nettlesome doubts about their colleague's on-the-job behavior. Cullen had worked for St. Barnabas for more than four years when the hospital quietly launched an internal probe into suspicions that someone was tampering with bags of intravenous fluid. He was reprimanded for contaminating an IV bag with insulin.

Used correctly under a doctor's supervision, the medication is a valuable lifesaving drug, but when used improperly, it can cause death through hypoglycemia—low blood sugar. Cullen was not a doctor and he had no authority to be acting on his own and fiddling around with insulin and IV bags. By January 1992, the sinister RN simply was not being called in to work, neither full-time shifts nor an occasional hour here and there. In effect, he was given his walking papers.

Hospital administrators didn't publicly disclose the internal probe, didn't contact police, didn't notify any state or other regulatory agencies, and didn't attempt to have charges filed in the courts against Cullen or anyone else for wrongdoing of any kind. Years later the hospital was still jealously guarding its secrets and admitted to the press only that Cullen left under a cloud, but would not publicly disclose the reason he became persona non grata at St. Barnabas.

After four-and-a-half years at the prestigious northern New Jersey hospital, the strangely moody nurse was free to seek new employment. And his record was clear.

Chapter 4

Dark Clouds

In February, the month after he was eased out or fired from St. Barnabas, Cullen began a challenging new job in the cardiology department at Warren Hospital on Roseberry Street, just east of a bend in the winding Delaware River in Phillipsburg, New Jersey.

Named for the county it was located in, Warren was a nonprofit community hospital with approximately two hundred beds and a reputation for efficiency and the high quality of its services and patient care. Administrators took special pride in the hospital's state-of-the-art cardiology unit, where the newcomer was assigned. The modern hospital in the small town of about fifteen thousand residents, just across the river from Easton, Pennsylvania, was a good place to work.

Cullen seemed to be a valuable employee, and he was appreciated by supervisors and colleagues for his readiness to step in and work an extra shift, or come in early and leave late. He was a workaholic who regularly put in anywhere from twelve to thirty-six hours of overtime per week. That swelled the paychecks, but left him tired, energy-depleted, and an impossible grouch when he was at home.

The family lived in a comfortable, well-kept home on Grand Street in Phillipsburg. By early 1993, however, his already disordered life was in absolute chaos, and the opening weeks of the new year were emotionally devastating. The alcoholic RN and the entire Cullen home were in turmoil.

On January 11, Adrienne filed the first of two complaints with the Phillipsburg Police Department, accusing Cullen of domestic violence. Adrienne's request for a restraining order was later denied by Warren County municipal judge Robert J. Ellwood Jr. The judge observed that her husband was guilty only of odd behavior, not of threatening violence.

On January 15, she filed for divorce. A week later Cullen was at work when he was served with divorce papers.

The marriage had been mired so deeply in the dumps for so long that there was no hope of salvaging it, and Cullen's long-suffering wife had at last decided it was time to give up and cut her losses. She cited the catch-all phrase of "extreme cruelty" as grounds for the action. In the divorce documents Adrienne described her husband's impossible behavior in embarrassing detail, including his fiddling with the thermostat in the winter, the humiliating trip to Disney World, his growing alcoholism; and his three-year refusal to share the marriage bed.

A few days after Cullen was served with divorce papers, Adrienne filed her second domestic violence complaint at the Phillipsburg Police Department. She also filed in the Warren County Municipal Court for a temporary restraining order against her husband because she was afraid that his access to medications at the hospital put her and the girls in danger. On January 25, a Phillipsburg police patrolman wrote in a report: "Ms. Cullen stated that her husband is an alcoholic, had done bizarre things such as placing pets in trash cans, has placed lighter fluid in other persons drinks in the past and recently requested funeral rates from the Finegan Funeral Home." The patrol officer added that the complainant "said her husband has never acted this strange before."

In the complaints the distressed homemaker also accused him of burning his daughters' books in the fireplace. The Al-Anon books were among those confined to flames. But one of the erratic husband's most frightful domestic shenanigans occurred when, according to his wife, he dropped his daughters off at a baby-sitter's home, and didn't return to pick them up for a week.

The harried nurse's inner demons were gathering, and on the last day of the month, he again attempted to end it all by suicide. Like his previous attempts, the effort to kill himself wasn't successful. Instead of a morgue or a funeral home, still very disturbed but very much alive, Cullen was driven to the Muhlenberg Regional Medical Center in Bethlehem and admitted to the behavioral-health unit.

After Cullen was released from Muhlenberg on February 5, he returned to the home on Grand Street, which he had so precariously shared with his wife and daughters, packed a bag, and left. The Cullens never lived together as a family again. His firstborn daughter was four-years-old; the youngest wasn't yet two.

Depression, the suicide attempt, the domestic feuding, and the added complication of the terminal illness of his brother, Edmond, had taken a horrid emotional toll on the embattled RN ever since the new year was ushered in—and the pressures weren't yet about to ease off

In early autumn, approximately nineteen months after Cullen began working in the ICU-CCU, he was plunged knee deep in trouble when Larry Dean told the Warren County prosecutor Thomas S. Ferguson and hospital authorities that the wispy RN, with the hangdog look, murdered his mother.

The retiree was visiting his mother, Helen C. Dean, a cancer patient who had undergone a colectomy, on the afternoon before she was to move into a nursing home for physical rehabilitation, when a skinny male nurse, who looked as insubstantial as a cobweb, sidled into her room. The interloper told him to leave while he tended to the patient. Larry Dean hadn't seen the man in his mother's room before. He was obviously a nurse, although unlike his colleagues on the ICU-CCU, who usually wore blue hospital scrubs, the stranger was dressed totally in white.

When the ninety-one-year-old woman's son returned to the room a few minutes later, she pointed to the nurse as he was leaving and angrily complained, "He stuck me."

Considering her age, Mrs. Dean was an exceptionally vigorous woman, who belonged to a family known for longevity. Before she was hospitalized for her operation, she lived on her own and had expected to return to her home in nearby Lopatcong Township after recuperation. She was bright-eyed and active, had a rollicking sense of humor, and her niece Sharon Jones, of Nazareth, Pennsylvania, later described her to a news reporter as "sharp as a tack." The old woman was hospitalized for a physical problem, and there was nothing wrong with her mind. Larry had no doubt that if his mother said she was given an injection, she knew what she was talking about.

The nurse had left the room when Larry Dean withdrew his Swiss Army knife from his pocket and trained a magnifying glass on his mother's right leg, where she said she was given an injection. A tiny puncture wound was plainly visible through the glass, on the inside of her thigh, exactly where she said it was.

Later that evening when the same nurse entered the room to clear out dinner dishes, the woman again told her son: "That's the man who stuck me."

Mrs. Dean and her son complained to other nurses about the strange man who gave her a shot. Larry, who learned after talking with nurses that his mother wasn't scheduled for an injection, told her oncologist what happened. The doctor confirmed that no injection was authorized.

Larry later identified Cullen to hospital authorities as the RN who administered the unauthorized injection. The nurse's name wasn't difficult for Dean and other members of the family to remember. By a quirk of fate "Cullen" was Helen Dean's middle name. Despite all the questions posed by the curious incident, except for talking with a few other health-care professionals on the ward, nothing substantial was done by hospital authorities about the complaint.

The apparent disinterest continued the day after the incident with the needle when Mrs. Dean became violently ill and vomited just as she was preparing for transfer from the hospital to a nursing home for physical therapy before returning to her own house.

Vomiting is a classic reaction to a digoxin overdose. Irregular or slowed heartbeat, heart palpitations, diarrhea, stomach pain, loss of appetite, unusual weakness or tiredness, drowsiness, confusion, fainting, or changes in vision are other side effects frequently experienced from overdoses of the drug.

Despite Mrs. Dean's advanced age, the irrepressible nonagenarian bounced back from the unexpected stomach upset, and a few hours after she originally was scheduled for transfer, she was loaded into an ambulance and driven to the Care Center of Brakeley Park in Lopatcong Township. She seemed to have rallied well and was enthusiastic about leaving the hospital, but her skin still had an unhealthy green tinge to it. The stomach upset had taken an obvious physical toll on the chipper old woman.

When Mrs. Dean was discharged from the hospital on the afternoon of September 1, 1993, she was listed in stable condition. She was checked into the medical-care facility at 1:15 P.M. and Larry helped her get settled into her room before leaving for her house to pick up something she wanted. Ten minutes later, while her son was away on the errand, she suffered a heart attack and died.

Larry telephoned the county prosecutor that night and

reported that his mother was murdered. He named Cullen as the nurse he believed had given her a fatal injection.

The bereaved son didn't let the matter drop, just because he had brought his suspicions about his mother's death to the attention of the prosecutor. He continued to dig into the mystery on his own, and learned that the nurse not only was not assigned as one of his mother's caregivers, he wasn't even scheduled to work on her floor. Yet the nurse had persisted in hanging around the old woman's room, as if he were monitoring her condition.

Curiously, about a year earlier, Cullen was one of the nurses for Mrs. Dean's ninety-six-year-old sister, Anna Smith, who died at Warren Hospital, on December 22, 1992. Smith was a patient at the Brakeley nursing home when she complained of not feeling well and was rushed to Warren by ambulance a few days before she died.

The elderly sisters weren't the first patients to die at Warren Hospital while under Cullen's care, or after he had ministered to them. But Mrs. Dean's unexpected death was apparently the first one to raise suspicions of possible foul play.

From the beginning of his nursing career, Cullen specialized on working with the most critically ill patients, and his colleagues were reluctant to raise any red flags without good cause when someone died on his watch. Just about everyone who worked with the morose nurse, who padded along the hallways and rooms as silently as cat's paws, thought he was strange. He simply didn't fit in—and he didn't try. He didn't take breaks for meals during his shift, and even when other nurses invited him to chip in and join them ordering take-out pizza, Chinese, or other food, he never took up the offer. He was polite, and always ready to lend a helping hand to colleagues when needed, but he didn't encourage unnecessary conversation or friendly chitchat. Cullen was a loner.

Like Eleanor Stoecker's loved ones at the Somerset Medical Center a decade later, the families of most of the elderly patients who died at the hospital in Phillipsburg grudgingly accepted the inescapable end of life and dealt with their grieving as best they could. There was no cause to suspect that something at Warren Hospital was seriously wrong—or that the lives of their loved ones may have been placed in deadly peril at the hands of one of the health-care professionals counted on to help nurse them back to health. The deceitful, homicidal RN stalking the halls at Warren Hospital took full advantage of that trustful acceptance, to kill.

Personal troubles also continued to pile up for the embattled RN during the next several weeks, as he was battered and bounced from one crises to another. The strain on his already fragile psyche was increasing from all sides. Much of the trouble was his own fault, because at the time he needed it most, he stopped taking medication prescribed for his long-running depression, and he stepped up the pace of his drinking.

A family case manager with the Warren County Family Division assigned to oversee the increasingly chaotic family relationships was sufficiently concerned about the destructive behavior that he urged the out-of-control RN to continue treatment for alcoholism and depression.

"Mr. Cullen requires on-going treatment for alcohol and depression," the caseworker wrote. "Of major concern is that Mr. Cullen states that he loves his children, and I believe this is the case," George Kulanko observed in a report to the court. "However, Mr. Cullen fails to recognize that suicide is the most severe and ultimate form of abuse/neglect, rejection and abandonment one could inflict on one's children." Kulanko recommended that Cullen should be permitted only supervised visits with his children.

The girls' protective mother was scared to death of the prospect of allowing them to stay overnight with their dangerously unbalanced father, and she put up a spirited legal battle to see to it that their visits were supervised and they were kept safe. She said she was afraid he would run off with his daughters, or "impulsively take his life and theirs." Her fears were given alarming credibility, in view of his dismal record reaching back to early childhood of repeated suicide attempts. Cullen temporarily lost visitation privileges with his daughters after his wife filed the domestic-violence complaints, but a judge eventually allowed him to have supervised visits, then to keep the girls overnight.

The domestic war of the Cullens produced a storm of paperwork in the local courts. The documents and in-court statements by Adrienne painted a dreary, at times extremely frightening, picture of life with a lunatic. They clearly showed that family members and relatives weren't the only ones who bore the brunt of his mean-spirited crankiness and hair-trigger temper.

Nasty fusses were an almost everyday event in the Cullen home before their separation. Tracing some of her husband's increasingly macabre and threatening behavior in the divorce papers, Adrienne said he often went to the basement late at night and abused their two Yorkshire terriers. "I was awakened many nights by the screams of these dogs," she wrote. "Charlie was in the basement 'training' and beating them if they did not listen to him." One time her husband became irritated at a puppy named Juliet after the pet peed inside the house and he zipped her up in a bowling bag. Pet hamsters and a ferret mysteriously vanished after Cullen tired of them. Adrienne later found the ferret in a trash can.

Cruelty to animals is a classic trait of serial killers, spree killers, and other especially savage sociopaths, studies by forensic psychologists and other students of the criminal mind show. Milwaukee cannibal Jeffrey Dahmer tortured and impaled frogs and cats on sticks; Ted "the Troller" Bundy boasted of tormenting small animals; "Son of Sam" killer David Berkowitz stuck pins in his mother's goldfish, and later shot a neighbor's dog; Lee Boyd Malvo, the teenage member of the "Washington Sniper" duo, hated cats and attacked them with slingshots; San Diego schoolhouse shooter Brenda Spencer set the tails of dogs and cats on fire; and Kip Kinkel, who murdered his parents, then shot up his Springfield, Oregon, high school, killed small animals and bragged about stuffing lit firecrackers into the mouths of cats, squirrels, and chipmunks.

A family court employee who interviewed Adrienne quoted her as saying Cullen liked animals, but when the novelty wore off, "he disappears them." His behavior blew hot and cold. At times he was attentive and loving to his daughters and family pets, and at other times he did horrible things like killing the ferret—or swallowed a handful of pills, then flopped onto the floor like he was dying. His wife finally got rid of the pets to keep her callous, alcoholic husband from continuing to mistreat or kill them.

In one of her court filings Adrienne shared her own personal diagnosis of the husband she had previously labeled a dangerous alcoholic, by describing him as a "borderline" personality. Quoting from a medical manual, she observed that many borderline personalities "'may show flashes of promise, stability and achievement, but these periods usually are either short-lived or dependent on the presence of a highly tolerant social system.'" Continuing, she related: "'The borderline patient goes round in circles, covering the same ground as before, getting nowhere and then starting all over again.'"

To anyone who knew much about her husband, the description did, indeed, sound a lot like him. She may have been onto something, although in his own court filings he denied most of the accusations and claimed his wife was lying and exaggerating in efforts to convince the court to keep him from his children.

The pressure on Cullen's already fragile psyche was increasing from all sides. As his emotions were frayed and his mental health was unraveling, he turned with savage force on the only people he could exert any control over: helpless patients.

The RN was a primary nurse assigned to help care for two elderly Phillipsburg grandmothers who died at Warren

Hospital within a few weeks of each other after their previously vigorous health unexpectedly deteriorated. Both
Lucy Mugavero and Mary Natoli were the daughters of Italian immigrants and worked hard all their lives.

The first to die was ninety-year-old Lucy Mugavero, who
was deeply loved by her family and would be remembered
as a kind, gentle old lady. Visitors had left for their homes,
and the hospital hallways and wards were quiet and bathed
in the steely gray of the nighttime gloom when Cullen
padded into the elderly woman's room and silently slipped
a lethal dose of the heart stimulant, digoxin, into her intravenous line.

Cullen had developed a murder technique that he followed often throughout his seamy career as a medical
murderer. Once he decided to kill, he usually waited until
visitors left for the night; then, while protectively cupping
a syringe in his hand, he would creep quietly into the
room and approach the patient stretched out on the bed.
The hidden syringe contained enough stolen medication
to throw the patient into a "code blue" emergency or stop
the heart.

Code blues, or "coding out," is hospital lingo for the
alarm sounded when a patient lapses into cardiac arrest.
When that happens, a highly skilled team of medical professionals, which typically includes a cardiologist, anesthesiologist, resident doctor, and intensive-care unit nurses,
rush to the patient to begin resuscitation attempts. Nothing
is more serious or critical on a hospital ward than a code
blue. Cullen was responsible for countless such emergencies.

If IVs or medicine bags were hooked up to the patient,
he inserted the needle into a port on the device. Then he
slipped back out of the room while the toxic medication
drained down through the plastic tube into the patient's
body, as it did with Mugavero. If there was no bag, he killed
by directly injecting the patient, as he did after the Mugavero
and Natoli murders when he took the life of Mrs. Dean.

Drugs were relatively easy to obtain early in his career,

by raiding drawers or closets where medications were kept for patients. Most hospitals didn't even keep close track of the drugs. In later years as electronic dispensing systems were adopted to tighten up medication surveillance and controls, obtaining unauthorized drugs became more difficult. Cullen worked out his own techniques for sidestepping the new electronic gadgets.

Grandma Mugavero was one of eight siblings who lived into their nineties, and included a brother who eventually topped the century mark, when she took an alarming turn for the worse and died on March 9, 1993. As a young woman and later as a wife, mother, and homemaker, she worked in a pocketbook factory and in the garment industry as a seamstress.

Her life was hard and she raised three children almost on her own, relatives later recalled, and even in her later years she was always available to her family for help and advice. She was a classic hardworking, self-sacrificing Italian grandmother.

Mrs. Mugavero was still relatively healthy for a woman of her age when she was admitted to Warren Hospital for tests and treatment of a minor lung ailment. On the night she died, the spunky woman told the wife of her grandson Phillip Mugavero that she wanted to come home. One of eight grandchildren, Phillip Mugavero was chairman of the Delaware River Joint Toll Bridge Commission, and a former mayor of Phillipsburg. His grandmother's sudden death was unexpected and came as a shock, but like other members of the family, the loss after such a long, fruitful, and giving life was accepted as natural. He figured she simply died of old age, and no one suspected foul play. There was no autopsy.

Mary Natoli was the next to die at the hands of the maladjusted misfit health-care professional. The eighty-five-year-old grandmother and retired silk-mill worker had symptoms of Alzheimer's disease and was a resident of the Brakeley Park Center nursing home in Phillipsburg when she was checked into Warren Hospital for tests and treatment for anxiety. She was feeling chipper and chatting with visitors and nurses. Then, according to an entry Cullen scribbled on her medical chart, he treated her with the antinausea drug Compazine because she was vomiting. Helen Dean would also vomit shortly before she died.

Cullen was working a day shift and before leaving his workstation and checking out at 6:00 P.M. he noted on Natoli's chart that the patient was "resting comfortably." Her condition suddenly worsened, then turned critical. A few hours later, on July 23, 1993, she was dead. The medication injected into her IV wasn't antinausea medicine. It was the same heart stimulant the RN used to kill Mrs. Mugavero. And like Mugavero, no autopsy was ordered because there seemed to be no reason to believe there was anything unnatural about Natoli's death.

While patients were dying unexpectedly on Cullen's watch, his lifelong depression was at its worst, and his private life was a depressing morass of domestic, romantic, and financial crises. Everything that could go wrong went wrong, and he was bounced from one frustrating and confusing predicament to another. He had trouble paying his bills, trouble with women, trouble with the law, and trouble with his mental health. When he lagged behind in his child support payments, he was dragged into court and a judgment was ordered against him.

Cullen's bizarre behavior with women was only making things worse, and when he developed an obsession with a female nurse he worked with, then refused to take no for an answer, he wound up trying to explain things that had nothing to do with mysterious patient deaths to police and to a judge.

Michelle Tomlinson had no interest in a romance with her weird colleague, but that didn't stop him from developing a morbid fixation on her and a manic desire to forge a significant relationship. She turned a firm thumbs-down when he attempted to give her an engagement ring, so Cullen began to stalk her. He followed her around, pestered her with repeated telephone calls, and left messages on her answering machine—even though she made it as clear as she possibly could that she had no romantic interest in the creepy thirty-three-year-old male nurse.

While the frustrated suitor was relentlessly pursuing Tomlinson, Lucy Mugavero died. Two weeks after killing the Italian grandmother, sometime in the early-morning hours before dawn, Cullen broke into the home of the reluctant object of his affection.

Tomlinson reportedly already had gotten back together with a former boyfriend, and she and her six-year-old son were sleeping when he shattered the glass in a window in the kitchen door of her Palmer Township, Pennsylvania, house in the middle of a crisply cold early-spring night in 1993. When the woman awoke, she discovered the door glass shattered, and other evidence that someone had been creeping around inside the house. Nothing was stolen, but some of her personal property had been shifted around.

The male nurse's menacing, off-the-wall behavior was chilling. The idea of someone prowling around her darkened house while she slept was every woman's nightmare. Tomlinson reported the eerie incident to the Palmer Township Police Department and a tap was placed on her telephone line.

Cullen phoned the woman later that morning and admitted he was the midnight skulker. He was proud of prowling around inside her house while she slept. "I wanted to check on you. You know, to make sure you were okay, that you did not try anything—like suicide," he blithely explained. The woman was no more interested in committing suicide than she was in carrying on a romance with the male nurse who was stalking her.

When police officers telephoned Cullen, he couldn't have been more cooperative. He drove straight to the police station, admitted he had a fantasy that he and his female colleague were romantically linked, and told investigators the whole story. Cullen submitted meekly while his fingers were inked, then rolled on a stiff white fingerprint card, and stood quietly staring into space while mug shots were taken. Then he was arraigned on felony charges, advised that he would be notified of a court date, and released.

It was Tuesday morning, March 23, 1993, just two weeks after the unexpected death of Mrs. Mugavero at Warren Hospital.

The emotional toll of the dreadful divorce and custody battle with his wife already had Cullen slumped on the ropes, and when his obsessive pursuit of the other nurse backfired and got him into trouble with the police, he was left woozy and staggering.

The day after his arrest, while he was still living in the brick Cape Cod, Cullen tried to deliver his own knockout punch and end it all with another suicide attempt. An ambulance crew rushed him to Warren Hospital, where he was treated by colleagues in the emergency room and the intensive-care unit. After his condition improved sufficiently to allow him to be moved, he was admitted to the Carrier Clinic, a 281-bed psychiatric hospital in Belle Mead, New Jersey. The clinic was one of two facilities in Somerset County that provided inpatient behavioral and mental-health services for such conditions as depression, acute anxiety, suicidal tendencies, and similar disorders. The other was the Somerset Medical Center in nearby Somerville.

Cullen eventually took two-months medical leave from his job while being treated at Carrier and at an older and larger New Jersey state institution in Parsippany, the Greystone Park Psychiatric Hospital.

While he was on leave, authorities at Warren Hospital notified him that they could offer only temporary work after he completed his psychiatric care. Hospital spokesmen explained much later that an employee couldn't be fired because of mental illness any more than he could be fired because he was recovering from cancer. That would be discrimination.

Police detectives contacted Cullen's supervisor at Warren and asked that he be kept away from Tomlinson. The hospital complied, and his schedule was organized carefully to ensure that he didn't work with the woman. Otherwise, the hospital took the attitude that the trouble between the two nurses occurred outside the work environment, and was not something the administration should overly concern itself about.

Cullen had been locked in a vicious divorce and custody battle, attempted suicide, broke into a woman's house, was arrested by police, corresponded with judges, interviewed by court-appointed psychiatrists, submitted to inpatient treatment by additional psychiatrists, advised by mental-health counselors, met with probation officers, and talked with lawyers.

Despite all the chaos swirling around him, the RN, known for having such a tenuous hold on his fragile mental health, was back at work as a critical-care nurse, a job that was widely recognized as one of the most stressful, pressure-intensive, and emotionally draining positions in the health-care field. He was still being treated for depression, and he was working all the extra hours he could sign on for at the same hospital where he was so recently rushed as an emergency-room patient.

Cullen and his estranged wife continued to skirmish bitterly over the terms of the impending divorce, and at one point, in what years later would stand out as an amazingly prescient observation, she expressed concern over his returning to work as a critical-care nurse so soon after release from two mental-health facilities.

Cullen was experiencing a critical money crunch, and apparently none of the mental-health professionals he dealt with, no one in the courts, and no one at the hospital stepped forward to apply the brakes when he threw himself so wholeheartedly into his work.

Expenses from his legal troubles and the latest suicide try exasperated his already serious financial burden. Under different circumstances his long work hours and high annual earnings would have supported an upper-middle-class lifestyle, but the harried nurse's finances were a mess. No matter how many overtime hours he worked, it was increasingly difficult to keep up with his child support payments, alimony, and other financial responsibilities. He had trouble merely paying his rent, even after moving out of the Cape Cod and into a more modest basement apartment on Shafer Avenue in another quiet, working-class Phillipsburg neighborhood. For a while he tried living off his credit cards, but in the end that only piled up new debts and made matters worse.

Soon after he moved in, his estranged wife complained to Phillipsburg police that she believed the new apartment was a danger to her children because it was a fire hazard and their father was known to slip inside the boiler room and light candles, then drink booze he kept in a footlocker. Fire code inspectors checked out the apartment for violations of fire codes or hazards. They didn't find a single violation.

The harried RN decided to represent himself in the criminal court case stemming from the harassment and stalking of his female colleague. Then he had a change of heart and filed an application in the Northampton County Court for a public defender. He listed expenses of more than $2,000 a month, without factoring in such necessities as food, clothing, shelter, transportation, and other personal costs for his own survival. The biggest chunk taken from his monthly pay was $1,460 for child support. He also listed minimum-balance credit card payments of $346, and $300 in monthly payments for psychiatric care. The request was denied.

He wasn't an easy client to represent, and when a lawyer bailed out of the case, Cullen wrote a scathing, somewhat meandering and confusing missive to the judge comparing the attorney's professionalism with his own professionalism as a nurse. In Cullen's tortured reasoning the lawyer came off a distant second best: "As a nurse I can only refer professionalism to me because of a difficult client refusing my services, or a surgeon half-way operating and then closing up and saying get another surgeon."

Cullen wound up pleading guilty in the Northampton County Court to a scaled-down second-degree misdemeanor charge of defiant trespass and was sentenced to one year of probation. He was also ordered to pay $220 in court costs and, in accordance with Tomlinson's request, was ordered to stay away from her.

Cullen offered a mealymouthed defense of his behavior at the plea hearing by saying of the complainant: "I was concerned for her well-being and her safety, Your Honor, and I have never in my life intentionally tried to inflict any distress or harm on anyone."

No one at the time came close to suspecting what a monstrous perversion of the truth the defendant was manufacturing with his outrageous cock-and-bull story. He also told senior judge Alfred T. Williams Jr. that he was undergoing counseling at the Family Guidance Center in Phillipsburg, and was hospitalized twice for depression. The treatment included his four-week stay at the Carrier Clinic, and three weeks at Gracedale in Northampton County.

A few days after the case appeared to have been settled, Cullen changed his mind about the guilty plea and filed an appeal. Once more representing himself, he filled pages with laboriously handwritten motions, with his unique misspellings and errors in grammar, insisting that he hadn't stalked the female nurse: "Their was a sexual intamate relationship between Michelle Tomlinson and myself," he wrote in one statement.

While all that was going on, Cullen was prowling the hallways and busily drifting in and out of patients' rooms at Warren Hospital, checking vital signs, hooking up IVs, passing out medication and generally tending to the critically ill.

Helen Dean died unexpectedly three weeks after he was convicted in the trespassing case.

Trouble was coming at Cullen from every direction, and he was bending, almost breaking under the strain. He recalled years later that he worried about the terrible things he was doing, the lives he was taking, the families he was cheating out of treasured experiences and memories, and about the noble, unselfish profession that he was betraying and so unfairly soiling. He considered getting out of nursing, but he knew that he could never find another job that would pay as well and money was a constant worry.

There was also the old lure of self-destruction, and he thought about using some of the stolen medications on himself instead of injecting it into the IVs and medicine bags of helpless patients. Curiously, although he had tried to commit suicide so many times in so many ways, he couldn't bring himself to use the same method he used so efficiently on other people to kill himself.

Digoxin, his drug of choice for committing murder, would almost certainly have done the job, and it was known to be a favorite of suicidal people. Another reputed Death Angel was believed to have used digoxin at a Toronto hospital in 1981 to kill eight babies, who were found with elevated levels of the drug in their systems. Yet, some quixotic glitch in Cullen's troubled mind—perhaps linked to the brother who died of a narcotics overdose—wouldn't allow him to use his favorite murder weapon to kill himself because he didn't want his daughters to know that he committed suicide with drugs or stolen hospital property.

So he was stuck with his troubles: the horrible, draining struggle over the divorce and his daughters, money problems, and the destructive fits of depression that had plagued him all of his life.

At the moment the most immediately disturbing and persistently vexatious of his troubles was the exasperating ruckus over the elderly Lopatcong woman's suspicious death. It continued to plague him, and Larry Dean, the patient's son, installed himself at the center of the tempest.

Dean's persistent complaints led to an internal investigation launched by the hospital administration, and to an inquiry by the Warren County prosecutor. At the family's request an autopsy was ordered on the old woman.

Larry Dean hired an attorney, talked with nurses, and when he got together with other family members, including his cousin Sharon Jones, they agreed that laboratory tests should be conducted on his mother's blood and tissue for the presence of a powerful heart drug, digoxin. Dean asked his lawyer to contact the prosecutor and request the test. But somehow, a family member later recalled, the request didn't reach the prosecutor. It was never passed on to the pathologists.

Warren County medical examiner Dr. Isadore Mihalakis was out of town, so the procedure was performed by another doctor. As part of an extensive toxicological scan ordered by Dr. Mihalakis, laboratory tests were conducted on Mrs. Dean's tissue, blood, and other body fluids for one hundred possible toxic chemicals, but it didn't turn up anything especially suspicious. Digoxin wasn't one of the drugs the blood and tissue were tested for.

Cullen was mentioned twice in the autopsy report, once by name, and the other time as the "male nurse" whose behavior was so unsettling to the patient and to her son. But the meticulously conducted necropsy was inconclusive.

Larry Dean remained convinced that his mother was murdered by the weaselly little nurse who crept in and out of the rooms of elderly or gravely ill patients, doing who knew what while they were helpless to resist. At her funeral the heartbroken son placed his hand on her coffin and tearfully vowed to find out exactly what caused her death, and if foul play was involved, as he firmly believed it was, to see to it that the killer was brought to justice. Then her body was laid to rest beside the grave of her husband, Mark Dean Jr. in the Fairmount Cemetery in Phillipsburg.

The investigation wasn't over after the necropsy, and detectives probing the troubling death even talked with Cullen's estranged wife, Adrienne. The alarming development added to her concern for the safety of her daughters whenever they were visiting with the ominously menacing man who was their father. "When homicide detectives came to my place of employment to speak to me about Mr. Cullen and an investigation regarding the poisoning of a patient," she wrote in a family court statement, "this has a bearing on my children."

Cullen and several other nurses who had contact with Mrs. Dean were questioned by investigators from the prosecutor's office about the suspicious death and he was hooked up to a polygraph. He was the only male in the group and the only nurse given a lie detector test. Like the autopsy, it was inconclusive.

Cullen and his female colleagues appeared to be in the clear, although both the medical examiner and prosecutor confirmed that no doctor had given orders for the shot injected into the woman's thigh the afternoon before she left the hospital for the nursing home.

Cullen's behavior was extremely troubling, because the investigation indicated that he was almost certainly the person who had given the injection to the patient—and he wasn't even her assigned nurse. He had his own patients to care for. But there was no solid proof that he had carried out such a serious violation of hospital protocol, and the twin inquiry sputtered out. The New Jersey Board of Nursing wasn't informed about Cullen's prominent role in the investigation into the suspicious death because the probe ended without any charges filed.

During the tumultuous months Cullen worked at Warren Hospital, his life had been a weird roller-coaster ride of personal and professional catastrophes. He was arrested and convicted of a misdemeanor after stalking and breaking into the home of a female colleague; he attempted suicide; his marriage broke up; he was given psychiatric treatment in two institutions; he became mired up to his hips in the mess over a patient who died shortly after she was injected with an unauthorized medication.

Yet, despite all the evidence of serious mental dysfunction and suspicions of serious criminal behavior at the hospital, no steps were taken to fire him and he continued to work with some of the most feeble, critically ill, and helpless patients. Although it would seem to be obvious that nurses with psychiatric problems might be dangerous to patients, no one filed a report with the New Jersey Board of Nursing about the unstable RN.

Unlike hospital authorities and local law enforcement, Larry Dean refused to wash his hands of the matter. He was devastated by his mother's suspicious death, and dissatisfied with the inconclusive results of the twin inquiry. Everyone involved knew that his mother was given an unauthorized injection of some medicine that wasn't prescribed for her; the puncture wound was evident on her thigh, and she identified the person who gave her the shot—an emaciated-appearing male nurse who was frightful and sinister-looking.

So, he continued digging into the suspicious death, talking with former colleagues of Cullen's, scanning his mother's autopsy report for clues, collecting boxes of documents and other files, and pressing everyone he could think of for more information. Dean even stored samples of his mother's tissue in his home freezer, so it would be readily available if the time ever came to take another, closer look at exactly how she died—and at whose hands.

The grieving, tenacious son complained for years that the hospital administration dragged its feet and provided little help, but his bulldog determination to bring his mother's killer to justice never flagged. He kept close track of Cullen's spotty career and recorded his every job change. He was constantly on the watch for new information or a fatal misstep that would prove the depraved and dysfunctional RN was a cold-blooded murderer.

Dean became Cullen's police inspector Javert, but he was no vindictive fictional sleuth pursuing the hungry thief Jean Valjean in Victor Hugo's classic novel *Les Misérables*. He was as substantial and real as the tombstone over his mother's grave at Fairmount Cemetery. And he made the fight to bring her killer to justice a personal crusade.

A few people who knew the Dean family may have clucked among themselves that he was letting his bereavement lead to the wrong conclusions and take over his life. He was wasting his time, they may have said, but he continued plugging away, doggedly seeking the silver bullet that would provide the breakthrough he sought. He was stubborn and hell-bent on setting the record straight. He refused to give up.

On a day honored by Americans in remembrance of the devastating 1941 Japanese attack on Pearl Harbor that dragged the nation into a world war, Cullen's attention was riveted on more personal matters. On Tuesday, December 7, 1993—more than a half century after the national tragedy in Hawaii—his divorce became final.

Family court judge William R. Albrech awarded physical custody of the couple's daughters to their mother. The order provided for Cullen to share joint legal custody with his ex-wife, the right to play an active role in decisions relating to the health and education of the girls, and to have unsupervised visits with them. The beleaguered nurse represented himself in the family court action.

Making the divorce official and awarding of a personal restraining order to keep Cullen away from Adrienne didn't mean an end to the bitter domestic skirmishing between the former husband and wife. The ongoing duel over child support and visitation with the two girls was particularly caustic. Adrienne was worried about the welfare of her daughters, and their safety, and in family court documents she outlined her concern about placing children in the care of someone with such unpredictable moods: "especially not as they sleep when they will be extremely defenseless and unaware." Observations about Cullen's alcoholism, repeated suicide attempts, volatile temper, and unpredictable behavior all found their way into the bulging file.

In a series of laboriously handwritten, frequently misspelled, and poorly constructed filings and letters to judges during the next few years, the scrawny RN denied various accusations and claims made by Adrienne in the divorce suit and in the ongoing contest over the children. Referring to his wife's open concern about his return to duties as a critical-care nurse so soon after receiving psychiatric care, he wrote: "No concern about my ability to handle stressful work or patients in a crital [*sic*] care setting existed."

His ex-wife was motivated by a selfish desire to keep him away from his daughters, he argued. Cullen said doctors at Greystone Park felt he was capable of returning to his job, and that their conclusion wasn't "something that would be recommended lightly. At no time," he declared, "did they not recommend or suggest that I could not return to (the) high stress field dealing with the care of sick adults, infants, adolescents."

Responding in another filing to the observation of a court-appointed psychiatrist that his frequent efforts to commit suicide were "the ultimate form of child abandonment," he admitted being bothered by depression most of his life, but he insisted that he wasn't a threat to the girls.

"That I have a history of depression is true, was true when I married Adrienne, served in the Navy, finished nursing school. The fact is I have never, even in 1993 when my depression was at its worst, never placed my children in danger, never stopped loving them, never cut them off emotionally," he wrote.

Claiming in another entry that his ex-wife didn't understand why he fought so desperately to increase visits with his daughters, he wrote in another entry: "The simple fact is that I love my children."

Adrienne hadn't forgotten the visit from detectives and was suspicious about the role her ex-husband may have played in Mrs. Dean's death, according to statements he filed as part of his plea to regain more generous visitation rights with his daughters. Even with a favorable report from a detective "and the coroner stating the death was cancer," he wrote, "Adrienne still does not believe."

Cullen could write just about anything he wished to write in his court filings, but he couldn't as easily plead his case to colleagues at the hospital. Even though no charges were filed against him in Mrs. Dean's death, and apparently no one yet thought there was anything amiss involving the deaths of the two Italian-American grandmothers months earlier, he had been cast under a permanent cloud of suspicion. He was closely watched, especially when interacting with patients.

The bizarre night-shift nurse, who mumbled to himself and floated through the cavernous hospital halls, frightened his female colleagues. He made them uncomfortable when he was around, and some of the nurses made no bones about their desire to have as little to do with him as possible. No one wanted to work with him.

On December 1, shortly before the year-end holidays, and about two months after he successfully humbugged the polygraph test, Cullen resigned from his job at Warren Hospital. He worked there for approximately ten months, nursing some gravely ill patients back to better health—while playing God and coldly selecting others for an untimely death.

Chapter 5

A Life in Free Fall

Wild violets, crocuses, blossoming dandelions, and other spring flowers were spreading brilliant splashes of yellow, purple, blue, and white in the woodlot fields, pastures, and parks around Flemington, New Jersey, when Cullen finally snagged a job there at the Hunterdon Medical Center. Fields and flower gardens in the "Garden State" were blooming and bursting with fresh new life. It was April, and the homicidal nurse had been out of work for four months.

The quiet Delaware River Valley community of Flemington in Raritan Township, with some four thousand residents, was even more small-town than Phillipsburg; it was more rural and comfortably insulated from the big-city problems of noise and air pollution, rush-hour traffic tie-ups, and rampant crime. It had all the advantages of small-town life with downtown parades, local beauty queens, and hay rides, as well as its own active artists community. Just outside of town the Flemington Speedway even offered the vicarious excitement of watching local boys test their driving skills against competitors from other nearby towns and cities. The shower of vegetables and other fresh produce that moved through the small farming communities in the rich, fertile Delaware River Valley were one of the reasons New Jersey is known as the Garden State.

For those who wanted more, the advantage of good highways offered easy access to the clutter of small and midsize cities of Allentown, Bethlehem, and Easton to Cullen's home in Phillipsburg on the New Jersey side of the urban scatter, a matter of no more than a few minutes' drive. Philadelphia, with its historical buildings, art museums, fine restaurants, and professional sports teams—the Phillies, Eagles, Flyers, and the 76ers—was a bare sixty miles away. Surrounded by rolling woods and farmland, Flemington was a perfect place to slow down and soothe badly frayed emotions.

Hunterdon Medical Center (HMC), named for the county it was in, was a comfortably appealing place to work. Located on the town's outskirts, Hunterdon Medical was a 176-bed nonprofit community hospital with its own family-practice-residency program for physicians. Facilities in the complex of modern buildings offered a full range of inpatient and outpatient health-care services, including an up-to-date cancer-care center and intensive/coronary-care unit.

Cullen passed through Hunterdon's normal vetting routine. His license was checked to make sure it was up-to-date, and his background to verify dates of previous employment. Everything reported back to the hospital was positive—or at worst, not negative. No black marks were turned up on his record. That wasn't surprising, since it was hospital policy not to delve too deep into the background of prospective employees. Cullen was hired and assigned to the ICU-CCU. As usual, he worked with some of the most gravely ill patients.

It seemed for a while that Hunterdon Medical Center, the friendly, efficient coworkers, and the fresh country air were good for him.

From all indications the self-appointed executioner

allowed death to take a brief holiday. Or at the very least he didn't immediately reach out to help the Grim Reaper in the dismal task of harvesting new souls. If the homicidal nurse indeed killed during his first year and a half at Hunterdon, the murders were accomplished with such cunning and guile that no one became suspicious enough to question the deaths openly.

The lapse in the violence, if that is what it was, may have been because the Death Angel was faithfully taking his medication, a lessening of financial pressures, a quieter, less tempestuous personal life, or any number of other factors. But regardless of what it was that temporarily quieted the murderous instinct, when he resumed his killing ways, the slaughter was more fierce and destructive than ever before. The brief respite from killing was like the calm before the storm.

About six months after he began working at Hunterdon, colleagues presented him with an award for his diligence and hard work. It read: "In appreciation for Grace Under Fire to Charles Cullen at (Hunterdon Medical Center) ICU. For all the night shifts you helped out on. Thanks!"

The pleased recipient later cited the award during one of his pleas in court seeking overnight visits with his daughters.

In June 1994 he even obtained a Pennsylvania nursing license to go with his New Jersey credentials. Licenses in both states were good for two years before renewals were required. Years later, authorities were unable to determine if he mentioned his conviction for defiant trespass in a space on the form asking applicants if they were ever convicted of a misdemeanor or a felony. A few weeks after his application was processed, it was destroyed in an accidental fire.

As it had when he returned to part-time work at Warren Hospital after treatment for depression, fear of possible lawsuits over accusations of discrimination also continued to work in the psychotic RN's favor. There was nothing in the application for the Pennsylvania license that inquired about mental illness. It would have been discriminatory to do such a thing, so a man with a criminal conviction and whose mental history clearly showed his propensity for lapsing into madness wound up with new credentials. He had a green light to practice nursing in two states.

Early in the new year of 1996 the old disturbing pattern of patients who appeared to be recovering or holding their own suddenly taking critical turns for the worse and dying on Cullen's watch began occurring once more. After the finalization of his divorce on December 7, 1994, there was only a brief respite before his life began to get complicated again. He was still fighting to win overnight visitation rights with his daughters when he became romantically involved with a married co-worker. Recalling the affair years later, Cullen said he had fallen in love with her, and claimed she talked about dumping her husband and marrying him. The rogue RN had a long history of difficulty coping with the emotional bumps and bruises that were part and parcel of his relationships with women, and of responding to the pressure with irrationally destructive acts.

On January 21, 1996, Leroy G. Sinn died in the Hunterdon Medical Center's ICU, after he was given an unprescribed dose of digoxin. The seventy-one-year-old patent attorney was a native Hoosier and graduate of the Indiana University School of Law, who lived in Massachusetts and Washington, D.C., before settling down in Hunterdon county's Tewksbury Township seventeen-years earlier. A father of four, and an elder at the Lamington Presbyterian Church, at the time of his death Sinn still maintained a private law practice.

On May 31, seventy-five-year-old Earl A. Young died of a digoxin overdose. The father of two daughters and a grandfather of three, Young had worked 15 years as a stock clerk at the Flemington Cut Glass store. An eight-year U.S. Navy veteran of World War II and it's immediate aftermath, he was born in Clinton, New Jersey and lived in a private residence in Flemington before moving into Cooper's Home for the Aged there in 1989.

On June 9, forty-nine-year-old Catherine Dext died after being administered an unprescribed dose of digoxin. A native of New York City, she had worked for eighteen-years at the Edna Mahan Correctional Facility for Women in Clinton, New Jersey's only prison for females. Dext began working in food services, quit after nine years, then returned in 1989, and in 1993 was promoted to supervisor, a position she held until her death.

On July 24, sixty-five-year-old Frank J. Mazzacco, Jr. died of a digoxin overdose. A former elementary and special education teacher at public schools in Trenton, who retired in 1989, Mazzacco had lived in New Jersey's capital city for 30 years before moving to nearby Lambertville.

On July 10, eighty-year-old Jesse W. Eichlin died after he was given an unprescribed dose of digoxin. Eichlin was a loyal member of the Quakertown Methodist Church and was there among his friends over the July 4 weekend when he passed out, was given CPR by a member of the congregation, then was rushed to the hospital. A man of the soil, Eichlin grew up on a Franklin Township farm and spent his life farming and working as a carpenter. He served as a scoutmaster of Boy Scout Troop 108, and for years was active with the Quakertown Volunteer Fire Company. Widowed by the death of his wife, Bertha, in 1997, he was the father of three and had four grandchildren.

Although four of the five patients died within a six-week period, they had all been seriously ill, were being treated in the ICU, and there seemed to be no reason to believe any of them may have been speeded on their way to the hereafter by a nurse, or by any other hospital employee.

Cullen had managed to keep himself reasonably clear of suspicion of serious wrongdoing at the HMC for almost two-and-a-half years, until October 1996, when his girlfriend told him that she was returning to her husband. Stung by the development, he reacted by resigning from his job at the hospital on the same day he learned the disappointing news. The disillusioned RN quickly realized that the impetuous act may have been a serious mistake. He liked working at the HMC, but when he asked for his job back, hospital authorities told him they were allowing his resignation to stand. Cullen later said he believed he was denied a second chance on the job in part because people at the hospital knew about the romantic affair.

By November he was working at Morristown Memorial Hospital in Morristown, New Jersey, closer to his childhood home. The hospital had a policy of conducting criminal background checks on all employees, but typical of the industry, reference checks were cursory. The process was basically confined to verifying dates of employment, and Cullen was cleared to begin his new job.

Although the population of Phillipsburg, where Cullen continued to live, was about the same as Morristown, the new commute between home and work brought Cullen back to the congested edge of the big-city urban sprawl radiating out from New York City that the peripatetic RN had known in his youth. Morristown was a big change from the soothing, rural calm of Flemington and Hunterdon County. Once more, the Big Apple was as close as the shrill siren of a fire engine or the wail of an ambulance rushing an accident victim or a patient with a heart attack to the Morristown Memorial Hospital emergency room.

Cullen didn't last a year in the new job. In August 1997, he was fired for "poor job performance." Like authorities at St. Barnabas, no one at Morristown Memorial bothered to notify the New Jersey Board of Nursing.

It was years later before Cullen told investigators he was fired for what he described as making an honest mistake when he stopped giving heparin, an anticoagulant, to a patient who was supposed to remain on the medication. During his brief stint at Morristown he was also twice written up, or given bad reports, by supervisors for other infractions. One time he got into trouble for tampering with oxygen settings on ventilators. The other time he didn't follow a doctor's order to discontinue a sedative for a patient.

The brief respite in killing while the homicidal RN worked at the hospitals in Flemington and at Morristown may have been because he was faithfully taking his medication, a lessening of financial pressures, a less tempestuous personal life, a sharp-eyed colleague or supervisor becoming alarmed by suspicious behavior, or by any number of other factors. But regardless of what it was that temporarily quieted the murderous instinct, when Cullen resumed his killing ways, the slaughter was more fierce and destructive than ever before.

His life had been in free fall for years while he continued his peripatetic travels between jobs in hospitals in the Garden State, and unemployment added to his woes. He was way behind in child support payments, and was running up huge credit card balances that he couldn't pay. His erratic behavior, already strange and troubling, became even more bizarre.

One of the few activities other than faithfully taking his antidepressant medication—which he wasn't very good at doing—that had a calming influence on him was being with his daughters and puttering around in a little backyard garden he planted at his basement apartment. He erected birdhouses, planted trees and flowers, weeded, watered and fussed over them, and the garden thrived. The monster, who stalked and cruelly murdered hospital patients at work, had a green thumb. Alone in his flower beds or playing with his daughters on treasured weekend visits, he nurtured and encouraged life.

During periods when visits by the girls were permitted, he climbed into whichever beat-up, old jalopy he owned and made the long round-trip drive every week or so between Phillipsburg and Roselle Park, where they lived with their mother a few miles south of his childhood home in West Orange. The girls often played in the yard while he fussed over his trees and flowers, or watched and listened while he tutored them in the mysteries of making plants thrive and grow.

He liked having animals around, but his behavior with pets continued to be strangely ambivalent. After acquiring a pet he treated them well initially, but eventually began to abuse them through either neglect or deliberate mistreatment.

Cullen was still quiet and withdrawn, and most of his neighbors who paid any attention knew they were most likely to get a smile or some other pleasant acknowledgment of their presence when he was among his flowers or building birdhouses. Gardening and feeding birds outside the Shafer Avenue apartment may have been one of his last anchors to sanity. The modest stone apartment would be his home for the next ten years, while he bounced from one job to another in seven counties in two states.

As the amateur gardener fussily tended to his tidy flower beds, he inexorably sank back into the depression and madness that had stalked him all of his life. As he grew more disturbed, his neighbors were more likely to be deliberately ignored than acknowledged with a friendly greeting, or to have him make ugly, mocking faces at them behind their backs as they walked away. At night neighbors became used to hearing the fuss when the RN streaked across the darkened lawn, yelling and chasing any house cat that showed the bad judgment of hanging around the apartments.

He didn't like the outdoors in the crisp winters as much as he enjoyed gardening in better weather, and often neglected to shovel the snow off his walks. Cullen became agitated and defensive when neighbors complained about the unshoveled snow. He claimed that no one liked him and the neighborhood was conspiring against him. He bought another ferret and had a dog for a while, until someone alerted animal-welfare authorities that he kept it chained outside for hours in bitterly cold weather and it was taken away from him.

In the summer and the winter he irked his neighbors with his habit of parking his car in front of their driveways.

Some of the older children in the neighborhood coined the nickname "Crash" for him because of his propensity for driving home with paint scrapes or fresh bumps and dents on his car.

He was out of work two months when he was treated in the emergency room at Warren Hospital for depression and got into a nasty confrontation with a doctor. The fracas erupted when the emergency-room doctor Howard Swidler told him he needed to provide a blood sample for tests. Cullen was going to be sent to the Greystone Park Psychiatric Hospital in northern New Jersey, and it was established policy that blood work had to be conducted on patients before transportation to the mental-health facility. Cullen noisily resisted before finally conceding and submitting to having a sample of his blood drawn. Then the patient was bundled into an ambulance and driven to Greystone Park in Parsippany. He was already familiar with the mental hospital and the routine from his earlier stay there following the suicide attempt stemming from his obsessive pursuit of his co-worker at Warren and his arrest in the trespassing case.

Greystone was a dinosaur out of the nineteenth century. Opened on August 17, 1876, as the Lunatic Asylum at Morristown, the sprawling old complex of cement and stone buildings was decaying inside and out. The state-operated institution had been plagued by security and other problems for years, while caring for a live-in patient population of about six hundred men and women. Sex offenders committed to the psychiatric hospital under the New Jersey statute named for Megan Kanka, a seven-year-old girl murdered by a convicted child molester who lived near her home, would be some of his new neighbors. Greystone wasn't a pleasant place, but for the next two months it was Cullen's home.

Cullen remained angry over the emergency-room confrontation, and after his release from Greystone he filed a complaint with the Phillipsburg Police Department accusing Dr. Swidler of forcing him to give blood, according to a report filed by the patrolman John M. Maczka. The harried RN claimed he was threatened with physical harm if he didn't cooperate, and finally submitted to providing blood because he was so afraid. No charges were pressed by police or prosecutors against the hospital, Dr. Swidler, or anyone else named by the glaringly dysfunctional complainant.

The fracas at the hospital wasn't the only time Cullen had filed a complaint with police that failed to produce charges against anyone. Another time, while he was battling fiercely with his wife seeking more generous visitation privileges, he claimed that someone was making threatening telephone calls to his apartment. He suspected it was one of his wife's relatives, Cullen said.

Bills for the increasingly agitated RN's psychiatric care added to acute financial pressures that were squeezing him, and soon after he was released from Greystone, he filed for bankruptcy. On the petition filed in May 1998, Cullen listed $66,888 in debts, including the costs for his psychiatric care. About one-third of the total, $22,000, represented his most recent bill from Greystone. Credit card bills accounted for almost $43,000. According to the petition, after all the years working extra shifts while compiling hundreds of hours of overtime, he didn't own much except a 1985 Dodge truck, a bicycle, a few dog-eared books, and videotapes.

Cullen took another big step back toward financial solvency when he landed his first job in Pennsylvania, a position with the Liberty Nursing and Rehabilitation Center in Allentown. He met all the qualifications established by the commonwealth for employment in a health-care facility. He had a current nursing license, met education requirements, and had written references from previous employers. Employers were not required by regulations to seek out the reason a prospective new worker left his or her last job.

Cullen signed on to work in the vent unit, where patients

are hooked up to ventilators to help them breathe. The new job fit right in with his practice of seeking night-shift assignments with some of the most distressed patients. A few of his colleagues were curious about why a nurse with his skills and experience would take a job for $16 an hour and make the daily round-trip drive from his home in Phillipsburg when several hospitals in the area were closer and paid better. Despite the curiosity the new RN appeared to be satisfied with the job.

It was his first nursing home assignment, and even though he was working in the vent unit, if the condition of full-time residents of the home or patients undergoing rehabilitation deteriorated sufficiently to indicate their lives were threatened, they were transferred to a hospital. For the first time since he began his nursing career, Cullen wasn't in a position to pick and choose among patients who were critically ill and whose deaths would be unlikely to arouse suspicion in deciding who would live and who would die.

His access to drugs that could be used to deliver toxic overdoses was also more limited. Cullen was up to the challenge, and that's what serial medical murder is to some killers who hide behind stethoscopes, hospital scrubs, and medicine carts to carry out their slaughter: a challenge. To get away with murder, then repeat the crime over and over again without getting caught—while outsmarting supervisors and other colleagues senior to them, as well as police and prosecutors—can be a heady experience for some people. Other medical murderers have admitted to the pride they took in the perceived superior cunning and guile that permitted them to kill repeatedly under the guise of being Angels of Mercy. When the time was ripe and the circumstances were favorable, Cullen found a way to continue killing.

Although eighty-three-year-old Francis J. Henry Jr. wasn't one of the new RN's vent unit patients, and had a different nurse, he shared a room with another man who was being cared for by Cullen.

The longtime retiree from the Leeds and Northrup manufacturing plant, where he worked as a salesman and inventory control specialist, was convalescing at the nursing home after treatment at the Lehigh Valley Hospital. He suffered a stroke while he was driving near his home in the Melody Lakes mobile home development in nearby Richmond. With the driver suddenly incapacitated, his car crashed into a utility pole. It was a nasty crash that shattered brittle bones and left the elderly man with a broken vertebrae and broken ribs. Henry's wife, Dolores, was also injured in the crash but recovered.

Henry's battered and swollen body was fitted with a protective brace described by doctors as a halo to stabilize his neck, and a tracheostomy tube was inserted down his throat to help him breathe. When he recovered sufficient strength to handle the move, he was dismissed from the hospital and sent to the nursing and rehabilitation center to recuperate.

Henry was a big, outgoing Irishman who interrupted his career at Leeds and Northrup to serve five years in the U. S. Army during World War II and rose to the rank of staff sergeant before returning to his old job. A Philadelphia native, he sang during services at various Roman Catholic churches in his hometown during his earlier years.

He was already suffering from Parkinson's disease before the accident, and even after transfer to the nursing home, he was semiconscious and experiencing a rough time. There seemed to be reason for optimism, however, and a senior nurse told family members she was hopeful he would eventually be able to walk again. Despite his breathing troubles, he could speak clearly when the oxygen tube was removed from his throat. As sick as he was, he managed to tell his wife, who was at his bedside, "I love you." The couple had been married thirty-seven years.

On the night of May 7, Henry began throwing up, inhaled

some of his own vomit, and developed fluid on the lungs. Early the next morning he was rushed back to Lehigh Valley Hospital. Doctors quickly determined that he was suffering from hypoglycemic shock, aspirations, and seizures that were traced to a precipitous drop in his blood sugar level.

Laboratory tests on samples of bodily fluids disclosed high insulin blood levels. That was extremely troubling because insulin is a powerful hormone that is the medication of choice for diabetes. Produced naturally by the pancreas, it enables the body to use sugar in food as a source of energy, but Henry didn't have a history of diabetes and his body was already producing all the natural insulin it needed. Insulin wasn't prescribed for him.

The drug can be a deadly effective killer and was the weapon of choice used in England by student nurse Beverley Allitt, who murdered four children and attempted to kill nine others at a Lincolnshire hospital in the early 1990s. Allitt craved the attention she attracted when she signaled a code blue and colleagues rushing to help in the emergency found her seemingly battling to save an infant's life. After conviction for multiple murders she was sentenced to thirteen life terms in prison. Britain has no death penalty.

Like the insulin used by Allitt and at times by Cullen, most medical serial killers have a special drug, substance, or compound that is their favorite killing agent. Orville Lynn Majors Jr. a licensed practical nurse at the Vermillion County Hospital in rural Clinton, Indiana, injected elderly patients he marked for death with potassium chloride. The drug is normally used to regulate heartbeat, but when the dosage is too strong or when it is given to the wrong patient, it can cause fatal heart rhythms. Potassium chloride is so lethal that it is one of a toxic mix of chemicals used for executions on death row in Texas.

Majors's victims were overwhelmingly elderly, and before the slaughter ended and he was arrested in 1997, so many patients had died on his watch that some of his colleagues were already whispering behind his back that he was a Death Angel and taking bets on who would be the next to die. In 1999, he was convicted of murdering six patients, and a mistrial was declared in a seventh case after the jury was unable to agree on a verdict. The soft-spoken nurse, who babied patients and called them pet names like "Punkin," was suspected in the deaths of many more during a killing spree extending through the mid-1990s. He was sentenced to six consecutive sixty-year prison terms.

Long Island Death Angel Richard Angelo favored Pavulon, a powerful, paralyzing muscle relaxant, although investigators found syringes and a stash of potassium chloride in his locker at work, and vials of another drug, Anectine, were discovered in his home shortly before his arrest.

Robert Diaz was a coronary-care nurse who killed patients in southern California hospitals with lidocaine, a drug designed to stabilize patients by correcting arrhythmia or irregular heartbeat. Dosages that were too strong could cause fatal heart attacks.

Insulin wasn't Cullen's killer drug of choice, but it could be effective. At Lehigh Valley Hospital, Henry's reaction to the outside overdose of insulin was alarming. His blood sugar level plummeted to twenty-five, a level that was so distressingly low that it could have caused him to lose consciousness and suffer brain damage. Normally, a person's blood sugar doesn't dip below seventy without outside interference—such as an injection of insulin. Diabetics use the hormone to combat high blood sugar, and insulin could cause that kind of drastic dip, with the effect peaking one or two hours after the injection.

Once clinicians identified the problem, and Henry was treated with an antidote, his condition leveled off and he was returned to the nursing and rehabilitation center, where he was placed on a morphine drip. Several days after that, he lapsed into a vegetative state, and his wife, Dolores, asked the nursing home to remove the feeding tube and take him off life support machines, she was later quoted as saying. He died on May 19, just a week after he left the hospital for the second time.

Injuries from the auto accident were listed on Henry's death certificate as the official cause of his demise. But laboratory tests conducted as part of the autopsy also detected the presence of insulin in his body and indicated that insulin poisoning may have been a factor.

No one wants to deal with ugly suspicions that a beloved family member may have died because of someone else's blunder, or because of a deliberate murderous act. Those are nasty, hurtful questions no one should have to confront. They tend to pile more pain on the hurts that have already been inflicted over the death of a loved one, but Henry's wife was pestered by fears that someone at the nursing center gave her husband a toxic overdose of insulin. She began thinking of that possibility from the time a surgeon telephoned her at three o'clock in the morning with the bad news about the sudden precipitous drop in her husband's blood sugar.

The possibility that a patient may have been accidentally or deliberately given a toxic dose of medication in the nursing home was a distressing development for Liberty. Some 16,400 nursing homes are licensed in the United States, and according to statistics provided by the federal Centers for Medicare and Medicaid Services, about 1.6 million people reside in the facilities daily. More than 3 million people are cared for in a nursing home at some time during a given year.

The baffling occurrence hinted at the kind of potential nightmare that no nursing home or hospital that is in the business of caring for the elderly, infirm, ill, or injured wants to occur at their facility. Residents of live-in facilities, like Liberty, come there for rehabilitation so they can someday return to their homes, or to be cared for while living out their twilight years in as much comfort and safety as possible. They don't come there to die because of a careless health-care worker's lethal mistake—or the even more ghastly act of someone who deliberately feeds them a toxic overdose of medication.

Administrators began probing Henry's troubling death, and they took their closest look at the night-shift nurse who was assigned to his care when he was believed to have been given the insulin injection: Kimberly A. Pepe.

Pepe was an attentive, efficient health-care professional with nine years of experience as a RN. She was shocked when she realized that she was suspected of committing a blunder—or worse—that may have cost the life of one of the patients under her care. In a near decade-long career as a nurse, she never before was suspected or accused of violating hospital codes or of any other misconduct that might endanger the health and lives of her patients. She had an impeccable nursing record.

The veteran nurse strongly asserted her innocence and pointed the finger of guilt at Cullen as a person who may have administered the insulin to the patient. He was the nurse for the elderly patient's roommate, she pointed out, and had easy access to her patient. Cullen was in and out of the room shared by the two patients numerous times on the night that Henry was believed to have been administered an insulin overdose.

But Pepe was the critically ill patient's night-shift nurse at the time, and nursing administrators at Liberty accused her of giving him the shot. It was her scalp that was in danger of being lifted. She was repeatedly asked by administrators if she gave insulin to the patient, and she always gave the same basic answer. She never gave him insulin, and she didn't check his blood sugar level because he didn't have a history of diabetes.

Despite her continued insistence that she had nothing to do with the patient's insulin overdose, she was suspended from her job. Then while continuing to proclaim her innocence, she was advised that she was going to be terminated because of a "medication error." The threat was effective, and on June 26, 1998, she quit before she could be fired, according to court documents filed in a wrongful termination lawsuit. She accused her former employer in the court action of gender discrimination, aiding and abetting discriminatory conduct, defamation of character, and intentional infliction of emotional distress. She suffered damages in excess of $50,000, she claimed.

Pepe also questioned her bosses about the hospital's plans for Cullen, who, she believed, should have been the target of the inquiry into Henry's death, and was advised that there were no plans to fire her former night-shift colleague.

In the legal complaint prepared and filed by Bethlehem attorney Donald Russo, Pepe contended that she was wrongly accused and that her male colleague, who was on his first job in Pennsylvania, was also on duty and had easy access to the patient. Cullen "was under suspicion for several serious matters," including improper handling of medications and the disappearance of medications at the time the man was being treated. "The evidence at the time clearly pointed to Charles Cullen as having been the nurse who administered the insulin to patient named in the suit as John Doe," she declared.

The complaint further stated: "At the time she was discharged, [Pepe] was not under suspicion by the [Liberty Nursing Home] for having taken improper actions with respect to medications, contrary to the cloud of suspicion surrounding Charles Cullen at the time." Yet, the nursing home intentionally overlooked evidence pointing to the likelihood that it was Cullen who administered insulin to the patient, it was alleged.

Although the patient was not identified by his real name in the lawsuit, Russo filed a subpoena asking for the medical and death records of Francis Henry Jr. The action was settled by the nursing home in 2001, but a gag order was part of the agreement in the case and details were not publicly disclosed.

The female nurse lived in Slatington, a small town just off the northeast extension of the Pennsylvania Turnpike, where everyone knew just about everyone else and reputations were important. She was also a fighter who was determined to safeguard her livelihood while protecting her professional standing, and she filed a complaint with the federal Equal Opportunity Employment Commission (EOEC) at the regional office in Harrisburg, Pennsylvania. The outraged RN, who took the hit for the patient's death, accused the nursing home of sex discrimination for assuming she was to blame, instead of investigating her male colleague.

Pepe contended in the complaints that her former colleague had equal access to the patient who died and that Cullen wasn't blamed, even though he was being watched by the pharmacy for stealing medication. Her work record was totally clean, while "Charles' record, however, was under suspicion for several serious matters," she claimed. Liberty Nursing and Rehabilitation was already conducting an internal investigation into suspicions that Cullen was stealing digoxin from the nursing and rehabilitation center, she said. She claimed he was suspected of misusing another drug, Lasix, as well as digoxin. The nurse accused the nursing home of refusing to take the concerns she raised about Cullen seriously.

Nursing home spokesmen disputed a significant portion of her contentions, and claimed that Cullen was not being investigated for any violations of hospital rules at the time Pepe left. At that time his record appeared to be clean. There was no reason to suspect her male colleague, and an investigation of Henry's toxic insulin overdose turned up no evidence that Cullen was involved, a spokeswoman said.

Staff members at Lehigh Valley Hospital telephoned Nurse Pepe three times on the day after Henry was taken there to ask if she had given him insulin, she recalled in the legal actions. She responded to the questions from the Lehigh Valley staff members with the same answers she gave to administrators at the nursing home. She firmly denied administering the drug to the patient.

Cullen outlasted Pepe at Liberty by only a little more than

three months. Although he managed to sidestep culpability in the probe into Henry's suspicious death, Cullen got
into serious trouble that couldn't be shifted to blame an
innocent colleague. He was working the graveyard shift,
11:00 P.M. to 7:00 A.M. when a noisy scuffle broke out in the
room of a ninety-three-year-old woman resident.

Allison Sechler, who was hired at Liberty at the same time
as Cullen and went through forty hours of orientation
with him, was just coming on duty when the fracas in the
elderly resident's room occurred. Her first impression of
her colleague during orientation wasn't especially memorable. He seemed to be competent and pleasant enough.
Then her close friend Kimberly Pepe became the scape-
goat for a tragedy that appeared to be directly traceable to
the male nurse, and her opinion of him drastically changed.

Nurse Sechler hurried to investigate the disturbance and
found the resident in obvious pain with a badly injured arm.
The frail old woman was unable to communicate, and
couldn't explain to the RN what had happened in the
room. Sechler had better luck when she talked with two
aides. They told her they saw Cullen entering the room
twice, both times while carrying hypodermic needles. The
last time he went in, the scuffle occurred, the old woman
was badly injured, and the floor was left in a mess.

While the elderly resident was stabilized and hurried off
to a hospital, where doctors confirmed she had a broken
arm, Sechler snatched up the woman's medical chart and
burst into the office of the nursing supervisor, Dawn
Costello. She began by pointing out that whatever Cullen
was trying to give the patient, antianxiety medication or
something else, the medicine was not prescribed for her
at that time of day. Then, according to a newspaper report
tracing the incident, she got down to the real nitty-gritty:
"This guy hurts patients and he needs to go right now," she
told her boss. "We cannot let him work another shift here."

Cullen couldn't deny being in the room, but he tried
to defend himself by blaming the resident for flying out

of control and flailing her arms. That was when he decided to give her an antianxiety medication, he said. After treatment at the hospital, the injured resident was returned to the nursing home wearing a cast. Cullen wasn't even one of the nurses assigned to her care, and within an hour or two after she was injured, he was fired.

The stone-faced male nurse, whose name had come up before when it appeared that something fishy was going on at the nursing home, was terminated officially for failure to follow proscribed procedures for administering medications and dispensing drugs to patients without doctors' orders and at unscheduled times. Authorities at Liberty notified the Pennsylvania State Department of Health about the investigation and said Cullen was terminated because of a medication error. The agency was charged with responsibility for regulating nursing homes, but did not have the authority to discipline individual nurses. No one notified the local or state police, or the Pennsylvania State Board of Nursing.

Once again the killer RN was unemployed, and looking for work. Since graduation from Mountainside, he had left five nursing jobs, survived suicide attempts, gotten into trouble with police for stalking a female colleague, seen his marriage shattered, filed for bankruptcy—and was questioned in the suspicious deaths of two patients.

Even though hospitals and nursing homes were reluctant to share reservations about forced resignations, firings, or deficient on-the-job performances by former employees, Cullen's bad luck with patients and other troubles had caused so much whispering among health-care professionals, and so much concern about his behavior, that it became difficult for him to find permanent employment in either Pennsylvania or in his home state of New Jersey.

Nevertheless, in November 1998, after less than a week of unemployment, he began obtaining periodic work at Easton Hospital in the nearby Allentown suburb of Wilson through a Harrisburg-based medical staffing agency called Healthforce.

Despite his near-invisible record of firings or forced terminations and other workplace disasters, Cullen had a lot going for him. The entire country was undergoing a serious nursing shortage. Thousands of fresh, new nurses graduate from schools every year, but most of them are female, and many of them eventually take months off to give birth. Sometimes they drop out of the profession for years to raise their children. Some leave and never return to the profession.

Licensed nurses must also keep up-to-date on a rapidly changing profession that requires knowledge of sophisticated equipment and techniques. Long absences from the job can leave a nurse—no matter how efficient, intelligent, and devoted to his or her profession—hopelessly behind.

Cullen could be an especially attractive recruit at hospitals because he was an ICU nurse, who was not only willing, but actually preferred to work evenings and overnights with some of the hospital's most critically ill patients. Furthermore, he anxiously accepted extra hours, or extra shifts. He no longer had a family life to interfere with his workaholic ways, and he gorged himself on overtime.

Even his hopscotching from job to job could be easily explained away or understood, because of the job stresses that are known to dog ICU-experienced and trained nurses. It wasn't all that unusual for ICU nurses nearing emotional burnout from the daily diet of agonized, dying patients and grief-stricken families to look around, figure there must be something better out there, and change employers. Often they simply wound up calling on their old skills and working in another ICU in a different hospital. In many, perhaps most, hospitals skilled ICU-trained nurses who will work the night shift are a hot commodity.

The Two Rivers Hospital Corporation was contracted with Health Med Inc. headquartered in Harrisburg and doing business as Healthforce, to provide registered nurses to Easton Hospital. Cullen became one of those nurses.

Following his long-established pattern, he started working full- and part-time shifts as a night nurse at Easton. Also, continuing to stick to the same pattern, he resumed working with some of the most seriously ill or injured patients. He was assigned to the ICU.

The cash-strapped workaholic nurse had a drawer full of unpaid bills waiting for his attention back in his apartment. So, continuing to utilize the temporary agency, when he wasn't busy at Easton, he also began filling in as a night nurse in the burn unit at the main campus of Lehigh Valley Hospital in Salisbury Township. Staff commonly referred to the institution by its initials, LVH, and it was a big operation. With satellite facilities in Allentown and Bethlehem, it was the biggest hospital in the region, and with a total staff from doctors and nurses to clerks and cooks of more than seven thousand, it was the largest employer in Lehigh and Northampton Counties.

Authorities at LVH contacted Liberty Nursing for reference checks on their new RN, and "no problems were indicated," a spokesman for the hospital later disclosed. Apparently, there wasn't a word said, or a confidence shared, about Cullen's role in two investigations at Liberty Nursing, or about his firing for violating the facility's protocol for administering drugs.

Even his gypsy travels, bouncing from one job to another for so many years, that might have sounded alarm bells in another profession, didn't raise any red flags or serious concern about his disordered employment record. Nothing had changed the dreadful shortage of nurses.

Administrators at Lehigh Valley Hospital had no reason to suspect that they may have been employing a renegade nurse who was a threat to the lives of his own patients and those of his colleagues.

"In case his heart stops," the nurse replied. A bony man with a sharp, peaked chin, a stubble of hair trimmed military close, and dressed in white hospital scrubs with white shoes, the nurse neither smiled nor bothered to modulate his voice with any inflection of sympathy. His attitude was totally cold, without the slightest hint of compassion. He may as well have been talking about replacing a defective spark plug or an engine that was misfiring in a beat-up old car.

Schramm's heart didn't stop—not then! But the elderly diabetic, who was hospitalized after suffering grand mal seizures at the Gracedale Nursing Home in Upper Nazareth Township, was critically ill. He had been a resident of the Northampton County–operated facility with diabetes and generally failing health before suffering the seizures and lapsing into a coma.

Born in Nicaragua to Moravian missionaries, the patient had worked hard and had lived an eventful, satisfying, moral life, and family members were hoping for the best. He rebounded from malaria and snakebites in Nicaragua, and survived service with the U. S. Army during the slaughter of World War II. After he was mustered out of the military, he went to work at the Saucon shipping yards for the Bethlehem Steel Corporation. A devoted husband and father of three children, he worked for years at two jobs to support his family, as a steelworker and at various times as a carpenter, artist, and musician. He was a talented, gentle man, who had a great capacity for love and a zest for life.

When he retired from Bethlehem Steel in 1976, after thirty-three years of work there, the beloved grandfather kept busy as a fisherman, amateur photographer, and with activities at the Nazareth Moravian Church, where he played for forty years with the trombone band. He was also head usher and a member of the Board of Elders at the church.

Three days after the incident with the hypodermic needle, Kristina Toth was sitting at her father's bedside when the same strange male nurse with the pale, ashen complexion drifted quietly inside the elderly man's fourth-floor room in the ICU, and without a word, he began to fiddle with the IV line. When she asked what he was doing, he tersely replied that he was giving the patient something to keep his heart beating.

Later that night the seventy-eight-year-old grandfather "crashed." Mrs. Toth was telephoned by a doctor who told her that someone had given her father the wrong medication. Routine blood tests revealed he had three times the therapeutic level of a heart medication, digoxin, in his system.

Early the next morning, on the last day of the old year, without recovering consciousness since he suffered the seizures, Schramm flat-lined and died. He lived only twenty-two hours, a bit less than a full day, after the digoxin overdose was discovered.

The anemic-looking, strangely disturbing male nurse, who shared such a troubling role in his care, had been employed in the hospital's ICU for about one month. He came on duty at 7:00 P.M. and worked through until early the next morning—the graveyard shift—while the elderly man was losing the battle for his life.

Disturbingly, the breath had barely left Schramm's body before the same nurse, who had been fussing with the IV tube, suggested to family members that they shouldn't bother having an autopsy performed. The elderly man wouldn't have wanted an autopsy performed because he had a living will, the nurse declared.

The family was attempting to cope with the shock and grief of their loss, but they weren't caught so off-balance that they allowed themselves to be talked out of an autopsy. They didn't need blood and gore to make them realize that something was seriously wrong and the beloved grandfather's death at that time and place may not have been preordained by his illnesses. Despite the retired steelworker's recent medical history and failing health, there seemed to be good reason to believe that his death might have been preventable and his life prolonged.

Schramm's relatives were concerned and upset over the elevated levels of digoxin detected in their loved one's system before his unexpected death. They didn't even know who ordered the initial digoxin screening that turned up the presence of the medication. The RN's attempt to dissuade them from seeking an autopsy was also exceedingly troubling. They made it clear that they wanted an autopsy conducted, but hospital authorities were already putting plans in motion to carry out the procedure. During the autopsy laboratory tests on the elderly man's vital fluids turned up a positive reading for digoxin.

Death was no stranger on Easton Hospital's ICU or in the critical-care units of any other hospital, but circumstances surrounding Ottomar Schramm's passing wasn't so easily explained away as the natural, inevitable end of a useful and satisfying life. Alarm bells were immediately sounded, and they were persistently demanding.

Easton Hospital authorities were predictably concerned about the unexpected presence of an unprescribed drug in the patient's system after his condition had become so critical. No one working in the ICU, or anywhere else in the hospital, seemed to have any idea how the digoxin came to be found in his blood.

The death of a patient after being given a lethal dose of the wrong medication was a serious matter that was tied directly to the reputation of the hospital in the community, and to the safety of the sick and injured people being cared for there. The hospital's credibility was at stake. Concerned administrators were determined to root out some answers, and to turn over every stone until they figured out who was responsible.

At 1:25 A.M. on New Year's Day, the hospital's on-call pathologist contacted the Northampton County coroner and asked the government agency to assume jurisdiction in a medical investigation into the death of a patient at Easton Hospital and to conduct an autopsy. The patient tested positive for digoxin, a drug that hadn't been prescribed for him, the concerned pathologist explained.

County coroner Zachary Lysek operated out of an office at the Northampton County Government Center in Easton that was about as sparsely staffed as it could be, with only himself and a secretary as full-time employees. But he had held the office for more than six years, knew his way around, and he swung into action, quickly putting procedures in motion to carry out the autopsy with an outside pathologist. He settled on Saralee Funke, an experienced professional medical sleuth with Forensic Pathology Associates, Inc. in Allentown.

Pathologists are trained to determine the causes of death, but forensic pathologists, unlike local doctors, go a step further and are trained to use law and medicine to investigate real or suspected murder, suicides, accidents, and other unnatural deaths. Dr. Funke was one of the best in the business, and she was well known in the Lehigh Valley for her professionalism and frequent appearances and testimony at murder trials. Her resume sparkled with testimony in locally notorious murder cases that featured nationally known professional witnesses, including Dr. Michael Baden, former New York City chief medical examiner, who later became chief medical examiner for the New York State Police.

Baden played a prominent role in a notorious New Jersey case of suspected medical murder a few years earlier, when he performed autopsies on five patients of Dr. Mario Jascalevich. The physician, who lived in Oradell, the same small North Jersey community that later became Zach Martin's home, was accused of poisoning patients at Riverdell Hospital in Bergen County. Known in the tabloid press as "Dr. X," Jascalevich was accused of killing patients with curare, a muscle relaxant used as a poison on the deadly blowpipe darts of South American Indians. After a sensational trial Dr. X was acquitted of all charges, and returned to his original home in Argentina, where he died a natural death a few years later.

Lysek didn't believe Schramm's death was an accident. If his suspicions were justified, a killer could still be roaming the quiet, antiseptic halls of Easton Hospital scouting out new victims. It was a chilling thought, and Lysek needed to talk to someone with experience and authority in criminal matters.

On a typically crisply cold midwinter afternoon shortly after taking the fateful telephone call from the Easton hospital pathologist, Lysek pushed his chair away from his desk, rode two floors up on the elevator, and walked into the office of Northampton County solicitor John F. Spirk Jr. The solicitor was a former assistant Northampton County district attorney, and Lysek trusted his expertise.

Northampton County Administration director James Hickey had followed Lysek into the office to talk with the solicitor about another matter, and he shared the stunned surprise with Spirk when the coroner unexpectedly announced: "We might have an 'Angel of Death.'"

The shocking statement hung in the air for only a moment before the door was slammed shut and the three men settled down to discuss Lysek's gut-churning disclosure.

Lysek brought his companions up-to-date on developments, and according to a later statement by Hickey, they decided that the main issue at that point was determining where the patient was when he was given the digoxin: at Gracedale, or at Easton Hospital. First assistant Northampton County solicitor Tony Blasko was soon admitted to the small group of men and women alerted to the possibility that a cold-blooded killer might be stalking the halls and wards at Easton Hospital.

While Dr. Funke was preparing to conduct the autopsy, Lysek ordered tests on all the samples collected from the patient at the hospital. He included tests on samples taken when Schramm was admitted so that it could be determined if the digoxin could have been administered at the nursing home. Authorities at Gracedale were further asked to provide him with a list of staff members who had access to the retired steelworker between December 1 and December 28 when he was taken to Easton Hospital. They were also told to secure all medications they had for Schramm, since it was possible that one of the bottles could have been mislabeled.

Inspection of the medicine bottles failed to turn up any evidence of mislabeling or of problems with the drugs that were inside, according to the coroner's later report. Nor did interviews with three nurses at Gracedale result in any evidence or indications that Schramm could have gotten his toxic dosage of digoxin at the nursing home. Gracedale wasn't yet completely off the hook, but the ball was clearly back in the hospital's court—and the autopsy was the most pressing immediate concern.

Full autopsies typically begin in a sterile, chilled, and fluorescent-lit hospital or county coroner's morgue, with the pathologist and assistants donning surgeon's paper gowns and sterile bootees as they prepare to strip away the body's secrets. Photographs are taken, and the body is weighed and measured to determine height. Then it is time for scalpels, bone saws, scales, and specimen bottles so that the organs exposed in the opened body can be studied and weighed, and samples taken of tissue, blood, and other bodily fluids.

A normal adult-human body contains about five quarts of blood. During the autopsy new samples were taken of the blood, of other body fluids, and of tissue. Gracedale was completely cleared of possible involvement when early toxicology tests revealed that the digoxin found in the elderly man's blood before his death didn't show up until two days after he left the nursing home.

It was months before all the samples collected during the examination were analyzed in sophisticated laboratory tests, but when the final results were in, they added damning confirmation of the earlier findings. Everyone's worst fears were realized. Ottomar Schramm died after being given a lethal dose of a drug commonly used to regulate heartbeat and improve the organ's pumping ability: digoxin.

Digoxin is a key element in a mix of four drugs that also include ACE inhibitors, beta blockers, and diuretics, which are used today to treat heart failure.

Although no surprise, finding further confirmation of digoxin poisoning was disturbing because the powerful heart stimulant was not prescribed for the patient. It wouldn't have been approved for him because he already wore a pacemaker. There was no legitimate medical reason for digoxin's presence. It shouldn't have been there.

When digoxin in its various forms is used in the wrong dosages or on the wrong patients, it can kill as easily as it can save or extend the lives of those whom doctors have prescribed it for. More than ten milligrams of the drug can be toxic for a healthy adult and stop the heart. More than four milligrams can endanger the life of a healthy child.

That doesn't mean digoxin is either a bad or a criminally dangerous drug, but there is no getting around the fact that it can have deadly side effects. It can cause nausea, visual disturbances, confusion, loss of appetite, and—at worst—cardiac arrhythmias and death.

Most pharmaceuticals have side effects that can range from the merely bothersome to potentially lethal. Just about anything that is ingested can become poisonous if it is overdone. People can die from drinking too much water, poison experts have pointed out. It is the dose that makes the difference. Like any other medication, knowledgeable caution with the use of digoxin—in the treatment of patients only in the dosages considered to be appropriate by physicians—is absolutely necessary.

Digoxin and chemically similar drugs are widely used to help weakened or injured hearts work more effectively and to treat rapid heartbeat, and are prescribed for approximately 3 million patients around the country. But the margin of error is razor thin. Recent research has raised serious questions about its safety, and lowered the ideal serum levels for men while indicating it may not be safe in any case for women. A study published in the prestigious *New England Journal of Medicine* on October 31, 2002, disclosed that researchers found that the use of digoxin actually increased the risk of death in women by approximately 23 percent.

The drug itself is derived from foxglove, an elegant plant with long spikes of thimblelike flowers and leaves that can be so toxic that it has been known through the ages by such menacing names as witch's gloves, dead men's bells, bloody fingers, and goblin's gloves. The tall, innocent-appearing plant may even have been among the flowers so assiduously tended to in Cullen's backyard, but whether growing wild or carefully nurtured in gardens, it has a long history of darker use. For centuries the close relative of snapdragons has been a staple of wisewomen, mountain grannies, desert shamans, Pennsylvania Dutch country powwowers, and other assorted herbalists who used folk medicines to cure or to kill.

The healing properties of digitalis in its original form became a staple of pharmacologists after a physician investigated an herbal recipe used by an old woman in the Shropshire region of England to treat heart failure.

When Dr. William Withering wrote about the folk healers' recipe of twenty or more different medicinal plants used to treat the ailment, he said he had isolated foxglove as the active herb actually responsible for the successful results. After conducting experiments of his own on the various parts of the plants, in 1785 he published his findings in his monograph "An Account of the Foxglove and Some of Its Medicinal Uses."

Dr. Withering's pioneering work led to his recognition as the discoverer of digitalis, and for more than two hundred years its use became the standard treatment for heart disease until ACE inhibitors were introduced in about 1990, and beta blockers became popular about a decade later. Long before ACE inhibitors began to replace digitalis,

Cullen had already developed deadly expertise in the use of the potent derivative of the deceptively beautiful flowering plant.

Foxglove looks much like a snapdragon, but it is so virulent in the wrong hands that it has been used through the ages as a favorite poison, as well as a lifesaving cure for heart disease and other ailments. In earlier days doctors and other health-care workers, as well as self-taught experts with knowledge of exotic herbs and fungi, who had homicide on their mind often turned to foxglove, deadly nightshade, death cap (*Amanita phalloides*) mushrooms, or other naturally lethal toxic plants.

That was then! Cullen had no need to scan woodlots, fields, or his own backyard for foxglove, deadly nightshade, or killer mushrooms. He realized early in his career that the medication derived from foxglove could be either a lifesaver or an assassin. Digoxin is sold under the names of Lanoxin, Lanoxicaps, Cardoxin, and Digitek, but its purpose is the same, helping a failing heart to pump blood and reduce the backup of fluid in the heart and other major organs, which can create breathing difficulties, swelling, and fatigue.

Digoxin, along with insulin, drugs such as norepinephrine, nitroglycerin, and a few other medications designed to increase the heart rate—which could be deadly when used improperly—were near-perfect killing tools. There was no necessity for gunshots to be fired, no screaming, no struggle, no bloody mess to clean up, and usually no need to try and explain things to suspicious doctors, police, or prosecutors. There was only the rapidly cooling body of a patient who had been seriously ill or injured and seemed to have died a natural death.

When Dr. Funke completed her report on the autopsy, she officially attributed Schramm's death to "aspiration pneumonia due to seizure with supratherapeutic levels of digoxin (nonprescribed)." Digoxin was clearly pinpointed as a possible contributing factor in the death.

"Neither a review of the available medical records nor

the autopsy itself indicates how Mr. Schramm received digoxin," she wrote. "On the basis of the contributing condition, manner of death will be listed as accidental." The pathologist's meticulous examination of the body had turned up no evidence of foul play.

Dr. Funke produced an intelligent, measured report based solely on medical evidence, and her conclusion was in keeping with the secrets uncovered in the examination. By itself the necropsy didn't tell the entire story or include certain outside circumstances surrounding the mysterious death of the Nazareth grandfather. The autopsy failed to turn up any clear-cut evidence of foul play, but the coroner wasn't ready to put the matter to rest.

Lysek later recalled that he was suspicious of the death from the beginning and wasn't comfortable calling it an accident. Discovering an unprescribed medication in a patient's system wasn't an everyday event. It was uncommon and—the coroner observed—"the levels were very high."

He continued pressing the inquiry by interviewing members of the hospital staff who were on duty at the time the medication was believed to have been administered to the patient. The results were disappointing. No one was prepared or able to provide the kind of information that would develop a solid, satisfying solution to the puzzle. The final autopsy report made no further mention of the mysterious male nurse, or what the coroner was told by authorities at the hospital.

On March 3, Lysek returned a telephone call from Kristina Toth, Schramm's daughter. She told the coroner about the strange male nurse who was carrying a syringe when he wheeled her father out of the hospital emergency room to take him away for additional tests. And she repeated the RN's reply about needing it to restart her father's heart if it stopped.

Posing the comment as a question, she said she wondered if the spindly male nurse who came for her father with the syringe was the same gloomy RN who tried to convince her that her father wouldn't have wanted an autopsy conducted because of the living will.

In notes made after the discussion and later included in records of his investigation, Lysek wrote that Toth said she probably couldn't identify the nurse, but wondered if he was the same one whom family members saw pushing her father away in the wheelchair. The grieving daughter decided to tell the coroner about the incident because it had been bothering her, she said.

The coroner advised her that he would forward the information to investigators at Easton in an effort to determine the identity of the mystery nurse, "and what his relationship was to the patient care of her father," he wrote in his report. The probe never turned up the RN's name.

Too many unanswered questions surrounding Schramm's death remained, and Lysek met with authorities to review the autopsy report. The coroner listed the cause of Schramm's death as inconclusive, but he was still dissatisfied. After the interviews with hospital staff members failed to disclose any breakthrough in the mystery, he changed the official finding of the manner of death to undetermined.

He also huddled with Easton's Medical Affairs director Dr. Eugene DiSalvo and Vice President for Administration Ed McDevitt and recommended an internal inquiry to try and figure out who administered the digoxin and if there were shortages or missing dosages of the drug. Lysek believed at the time that the hospital seemed to be best equipped to unravel the mystifying puzzle over how the digoxin overdose came to be administered to the patient, according to notes of the meeting he attached to the autopsy report. Responsibility for continuing the search for answers had been effectively passed to the hospital. The ball was in Easton's playing field.

While the internal investigation plodded fitfully along, Lysek continued to be tormented by fears that a self-appointed Angel of Death was stalking the hospital wards.

He remained troubled even after what would eventually become a frustrating eight-month inquiry sputtered out and, in February 2000, ended without turning up an answer. There were no significant findings, and investigators were unable to determine who administered the digoxin to the patient, Lysek later recalled he was told. Hospital authorities advised him that the results of their inquiry were inconclusive. No documentation of Easton's internal probe was provided to the coroner.

Despite his persistent suspicions and dissatisfaction with unanswered questions, Lysek never called for a coroner's inquest to determine responsibility for the death, and neither of the twin investigations turned up sufficient evidence of wrongdoing to convince Northampton County district attorney John M. Morganelli to investigate. Lysek talked with the DA shortly after Schramm's death, and also after the autopsy report was completed.

Webster's New World Dictionary, Second College Edition, defines the word "coroner" as "a public officer whose chief duty is to determine by inquest before a jury the causes of any death not obviously due to natural causes."

Northampton County, with a population of around 258,000, was neither one of the largest nor one of the smallest counties in Pennsylvania. It was somewhere in the middle, but in the more than six years Lysek had served as coroner, he never before held an inquest. A coroner's inquest was the only legal proceeding Lysek was empowered to use. Inquests are major legal procedures, complicated judicial inquiries conducted with the assistance of a jury. The inquisitions can be time-consuming and expensive, but they can also be used to shake loose sensitive information from reluctant sources that might otherwise never come to light.

Coroner's inquests are similar to proceedings of the grand jury, with evidence carefully examined and presented to jurors. Witnesses are called to testify, and nurses at the hospital could have been subpoenaed by the coroner to take the witness stand. Unlike a grand jury's proceedings, which are conducted in secrecy, coroner's inquests are held in public.

In bypassing a formal inquest Lysek made the decision he felt was the right decision to make at the time, but it would come back to haunt him. Despite all the tongue-twisting back-and-forth gobbledygook that speckled official reports and inquiries, no one really knew for sure how or why Schramm died exactly at the time he died. They didn't know if his death was the natural end of a richly satisfying life, or if someone deliberately gave the old man a helpful nudge into the abyss.

Increasingly disturbed over the manner of the family patriarch's demise and the inability of authorities to pin the blame on whoever was personally responsible, in April 2001—more than two years after Schramm's death—his widow, Lorraine, filed a damage suit against operators of the not-for-profit hospital in the Northampton County Court of Common Pleas.

It was claimed in the filing that he died from an overdose of digoxin, although the drug was not prescribed or listed on his medical chart as a medication for him. The civil damage suit was a bit like the first snowflake of the season. It took a while for others to show up, but when they finally did, a blizzard of filings would shower the courts in two states.

Long before the lawsuit was filed, Cullen left his job at Easton. The bad-luck nurse and the hospital severed ties about three months after Schramm died. When reporters tried years later to determine if Cullen was questioned during Easton's internal investigation, and pin down the circumstances that led him to discontinue working there, hospital spokesmen wouldn't say.

After severing his ties with Easton, Cullen began working exclusively at Lehigh Valley Hospital. Cullen was a burn unit nurse when twenty-two-year-old patient Matthew L. Mattern died at LVH on August 31, 1999.

A graduate of the Columbia-Montour Area Vocational-Technical School, the young Shamokin man worked for

Bloomsburg Mills, when he was severely burned in the crash of a car and a tractor-trailer on August 11. He was having a rough time of it in the hospital burn unit. Suffering from the burns was made worse by an agonizing round of infections followed by repeated surgical procedures—until a homicidal nurse stepped in and ended it all with a fatal injection of digoxin. Cullen slipped the fatal drugs out of the hospital's medications stock without signing for them.

Cullen's former wife had good reason to be afraid for herself and her daughters because of her husband's access to medications while he was working at Warren Hospital. He was already killing patients with stolen drugs, which were designed, developed, and manufactured in modern laboratories to save or extend lives.

Lucy Mugavero, Mary Natoli, and Helen C. Dean, who died at Warren Hospital in 1993, were all killed with digoxin. Then the autopsy turned up a high level of the same substance in Ottomar Schramm's body after he died at Easton. Only one person knew at that time that the mysterious occurrences were no coincidence.

Early Monday morning, January 3, 2000, Cullen again tried to kill himself. Neighbors were getting used to the curious loner's botched efforts at self-destruction. One time, after moving in, he deliberately left the gas on in the basement apartment. Another time he tried to kill himself with carbon monoxide by sitting in his car in the closed garage while the engine was running. In his latest effort he turned again to carbon monoxide as his tool of choice. The colorless, odorless gas is such an effective killer that year after year it has been recognized as the number one cause of poisoning in the United States and it is a favorite tool of suicides. Cullen might have been successful in his latest attempt, if it wasn't for an alert neighbor.

The scrawny loser prepared carefully for his self-destruction. He began by removing the batteries from smoke alarms and carbon monoxide detectors, stuffing insulation inside the heating vents, and sealing the doors to his apartment. Then he lit charcoal in a Japanese-style hibachi, placed it inside his dry bathtub, where it wouldn't start a destructive fire that could damage the building, and settled down to die of carbon monoxide poisoning.

Karin Ziemba, who lived upstairs from Cullen, became concerned when she noticed what she thought to be a strong odor of kerosene coming from the basement apartment, at about 9:00 A.M., and threw a monkey wrench into his suicide plans. The reclusive nurse didn't socialize with any of his neighbors, but she probably got along with him as well as anyone. They occasionally exchanged a few words of casual chitchat, and if there was a problem in her apartment that she needed a man to take care of when her fiancé wasn't around, Cullen would walk upstairs to take care of the emergency or make minor repairs. He even gave her candles and other little presents for Christmas.

Ziemba knew that her neighbor was a troubled, lonely man, and was worried that something was wrong. Deciding to investigate, she walked downstairs and noticed that towels were stuffed under Cullen's door. She knew he was home, and it wasn't difficult to put "two and two together," and realize that something was seriously amiss. After banging on the door and getting no response, she telephoned Phillipsburg police.

It was a few minutes after 9:00 A.M. when patrolman Bernard Kelly III arrived at the apartment. The policeman forced open a screen door, then began banging away on the inside door until it was opened by the thirty-nine-year-old occupant. Kelly and a partner could smell the burning charcoal, and they asked the stone-faced little man standing in the doorway what was going on.

In the subsequent police report Cullen was quoted as replying that the heat wasn't working and he lit a fire to keep warm. When the police officers walked inside, they found a spartanly furnished apartment with almost no furniture. The most prominent decorations were samples of artwork

Cullen's daughters had created at school and which he had taped to walls and the refrigerator.

More disturbingly, they discovered that the air ducts were stuffed up, the batteries were removed from the smoke detector, charcoal in a hibachi was smoldering in the bathtub, and the apartment was full of carbon monoxide. Cullen had a dog at the time, and he moved it safely outside before closing up the apartment and lighting the charcoal.

It was obvious that the occupant was attempting suicide, but Cullen told the police officer that he was merely trying to keep warm. Kelly knew better, and he said so. The plain-spoken lawman pointed out to the skinny waif, with the hang-dog look, who was standing just inside an apartment full of carbon monoxide, that he was a nurse and surely knew better.

". . . I know he is smart enough to realize the danger in what he had just done," Kelly later wrote in the report. "He is a R. N. and works at Lehigh Valley Hospital Burn Unit."

When Kelly and his fellow officers learned from talking with neighbors that Cullen had tried suicide before, they advised him that he needed counseling and they were going to arrange for him to get help. Cullen asked not to be taken back to Warren. He explained that he had filed a lawsuit against the hospital and some of the doctors that was still in litigation. So he was driven instead to the Warren County Crisis Center in Phillipsburg, and turned over to counselor Lisa Cooper, who dealt with him after the previous suicide attempt.

The dangerously depressed RN was back in his apartment the next day, and so were police. Officers went there looking for him after they were notified he left the crisis center without permission. Curious neighbors watched sympathetically as the narrow-chested little man was led out of his home in handcuffs and helped into the backseat of a police car so he could be driven back to the crisis center for treatment.

It was all so very sad. Years later Ziemba described him as "a gentle soul" to a newspaper reporter. "Was he normal? No!" she conceded. "But he wasn't mean."

By February, Cullen was back on the job at Lehigh Valley Hospital and just as dangerous to the frail, vulnerable patients he was trusted to care for as he had ever been. Late in the month, either February 20 or February 21, and only a day or two before his fortieth birthday, he tried to kill Stella Danielczyk by injecting her with a toxic dose of digoxin. Police investigators, who eventually looked into the incident, were uncertain of the exact date.

Danielczyk was well known around her home in Larksville, where she and her husband operated Wilkie's Café and Restaurant for many years. After they gave up the business, she continued working for several years as a waitress and in the garment industry as a sewing-machine operator.

The seventy-three-year-old grandmother had been in the hospital for three weeks with dreadful burns suffered when her clothing caught fire while she was cooking in her kitchen on January 26. She was burned over 60 to 70 percent of her body, but she was putting up a fierce struggle for her life. She survived the first murder attempt, so the homicidal nurse waited about a week, then tried again. On February 25, he gave her another injection of the powerful heart stimulant. The plucky mother of two sons and two stepdaughters died the next day.

With all the turmoil swirling around him, and all his money troubles, Cullen had made arrangements with other family members to take care of his terminally ill brother long before the latest suicide attempt. Charles rode along while Edmond was taken by ambulance to the home of a married sister and her husband, who cared for the terminal cancer patient for a while. As the ailing man continued to waste away, they were unable to continue caring for him and he was moved to the home of another sister.

Cullen sincerely seemed to sympathize with his brother's suffering and did what he could to help prepare him for his imminent death, but he never talked with his family about his own mental-health problems. If he was asked about his depression, he refused to discuss it. It was his problem— not theirs.

Despite the chaos of the previous year, Cullen applied for and was granted a renewal of his New Jersey State Nursing License. He filled in a question on the 1999 licensing form inquiring if any health-care facility had ever taken action against him that could affect his employment, by answering no. The response was a deliberate lie that made no mention of the past few turbulent months, his role in two investigations while he worked at Liberty—and his firing from the nursing home for improperly administering medications to patients.

The whispers and furtive glances from other nurses had started again, and it was time to move on. In April 2000, Cullen left his job at LVH and began looking around for a permanent position with another hospital.

Chapter 7

A Code of Silence

Lord, please help me to bring
Comfort where there is pain
Courage where there is fear
Hope where there is despair
Acceptance when the end is near, and
A touch gentle with tenderness, patience, and love.
                                        —Popular nurse's prayer,
                                        author unknown

The applicant for a job at St. Luke's Hospital in the Bethlehem, Pennsylvania, suburb of Fountain Hill was impressive.

At a time when hospitals all around the country were chronically short of nurses, a veteran RN with Cullen's six years of experience in some of the most respected medical facilities in the two-state area of Pennsylvania and New Jersey made the slender RN look like a good catch.

It also helped that the prospective employee was an experienced critical-care nurse, who had worked in burn units, ICUs, and CCUs with some of the most seriously ill or injured patients being cared for in the hospitals where he was previously employed. And while many other nurses preferred not to work nights, if they could help it, he loved the graveyard shift.

Performance records were requested from the Lehigh Valley Hospital, where he worked most recently, and from the Liberty nursing home, where he was employed in 1998. The check with former employers reportedly didn't turn up a single black mark on his record.

The matter of how his performance records were checked and the nature of the response would eventually become a matter of controversy. Like so many things about the speckled career of the sinister RN, many of the facts and figures—and the dark deeds attributed to him—were murky, convoluted, and so tangled by that time that they were almost impossible to sort out.

Whatever the exact circumstances of the reference check might have been, Cullen got the job. That would have been a worthy accomplishment for any nurse, because St. Luke's had a long, proud history of service to the community and was so respected for the quality care it offered to patients that it was named as one of the top one hundred hospitals in the country. It was a first-class medical institution that operated its own nursing school. The hospital administration was especially proud of the facility's state-of-the-art heart treatment center and record of caring for coronary-care patients, which was recognized with several national awards.

St. Luke's was also an impressive place to work, the hub of a system with four hospitals, a host of clinics, testing centers, and other facilities, which combined provided paychecks for more than five thousand people. The main hospital, with its satellites, was one of the largest employers in the Delaware Valley. The national magazine *U.S. News & World Report* named St. Luke's to its "Best Hospitals" list for patient care for six consecutive years. Cullen was going to work in the main hospital at the center of the rapidly expanding health-care network.

In June, approximately two months after leaving Lehigh Valley Hospital under a cloud, the deeply disturbed and homicidal RN assumed full-time duties in the CCU at St. Luke's. It was his eighth job since graduating from the Mountainside Hospital School of Nursing in 1984.

Time and again after the furtive mischief maker got into trouble and was fired or forced to resign, former employers were so fearful of being accused of violating his rights that they never passed along so much as a hint to colleagues at other hospitals of his suspicious character and behavior. Most hospitals are privately operated and companies run a strong risk of being sued for defamation if they discuss investigations that never lead to the formal filing of criminal charges. Consequently, new employers could only assume that the new nursing applicant had left his former jobs in good standing.

Most hospitals would do little more than confirm the dates of employment for former workers, and didn't pass along either positive or negative recommendations. It was standard operating procedure. They were afraid to go further because of the danger of slander suits. Regard for patient safety came in a poor second compared to concern over the possibility of being sued for slandering an inept or potentially criminally inclined nurse.

The RN with the woebegone manner and the thirst for blood was troubled throughout his life with depression, but he knew that killing his patients was a gross violation of the "Florence Nightingale Pledge" that he had recited when he graduated from nursing school. Assuming the dark mantle of a Death Angel and deliberately taking human life was simply wrong. Murder was the most serious criminal act he could commit—a violation of society's most jealously protected taboo.

Sometimes—possibly because he was taking his antidepression medication, because the turbulence swirling around him throughout his life had quieted and temporarily calmed, or perhaps a combination of both—there were periods when he managed to fight off the demons that so insistently urged him to kill.

He may have been experiencing one of those periods during his first several months at St. Luke's, when his disciplinary record was lily white. But like a man living in a dark dreamworld of slimy, fearsome, crawling things, he was hopelessly trapped in the continuing nightmare.

Inexplicably, early in 2001 he once again began to peer through patient files and charts, meticulously studying their condition and the medications they were prescribed, while seeking out the most frail, the oldest, and the most critically ill. Patients with multiple organ failure, and those who signed "do not resuscitate" (DNR) orders, were almost certain to attract his attention. He was looking for patients whose sudden deaths would be least likely to raise suspicions of foul play.

After nearly a decade-and-a-half of stalking hospital critical-care units for victims, Cullen was uniquely skilled in the art of murder. He worked purposely and quietly, with coldly methodical determination and cunning that was honed to perfection after so many years of practice.

Occasionally a patient was selected on impulse. It simply appeared to be the right person in the right place at the right time. Regardless of whether the condition of patients was carefully studied beforehand, or the decision was impulsive, those he selected were marked for death. When he felt it was time to act, he carried out the murders dispassionately, as if he were pulling out one of the pesky weeds in his backyard garden.

At the sprightly old age of ninety, John P. Gallagher had been a widower since his wife, Catherine, died in 1991. The Gallaghers were childless and he had no family left to look after him, but he was such a delightful old man that his regular visits to Lump's Center Street Deli in Bethlehem were highlights of the day for the customers and staff. He lived just around the corner, and he was a regular at the deli, dropping in every day for a cheeseburger, fries, and coffee. He also made regular rounds of nearby stores and clubs, where he bought shots of whiskey to keep him young and tried his luck playing the lottery. Most of the time he wore his favorite pink tie, and on long trips of three or four blocks or more, the old man drove his spiffy red-and-black 1977 Ford Mustang.

By the time he was checked into St. Luke's after falling and breaking a hip, Julie Sanders, co-owner of the deli with her husband, Dave, had taken over the job as the elderly man's caregiver. Julie Sanders replaced the family Gallagher had lost simply by growing old.

Gallagher was retired from Bethlehem Steel Company, where he worked for forty-four years—most of the time as an inspector—but many of his colleagues and longtime friends had already died, moved away, or were too frail to get around much. After he wound up in the nine-bed CCU at St. Luke's, Julie was his most faithful visitor. She stopped by to see him every day.

On February 11, five days after he was admitted to the hospital and almost a full decade after he was widowed, the former steelworker followed his wife in death. His death was a shock because he had seemed to be on his way to re-covery, and was already talking about returning to his home and his daily routine.

Cullen was lending a helping hand to the Grim Reaper at St. Luke's, when death made a more personal visit. The brain cancer that had been eating away at his brother Edmond finally claimed his life. The family's last surviving male, the RN contacted a mortuary and paid for a low-budget cremation without a religious service. With "Butchie" taken care of, the quiet, unassuming night nurse returned to business as usual—gorging himself on murder.

After suffering a massive heart attack on June 22, Irene Krapf was flown from the St. Luke's annex in Min-ersville in the Appalachian Mountain coal country to the hospital in Fountain Hill for pacemaker surgery after suf-fering congestive heart failure. The Schuylkill County woman had barely arrived at the main hospital before the blood-crazed coronary-care nurse loaded a syringe with ten cc's of digoxin and gave her a fatal injection. A mother of eight, a grandmother and great-grandmother, Krapf died only fifty minutes after she was checked in as a patient. Cullen was her only nurse.

The seventy-nine-year-old woman had lived a rich, full life that kept her busy with her large family, and in earlier years with the People's Taxi company, which she and her husband operated out of their home in the small town of Tamaqua. She worked as the secretary until her retirement in 1977.

William M. Park was a hard man to kill. The seventy-two-year-old native of South Korea provided what may have been the most daunting challenge of Cullen's appalling career as a medical serial murderer who staked out hospital critical-care units as his special killing ground. A retired, self-employed upholsterer who lived with his family in nearby Lehighton, Park was a survivor and a grizzled veteran of the Korean War. He served for twenty years during and just after the conflict, reaching the rank of major with the Republic of Korea (ROK) Army's military police.

He had already survived many crises in his life and there was reason for optimism and hope that the spunky old warrior would bounce back and return home to his family after treatment in St. Luke's CCU for heart failure. One of his nurses decided differently. After looking over the charts and other medical records of the grievously ill war veteran, the self-appointed Angel of Death made a fateful decision: it was time for the patient to die.

Cullen wasn't one of those serial killers who kept trophies and written or taped records of his dark deeds, but he eventually recalled that he tried three to five times to kill his helpless, unsuspecting patient with nitroglycerin, norepinephrine, or other similar drugs that are commonly used in the treatment of heart disease. Park gamely fought back every time until Cullen went back to the drug that was his weapon of choice throughout his career as a killer nurse: digoxin.

Park struggled against the persistent and silent assault for more than a week, steadily growing weaker rather than stronger while puzzled doctors sought to save his life, and family members reluctantly began to lose hope. The bone-thin, stone-faced, taciturn nurse was in Park's room, watching and listening, when the doughty old Korean War veteran lost his final battle and expired.

Cullen liked to be present when patients he helped give a final nudge into the afterworld died. He took necrophilic pleasure in hanging around so he could be a silent witness to the shock and grief that swept over families as their loved one took his or her last breath. Hovering on the periphery of the grief, he watched and listened, unobtrusively keeping to the shadows in the corners of the room, within the sight and sound of the gathered relatives and friends while they wailed and faced the grim reality that a vital member of their family was gone forever. There was a dreadful realization with the passing that their own lives were changed forever and nothing would ever be the same.

Paul Galgon was a hoot, an irrepressibly funny man who used his sense of humor and zest for life to make a living in radio and became one of the most popular and widely known on-the-air personalities in the Lehigh Valley. During the 1960s and 1970s, he supported his family by "acting up" on the air with WKAP-AM as half of the popular Allentown radio show "Dopey and Paul—Two on the Sunny Side." For a while he took a lesser-known back-row seat in the entertainment business, running a movie projector at a theater in Bethlehem.

By the time the year 2001 was winding down and people in the Lehigh Valley were preparing for the year-end holidays, the former radio personality was seventy-two, and had heart trouble. On December 4, he was checked into St. Luke's Hospital with breathing problems. A short time later he underwent routine surgery to have a pacemaker implanted in his chest, then was moved back to a bed in the CCU to recover. He was doing well until he fell out of bed, and his condition began to decline.

Cullen was working the CCU night shift and he smelled blood in the water. To a skilled predator like the homicidal RN, a patient who was in trouble and fighting for his life was the perfect prey. Cullen injected a dose of his favorite killer drug into the ailing man's medicine bag. Digoxin and pacemakers worked together like oil and water—they don't mix. Galgon nearly died, but he had a tremendous will to live—and with the expeditious help of the medical team at St. Luke's, he rallied. The outlook had begun to brighten a bit by December 28 when the killer nurse gave him another dose of digoxin. Nine hours later Galgon's kidneys gave up the unequal struggle and he died of renal failure.

The Lehigh Valley was blanketed in midwinter snow, vehicular traffic was inching cautiously along icy roadways, and smoke was hanging low over the chimneys of houses and factories when Samuel Spangler was admitted to St. Luke's Hospital for a blood transfusion. The eighty-year-old grandfather worked hard all of his life, putting in thirty-four years in the bottling department of the Lehigh Valley Dairy in Allentown, where he was a supervisor and foreman, then another thirteen years as a machine operator at the Stroh Brewing Co. in nearby Fogelsville. He also served for a time as assessor for East Allen Township.

Spangler had cancer and trouble with his liver, but he had undergone previous blood transfusions and returned to his home feeling chipper as ever. He was devoted to his family, and going home, where he was surrounded by the people he loved most, always perked him up. This time after being admitted to St. Luke's, he suffered a slight heart attack that led to his transfer to the CCU.

After a few days of treatment there seemed to be good reason to believe that the plucky old man would recover from the setback and return home as he had before—except one. He had the dreadful misfortune of being old, frail, and landing in the CCU in January 2002 while Cullen was prowling the hallways and wards with murder on his mind. After scanning Spangler's charts and medical history, the predatory nurse slipped an unprescribed dose of nitroprusside into the patient's IV or into his medicine bag. Years after the fact Cullen and investigators were a bit fuzzy about exact details of such things, but there was no confusion over the results. Nitroprusside is used to reduce blood pressure and dilate blood vessels. Used properly, it can work medical miracles; when used improperly, as it was used by Cullen, it can kill. Spangler died a few days after the drug was injected. He was grieved by Alverta, his wife of nearly sixty years, by three children, two grandchildren, other family members, and friends.

Daniel George spent his professional life making people feel good. Unlike Galgon, instead of sprightly radio chatter and images on a movie screen, George depended on good food and efficient, cheerful service to produce smiles and satisfaction. He was a well-known restaurateur, who operated George's Foodliner in Bethlehem's busy Westgate Mall for forty years, and Danny's Restaurant & Lounge in nearby Northampton County's Hanover Township for thirteen years.

The eighty-two-year-old World War II navy veteran, father of three daughters and doting grandfather, was a gregarious, friendly man. He was a devoted Mason and belonged to the Bethlehem Masonic Lodge, the Lehigh Consistory in Allentown, the Rajah Temple Shrine in Reading, and the Royal Order of Jesters. His life was busy and filled with family and friends.

George was admitted to St. Luke's for coronary artery bypass surgery, and family members were looking forward to his recovery when a male nurse with skin that was as pallid and sickly white as a three-day-old corpse injected digoxin into his IV line. George died on May 5.

On June 2, almost a full month after Daniel George's death, seventy-six-year-old Edward O'Toole died. The

Death Angel injected the paralyzing agent vecuronium into his antibiotic intravenous bag. A bachelor, O'Toole worked twenty years as district sales manager in Pennsylvania for the Clifton, New Jersey–based A. O. Smith Water Heater company, before retiring in 1990. Like George and Judge Yengo at St. Barnabas, O'Toole was a navy veteran from World War II, who was destined to be murdered by a much younger former submarine sailor, who served during the Cold War.

Cullen was caught up in a runaway orgy of homicide. Wherever he ventured on the hospital wards and in patients' rooms, death trailed along closely behind. The skilled, experienced caregiver, who was entrusted with the lives of the feeble—the most dependent and the least able to protect themselves—had become their worst nightmare. While patients struggled, gasped for breath, and fought desperately to live, the nurse assigned to their care was doing everything he could to bring their lives to an end.

He was never the "Mr. Personality" of the St. Luke's nursing corps, and kept to himself most of the time, but there were exceptions. Some of the other RNs joked about his workaholic ways—and about his practice of sitting down so infrequently while he was working a shift that they lightheartedly poked fun at him about "doing laps" around the CCU. He took the friendly teasing well, and occasionally joined his colleagues on special outings. One time he accepted an invitation to join other nurses when they got together to see a show at the State Theatre in Easton. He even gave a baby gift to one of the women who had recently given birth.

But after killing so regularly and so efficiently without getting caught for so long, he began to get careless. There were simply so many code blues on his watch, especially after he had worked at St. Luke's for eighteen months or so, that other RNs could hardly help but wonder if something was seriously wrong on the CCU.

Dealing with code blues went with the territory for

nurses working on CCUs, ICUs, and anywhere else where the most critically ill or injured patients were being treated. Ten or eleven code blues on the nine-bed unit in a month weren't unusual, according to at least one nurse. In a confidential interview with a reporter, the RN said that the CCU was suddenly experiencing about twenty to twenty-two code blues per month.

For several months code blues on the CCU were keeping nurses and doctors at St. Luke's on the run. The situation was as perplexing as it was frightening. A day-shift nurse might check out at the end of her workday, feeling good that a patient seemed to have turned a corner and was apparently on the road to recovery. It was a nice feeling to know that the nurse had made a difference. Then the grim night-shift nurse, with his close-cropped hair and the methodical, unemotional manner, would take over, and a short time later the patient's heart rate and blood pressure would escalate. He or she would lapse into a code blue.

The frequent lack of warning was one of the most distressing aspects of the emergencies. Experienced critical-care and coronary-care nurses are alert for warning signs that can signal an impending code. Nurses know when a patient's blood pressure has slumped dangerously low, when their urine output has dropped, if they're having breathing troubles, or if they have become suddenly nauseous. Under normal circumstances, when things are running smoothly, only rarely does a patient's coding come as a total surprise.

While Cullen was on duty, the condition of patients whose vital signs were normal, and who seemed to be doing well, inexplicably worsened and they slipped into code blues. Often the emergencies occurred in the late evening or early morning, during the hours the lethal RN preferred to work, and which were the worst possible time to code out. The staffs at most hospitals tend to be leaner at night with fewer nurses on duty in ICUs, and one or more of the doctors—key members of the response team—might be catching a few minutes of shut-eye. So the response time is likely to be slightly longer, and even a minute or two can make a difference between life and death.

The medical crises were experienced by patients while Cullen was on duty or shortly after he ended his shift far too often to write them off merely as coincidences. Even nurses on other units began to wonder and to talk guardedly among themselves about the alarming number of code blues on the CCU, and about the night-shift nurse who seemed so often to have been around the patients just before the emergencies were sounded. Nurses rushing to respond to CCU code blues began to wonder if Cullen's behavior wasn't perhaps more sinister than simply quirky or odd. It wasn't unusual for the wispy little RN to join in the rush to the room of a code blue; then while other RNs were working over the patient, he'd busy himself cleaning up. Often after gathering up all the medical clutter that littered the room during the frenzied effort to save a patient's life, he even carried away the trash that was dropped into containers.

Other nurses began to give him furtive, nervous, uncomfortable looks, as if something were bothering them. The same old whispers that had trailed after him as patients died unexpectedly at other hospitals started again. Colleagues, who had previously written him off as nothing more than an oddball, seriously began to wonder if there might be a more ominous element to his weird behavior.

When another coronary-care nurse informed supervisors that she found unopened heart medications in a hypodermic-needle-disposal safety bin for used syringes, known as a "sharps box," they began looking into the violation of security measures established to control and monitor hospital pharmaceuticals. The next day the concern turned to alarm when a second cache of bottled medications was found in the same place—the CCU's sharps box. Both discoveries turned up stashes of unopened arrhythmia and blood pressure medications, procainamide, and sodium nitroprusside. Like digoxin, procainamide is prescribed for treatment of irregular heartbeat. Sodium nitroprusside lowers blood pressure by dilating blood vessels, but must be administered with extreme care over time because if too large a dose is given over too long a period, it can produce a deadly by-product, cyanide. Consequently, when sodium nitroprusside is prescribed, it usually is administered intravenously.

Supervisors scanned medication records, checked patient charts, and talked with employees, trying to get to the bottom of the mystery. It appeared the medications were stolen from the locked medicine room, which was closed to most employees but was accessible to nurses. Some of the medications discovered in the sharps box hadn't been prescribed for any of the patients on the CCU.

The hospital hired a lawyer to spearhead the investigation into how the drugs got into the disposal box. The name of the same RN kept cropping up, and investigators concluded that Cullen was responsible.

Recalling the concern and turmoil months later, Cullen said, "Everybody was acting very weird at St. Luke's," and he knew something was going on. The supervisor would come in and go into the med room, and Cullen believed the hospital was trying to narrow down suspects in the missing medications to him. The last night he worked there, he went into the room and threw away more medications.

Cullen was called on the carpet and barred from contact with patients. When his superiors attempted to question him about the unopened medications in the needle bin, he was uncooperative. He stubbornly refused to submit to more questioning or to have anything more to do with the inquiry, and he was allowed to resign instead of being fired. He was ordered to bundle up any personal effects from his locker; then hospital security personnel escorted him off the property. His last day at St. Luke's was June 7, 2002, his fifteenth wedding anniversary.

After the ominous RN, whom other nurses called "Charlie," was led off the hospital grounds, there wasn't another code blue on the CCU for six weeks. Nor were caches of unopened drugs found again in the sharps box. Nurses continued to do their jobs, caring for seriously ill patients, and the excitement that had been rippling through the unit gradually subsided.

That didn't stop the questions or the whispering among Charlie's former colleagues, who were curious about what he was doing with the drugs. The medications weren't the kind that addicts would use to get high, and the amounts were too small to bother trying to sell on any black market. So, what was he doing with the drugs? More ominously they began to wonder: did the quiet RN they called Charlie and the stolen drugs have anything to do with the unprecedented rash of code blues during his shifts on the CCU?

Some worried that Cullen might have injected toxic doses of medication into drip bags mixed by the hospital pharmacy and stored in a refrigerator in the CCU medicine room. There was ample room in the bags to add more medicine, and the ports on the devices could be used to hide evidence of tampering. Of course the medicine room was accessible to nurses, and the possibility that the bags may have been used to poison patients was chilling.

Although some of the excitement subsided on the hospital wards after Cullen left, St. Luke's authorities still had questions that needed to be answered. While Cullen worked in St. Luke's CCU, 250 people died there. Experiencing a certain number of deaths among patients who were so ill was sad, although not especially alarming. But it was a different story, if someone was helping push patients into the abyss. Investigators pressed ahead with an inquiry into the deaths of nearly seventy patients.

Cullen lasted at St. Luke's almost exactly two years. This time when he walked away from his job, unlike previous experiences when he was fired or forced to resign, he left behind a serious blemish on his professional nursing record.

On September 3, almost three months after he was forced to quit, St. Luke's reported the "probable" unprofessional conduct of their rogue nurse to the Pennsylvania State Nursing Board and recommended an investigation. In the fifteen trouble-plagued years since Cullen graduated from nursing school, it was the only time that any of the nine health-care facilities he worked at ever reported his bizarre or criminal behavior to a state nursing board.

Investigators from the state regulatory agency interviewed Cullen, and he denied any wrongdoing at the hospital. Faced with the RN's flat-out denial that he did anything wrong, and without any other solid evidence to prove that he was a liar or harmed patients, the nursing board took no disciplinary action. It was a close call, but the diabolic RN seemed to have wriggled free and retained his license to continue practicing the profession that he was so appallingly betraying.

Set adrift once more, he turned his eyes back to Allentown, where he once worked in medical centers and a nursing home, and applied for a job at Sacred Heart Hospital. With a professional record still seemingly intact, and his reputation unblemished by negative responses to inquiries from human resources functionaries, he was hired by the Catholic-operated hospital.

Newly hired RNs, regardless of their experience, began work at the Catholic hospital with an eight-week orientation period aimed at helping them fit into the organization while supervisors assessed their skills and performance. During the orientation "new hires" were not permitted to work alone, and were always accompanied by a mentor. Cullen didn't last through the orientation before he was unceremoniously given his walking papers. The new hire worked for the hospital in Allentown for only 16 days—and he was never allowed to care for patients without a mentor by his side.

The nervous whispering and guarded sidelong glances began as soon as the newcomer showed up at the hospital. His old nemesis from the nursing home, Kimberly Pepe, was already working at Sacred Heart. Hospital authorities never revealed if she was one of the nurses who participated in an ultimate showdown with administrators—or if she played a vital role in the rumor mill that helped make the strangely disturbing newcomer's colleagues nervous and turned them against him.

But a report in Allentown's *Morning Call* newspaper quoted "sources" as saying nurse Pepe gathered several of her co-workers together and they informed Sacred Heart administrators that Cullen had been under suspicion elsewhere of serious misconduct and was a danger to patients. The nurses reportedly presented the hospital's human resources director with an ultimatum: Either Cullen went, or they went! The nurses didn't cite any specific incidents occurring at Sacred Heart for demanding his termination, but made it clear they wouldn't work with the creepy male RN.

Management made a practical decision to keep the employees who had already proven themselves and were valuable members of the nursing staff, instead of sticking their necks out for a single newcomer. Sacred Heart didn't bother to notify the Pennsylvania Nursing Board about the termination, the mini-revolt or any suspicions about Cullen's lack of trustworthiness around patients. A hospital spokesman later said the incident was simply interaction with employees, and it was believed there was nothing to report.

"Interpersonal problems" that developed during the RN's orientation were the official reason listed by administrators at St. Luke's for terminating the new employee after less than three weeks at the hospital. The "ten-dollar words" were bureaucratic gobbledygook that were apparently considered a nicer way to describe the reason for dumping him than spelling things out in plain everyday language and simply noting that other nurses didn't want to work with him. They didn't want to work on the same wards, or in the same hospital, because they were afraid of what he might do to patients. He was a dangerous creep.

Cullen had at last run out his string in the tri-city Allentown-Bethlehem-Easton metropolitan area of eastern Pennsylvania. So, he packed up his nursing gear and headed back to the Garden State, where everything had started. He landed a job at the Somerset Medical Center in Somerville, New Jersey.

The 355-bed acute-care and teaching hospital in the central area of the state was nationally accredited and a clinical affiliate of the University of Medicine and Dentistry of New Jersey. It had a sparkling reputation for emergency, medical, surgical, behavioral-health and rehabilitative services, and with approximately six hundred people on its medical staff had a near two-to-one employee-to-patient ratio.

It was Cullen's tenth job and the ninth hospital he worked at since graduating from the Mountainside Hospital School of Nursing in 1987. With all of his bouncing from job to job, he had never ventured outside an approximate forty-mile radius in New Jersey and eastern Pennsylvania when looking for work. The Somerset Medical Center was within that radius—and only eight miles from the Carrier Clinic, where he had been treated after one of his breakdowns and suicide attempts.

Chapter 8

Death on the Graveyard Shift

Cullen managed to clear out of eastern Pennsylvania ahead of the posse, but he wasn't forgotten. Like a modern-day Typhoid Mary, everywhere the spooky, taciturn nurse moved in the Lehigh Valley's medical community, he left misery, death, and nasty suspicions behind.

Intensive or critical-care units, burn units, coronary-care units—all were his special killing fields. Wherever the sickest or most grievously injured patients lay in hospital beds, surrounded by a bewildering electronic and plastic forest of softly beeping heart monitors, ventilators, IVs, and medicine bags while they struggled for breath and hung on tenuously to even the tiniest thread of life, the self-appointed Death Angel staked out the territory as his hunting ground. It was a familiar and protective environment.

Cullen's guile, cunning, and experience, the public's natural trust in his profession and his intimate knowledge of systems for keeping track of medications, were all put to effective use to continue the killing. Hospitals were the night-shift nurse's sheltered sanctum sanctorum, where he could move at will, stealthily seeking out and exploiting weaknesses and gaps in the safety systems that allowed him to prey on the weakest and most vulnerable victims.

Perhaps more than anything else that contributed to his ability to stay under the radar and keep his work record near spotless while stealing the lives of patients in two states was the overcaution of hospital administrators worried about possible lawsuits. Constantly they reacted to fears of being sued for defamation of character or some similar supposed breach of personal rights. Without revealing a negative word to a prospective future employer about Cullen's connection to suspicious patient deaths, stolen and misused medications, or other serious violations of hospital protocol, they merely passed on the bad apple and allowed the slaughter to continue.

A former employer of the nurse contacted by human resources personnel at the Somerset Medical Center was typical. Information was restricted to the dates of his employment, and no information was added that would lead authorities at the hospital in New Jersey to think that there could be anything wrong with the RN or that there were any questions about his past behavior with patients. A check on his New Jersey nursing license also failed to turn up anything negative.

Cullen didn't list Sacred Heart Hospital on his résumé when he applied for a nursing position at the Somerset Medical Center, but his past was already catching up to him.

Nurse Pepe filed her wrongful firing suit against the Liberty nursing home, naming him as a suspect in the insulin poisoning of Francis Henry, after Cullen began working at the medical center in Somerville.

Storm clouds already forming at St. Luke's, before he resigned under fire, also opened up with a shower of fat, oily drops of black rain when coronary-care nurses began hearing stories about their former colleague from RNs at other hospitals where he had worked. Nurses who remembered Cullen from the burn unit at Lehigh Valley

Hospital confided that they had noticed strange occurrences that were disturbingly similar to the experiences of his coworkers at St. Luke's. Patients would be holding their own; then Cullen would come on duty and their condition would suddenly worsen and they would die.

An ominous occurrence on Cullen's last day at St. Luke's before he was escorted off the property may have been the straw that broke the proverbial camel's back and caused the troubling suspicions of a group of critical care nurses to jell and convince them they had to act to protect their patients. An RN spotted him leaving the room of one of her patients, and when she asked what he was doing, he replied that he had changed the seventy-eight-year-old man's antibiotic IV. That was disturbing, because there had been no alarm indicating the IV bag was empty. The uneasiness turned to serious concern later that day when the elderly patient, who had been scheduled for discharge to a rehabilitation center, went into cardiac arrest and died.

The troubled RN and six of her colleagues, who were already worried that someone might be intentionally harming patients, talked things over and came to the frightening conclusion that their former oddball colleague might be a serial killer.

One of the nurses boldly took the initiative and launched a personal study of patient deaths in intensive care during a six-month period between January and June 2002. Records showed that Cullen worked 21.5 percent of the total hours the ICU was operating, but was on duty when 56.7 percent of the deaths occurred. Then listing the 67 deaths that occurred on the ICU during the six-month period, the inquisitive RN compared them against the shifts Cullen worked. The results were startling! Thirty-eight of the 67 patients died on his watch.

The identity of the amateur sleuths was jealously guarded and years later still wasn't publicly known, but they passed on the distressing information to hospital administrators. That was just the beginning.

One of the RNs telephoned the Pennsylvania State Board of Nursing with the suspicions. Another contacted authorities at Sacred Heart and passed on the ominous conclusions about the new hire there.

Quietly, through a third party, the nurse whose patient died after she spotted Cullen leaving the old man's room, informed Northampton County coroner Lysek about the disturbing goings-on at St. Luke's Hospital and the nurses' belief that a rogue nurse named Charles Cullen had been administering inappropriate medication to patients.

Lysek had never forgotten the frustrating investigation into Ottomar Schramm's death, and at last he had the name of the nurse he tried so fruitlessly to obtain years earlier. But St. Luke's wasn't in Northampton County. The hospital was in neighboring Lehigh County, so Lysek told the nurse she needed to take her information to the coroner there, Scott Grim.

Lysek, however, stayed involved and took a lead role in efforts to unravel the tangle of suspicions and accusations surrounding the ominous male nurse. He had waited a long time for answers, and one of the first things he did after receiving the tip was to telephone Easton Hospital to ask about Cullen. An administrator told him that the male nurse had never worked there.

Hospital spokesmen said months later that there was no deliberate intent to mislead the coroner, and the negative response to the question was accidental. Technically, Cullen wasn't a hospital employee, even though he worked there through a Harrisburg-based personnel agency. Deliberate or accidental, it was one more example in a long series of the kind of small and large blunders and oversights that helped keep the Death Angel in business for so long.

Lysek arranged a meeting, and he and the nurse sat down with Grim and Lehigh County DA James B. Martin to talk things over. The nurse and her colleagues had meticulously prepared their information, and she turned over a list to the law enforcement officials with names of sixty-seven patients who died on Cullen's wards, along with the dates of the deaths.

A few days after the conference, Martin opened a criminal investigation. With the cooperation of their tipster from St. Luke's, Martin and Lysek also recommended to the Pennsylvania state police that the law enforcement agency launch its own probe into Cullen's behavior at the hospital. A team of experienced detectives was assigned to the investigation.

The nurse told the detectives about the stolen medication, and insisted that they needed to come to the hospital to talk with her colleagues and look into the matter. The investigators were confronted at the hospital by a group of angry, worried nurses who said they suspected a former colleague caught mishandling medications may have used the drugs to murder patients in the critical-care wards. They were especially upset because they didn't believe the hospital had lived up to its responsibility to help bring the killer to justice, and had instead passed him on to other institutions to deal with.

Pressure in the case was rapidly building, and on September 3, 2002, St. Luke's President Richard Anderson wrote to the Pennsylvania State Nursing Board about what was described as Cullen's "probable unprofessional conduct." The hospital executive said the RN was believed to have stockpiled and wrongly diverted arrhythmia and blood pressure medications, but it wasn't known what he had done with them.

Anderson also pointed out that a review had been conducted of all the deaths that occurred at the hospital on the weekend that Cullen ended his employment there. "Medical records do not show that the deaths are attributable to anything but natural causes," he wrote. "However, the possibility of improper use of the drugs found in the sharp disposal container cannot be entirely ruled out."

The hospital official recommended the state regulatory agency launch an investigation. At the time the letter was written, St. Luke's didn't know about the state police investigation that was already underway, and didn't learn about the probe until January 2003.

Thanks to the coronary-care nurses who took it on themselves to alert law enforcement authorities and other agencies, by the time the state nursing board responded to the tip-off from St. Luke's and launched an inquiry into Cullen's behavior, multiple investigations—including the state police probe—were already under way. The nursing board joined other agencies in the investigation of Cullen's activities five weeks after he began working at the medical center in neighboring New Jersey.

Over the next several weeks investigators gathered and scrutinized the records of scores of patients who died in St. Luke's CCU during the final six months Cullen worked there. It was a daunting job that required investigators with a certain amount of expertise and experience with the medical profession. They had to know the language, and have some familiarity with medications, their side effects, various treatment modalities, and specific illnesses. Even some of the most skilled and experienced homicide detectives could be confused or miss something important because of unfamiliarity with medical matters.

State police detectives, working in tandem with the Lehigh County probe, realized they needed special medical expertise to interpret the information recorded in patient charts and records, and they hired Dr. Isadore Mihalakis. The same forensic pathologist who ordered work on the Helen Dean death inquiry, Mihalakis began scrutinizing the records.

Concerned by the awful suspicions and the activity of law enforcement agencies, St. Luke's hired their own outside specialist to look into the ominous cluster of patient deaths. The hospital selected Dr. Shashank Desai, an eminent cardiologist from the University of Pennsylvania, to check allegations Cullen inappropriately administered medications and to review medical records of sixty-seven patients for "inexplicable" clinical events or outcomes. The patients died in the hospital's CCU during the last six months Cullen worked there.

As the intertwining inquiries picked up steam, seventeen nurses who worked on CCU and ICU wards when patients died were eventually interviewed, and were asked about their former male colleague's behavior. The nurses had some curious stories to tell, and one RN remarked that "there were a lot of deaths on the unit," while Cullen worked there. "The deaths have dropped significantly since his departure," she said.

The most bizarre recollections, shared by several of the nurses, were of their former colleague's overzealous approach to cardiopulmonary resuscitation. Instead of leaning over a patient like his peers and working together to get the heart beating again, Cullen responded to code blues by leaping onto the bed and applying vigorous chest compressions. When other members of the medical team criticized his style, according to one nurse, he responded, "I got it pumping, didn't I?"

While investigators were peering into Cullen's past activities in the Pennsylvania hospital, he was settling into his new job at the Somerset Medical Center in New Jersey. And it was back to business as usual—caring for and killing patients who were critically ill or recovering from surgery. Somerset was about to become the scene for the worst outburst of murder in the Death Angel's ghastly sixteen-year career. Eleanor Stoecker may have been the first to die.

Eleven days after the murder of Mrs. Stoecker, the homicidal RN roaming the facility's intensive care unit struck twice, claiming the lives of seventy-four-year-old Joyce E. Mangini and eighty-nine-year-old Giacomino J. Toto. The patients died on February 23, only hours after Cullen's forty-third birthday.

Mangini was being treated on the Somerset ICU when Cullen gave her an injection of Pavulon. The powerful muscle relaxant used to kill Mangini is sometimes

prescribed for critically ill patients hooked up to ventilators. Cullen was assigned for a while as her primary
nurse after her admission to the hospital on January
24, but she was not his patient on the night she died. A
Raritan, New Jersey, homemaker, Mangini loved to cook
and crochet.

Toto was a retired vegetable farmer and mechanic with
a reputation for being able to fix just about anything that
was broken, from cars to furnaces to washing machines. A
father of five, the Bridgewater man operated Toto's Vegetable Farm in Somerset for years before his retirement.
Cullen had been assigned as his primary nurse since he was
admitted to the intensive critical-care unit with heart problems on February 12. A longtime New York Mets baseball
fan, he was killed with an injection of Pavulon.

On March 11, John J. Shanagher died in the ICU after
Cullen administered an injection of norepinephrine. In
many ways, the eighty-three-year-old retiree, called Jack by
family and friends, could have been a model for "Mr. Average Man," if such a person ever existed. The father of a
son and three daughters, a grandfather and great-grand-
father, Shanagher was devoted to his wife, Theresa, and to
their family. They were the center of his life, and while his
children were growing up, he worked two jobs in order to
give his family the very best of everything he could provide.

Shortly after midnight, every morning, he was out of bed,
getting ready to report at three-thirty to O'Dowd's Dairy,
where he worked until about 11:00 A.M. or noon. After
spending a few hours at home and resting up, he headed
for work at his second job with the U. S. Post Office and
put in another five hours. His son, John Michael Shanagher,
was in college when O'Dowd's closed, and the hardworking family man became a full-time mail carrier.

Although the families didn't know each other, the
Shanagher brood spent much of their childhood in Montclair, where Cullen attended nursing school, a few minutes'
drive south of Cullen's home in West Orange. The

Shanagher children knew other youngsters who attended school with the skinny little loner.

A U. S. Army veteran of World War II, Jack Shanagher wasn't a man who liked attracting attention, but sometimes talked with family and close friends about his experience helping to liberate inmates of concentration camps while the conflict was winding down in Europe. He was justifiably proud of his service with the Eighty-second Airborne, and the fighting force's unique experience as the only American Army division in history to serve under a foreign commander. The Eighty-second was under the command of British field marshal Bernard Law Montgomery, and it remained in combat over a wide area of Europe until the end of the war.

John Michael, Shanagher's son, still talks about his quiet, unassuming father as "the Forrest Gump of World War Two. Wherever you turn around," he said, "my father was wandering around Europe."

After retirement from the U. S. Postal Service in 1981, Shanagher and his wife moved to the Jersey Shore. A Yankee fan, the retiree watched his baseball team on television, and busied himself fixing things for his wife and doing occasional handyman jobs for neighbors. When the aging processes made it too difficult for the couple to continue handling things on their own, they moved in with their son and his family in Bridgewater. Shanagher's adoring grandchildren called the unassuming, gentle little man who had begun to show the debilitating effects of Alzheimer's, "Papop." In November 2002, after he fell and the family decided they could no longer provide the care he needed by themselves, he was moved into a nursing home a few blocks down the street from their house.

The following March after he developed a blood clot on his leg, he was taken to the emergency room at Somerset Medical Center, then transferred to the ICU. Doctors discussed a surgical procedure with his son, but John Michael was against it, so the elderly man continued to take blood thinners. By the second week of March he was expected to return to the nursing home in a couple of days.

But Cullen had his own plans for the beloved patriarch. Eight days after Shanagher was admitted to the hospital, the lethal nurse slipped into his room and injected him with the powerful drug that increases heart rate and blood pressure.

The Shanaghers were a close family, and every day—without fail—while he was in the nursing home, then the hospital, at least one of them visited with the patriarch for a minimum of two hours, often three or four. They were determined to make it plain to the devoted family man that he wasn't abandoned by the people who loved him most. Despite the Alzheimer's, he recognized his son and other family members, and most days he was able to talk with them and understand the conversation.

On Monday, March 10, his wife, son, and daughter-in-law all visited with him, and John Michael stopped by the hospital twice to talk with his father. During a late-evening visit they were chatting when Shanagher began saying that he needed to use the toilet, and a male nurse walked in and volunteered to help the confused old man in the bathroom.

Early the next morning, sometime around six o'clock, John Michael received a telephone call from the hospital, informing him that his father had died. The news was an appalling shock, because the elder Shanagher had seemed to be physically strong and doing so well. But he was old and sick, so his son reluctantly accepted the death as part of the natural cycle of life. Parents die, and the people who love them have to cope with the loss. John Michael drew some comfort from the thought that God decided his father and the family had enough of suffering, so He reached down and took the ailing old man before things got worse.

Before Jack Shanagher's death the worst tragedy to visit the family was the loss of their daughter, Linda, who died in 1962 of congenital heart defects when she was twelve. More than forty years later, Jack Shanagher was laid to rest beside the grave of his daughter.

Looking back, months after the early-morning telephone message from the hospital, the grieving son was still wondering if the caller was the same death-dealing male nurse he later learned had accessed the elderly man's medical chart late the previous night, then injected him with a dose of unprescribed medication. By the time Shanagher died, Cullen's instinct for murder was raging. He was killing approximately one patient per month.

Eighty-year-old Dorothea K. Hoagland was admitted to the ICU on April 6, and died a few hours later. Cullen injected her with the same drug he used to kill Shanagher. The Middlesex, New Jersey, woman was a patient at the hospital for three days.

On May 5, 2003, Cullen switched drugs and injected Melvin T. Simcoe, a sixty-six-year-old corporate manager, with sodium nitroprusside. It was the same blood-diluting, anti-hypertensive drug used more than a year earlier to kill Samuel Spangler in St. Luke's ICU. Simcoe, of Green Brook, New Jersey, a father of four, was admitted to the hospital on April 7, and transferred a few days later to the intensive-care unit for treatment of pneumonia.

The killer turned back to norepinephrine to kill twenty-one-year-old Michael Thomas Strenko, the patient believed to have been the youngest victim in the extended orgy of murder. In many ways Strenko lived a typical boyhood, delivering the local newspaper, the *Courier News*, watching professional wrestling on television, and like the much older Jack Shanagher, cheering his favorite baseball team, the New York Yankees. He was a 1999 graduate of Manville High School in Manville, where he lettered in soccer and in track and field. Strenko later attended Raritan Valley Community College and was a computer science student at Seton Hall University.

The boy in a classic nuclear family, he had an older sister,

Melissa, and was a cutup who loved to do comedy impressions. Framed school pictures of the brother and sister lined the wall along the staircase of their neatly kept two-story family home, with the photos when they were youngest at the top, moving to the most recent at the bottom. His high-school graduation photos showed a handsome, confident young man who seemed to have a lifetime ahead of him.

Strenko was proud of his athletic physique and spiked hair, and grew up in a loving home, drove his car with the stereo booming, and savored the thrill of climbing on roller coasters for daredevil rides. Shortly before his hospitalization he confided to his parents, Thomas and Mary Strenko, that he was thinking about giving his longtime girlfriend an engagement ring. His life was exciting and full.

A malfunction of the immune system that causes the body to attack its own red blood cells, and is known as autoimmune hemolytic anemia, landed the strapping 175-pound six-footer in the hospital to have his spleen removed. It was a serious ailment, but not a condition that couldn't be controlled with medical treatment, and was normally fatal only in unusual circumstances.

Strenko was familiar with the dangers and the limitations of the ailment, which drained his energy and turned his skin and eyes a sallow yellow. He was taking steroids to treat it, when he passed out in the parking lot of Fisher Scientific, where he worked in the shipping department. His collapse was a shock because he was feeling so good only a few days earlier that he stopped by his parents' home to pump iron. The steroids were adding bulk to his body.

The young man was admitted to the critical-care unit on May 8, and wasn't there for quite a week before he began having serious trouble. Six days after he was admitted, he nearly died and doctors were called in to resuscitate him. He survived that crisis, but unknown to the patient, his family, his doctors—and most of his nurses—he was marked for death.

Strenko was sedated and hooked up to a ventilator after

surgeons removed his spleen, but his blood pressure and heart rate were normal two days later when his exhausted parents left the hospital to get some sleep after hovering at his bedside for thirty-six hours straight. He was free of fever, his vital signs were good, and even his skin was beginning to look more normal.

By the time Tom and Mary Strenko returned to the hospital at about 10:30 P.M., their son's blood pressure was plunging and he was taking an inexplicably sudden turn for the worse. Shortly after midnight he coded—twice. It was the early-morning hours of May 15, and doctors and nurses, responding to a code blue, were working desperately to resuscitate him one more time.

His distressed family members were in the waiting room when a strange, sallow-faced male nurse sidled quietly up to them and began to give them unsolicited, unwelcome, and brutally graphic advice about what was going on and their son's meager chances of surviving the current crises. Staring into their eyes, he said their son was gravely ill, and patients as sick as Michael Thomas often didn't survive. The RN talked about the drugs doctors were using and went into other details that the anguished, fearful couple simply didn't wish or need to hear at that time. Mary Strenko told him to leave, and he turned and left.

The weird male nurse, who liked hanging around to watch and listen to grieving families, knew a lot about what was going on inside their son's room, because soon after beginning his overnight shift, he had stolen a dose of norepinephrine, a drug used to increase heart rate and blood pressure. Then he injected the young man with the unauthorized medication.

Shortly before 2:00 A.M., Mary Strenko walked into her son's room and stopped the resuscitation efforts. The pounding and the thrashing about was too violent, and he had undergone enough pain. Michael Strenko died in the Somerset Medical Center's intensive-care unit at about 2:00 A.M., in the same hospital where he was born.

An autopsy conducted at the medical center attributed the cause of death to his blood ailment, autoimmune hemolytic anemia.

Chapter 9

Gathering Souls

The year 2002 was probably the most perilous year in Cullen's sordid career as a medical serial killer—until 2003. The days of 2002 were filled with investigations of patients' mysterious deaths that he was suspected of playing a hand in. District attorneys and coroners in two counties were pulled into investigations, state police launched two probes, and an internal inquiry at one hospital led to his forced resignation. Other RNs banded together at two different hospitals to demand his termination and several nurses personally urged administrators, law enforcement agencies, and state-regulatory bodies to investigate suspicions that he was deliberately harming patients.

Then just as it looked like the rope was tightening around his neck, he slipped the noose once more and seemingly walked away unscathed. Suspicions weren't proof, and no one turned up the kind of solid, concrete evidence of misbehavior they believed was needed to file charges accusing him of murder or other serious criminal offenses.

Without autopsies on patients who had died weeks or months ago, investigators were left with little to do except examine records in efforts to develop evidence of suspicious deaths or criminal activities.

After weeks of scrutinizing the medical records of patients who died in critical-care units while Cullen worked as a nurse there, Dr. Mihalakis reported he was unable to establish a pattern. Dr. Desai also failed to find evidence that any of the deaths examined during months of studying the patient files were due to other than natural causes.

State police investigators apparently didn't learn of the murder accusations stemming from Francis Henry's death and Nurse Pepe's firing at the Liberty nursing home, or of the persistent claims by Mrs. Dean's son that she was given a fatal injection of unauthorized drugs at Warren Hospital. "Nothing prosecutable" was turned up in the Pennsylvania state police probe to link Cullen firmly to the alarming string of suspicious deaths in the St. Luke's coronary-care unit, according to a senior officer.

Even the Pennsylvania State Board of Nursing struck out after checking out his work history and confronting him with allegations he had hidden drugs. Cullen denied he did any such thing. The board's investigator gave a copy of his findings to the state police, but the regulatory agency didn't call for a formal hearing in the case.

Cullen's modus operandi of working on critical-care wards and consistently preying on the sickest patients had continued to provide him with great camouflage. The deaths of a certain number of patients being treated in CCUs were expected and were a sad fact of life. If patients weren't very sick to begin with, they wouldn't be in coronary care.

Martin wrote a letter notifying the hospital that his investigation was closed, and he had no plans to prosecute anyone in connection with the probe. During the nine-month-long inquiry, no autopsies were conducted, and no toxicology or physical evidence was gathered that could be useful in a confrontation with Cullen. He was never called in by police or prosecutor's officers for questioning. The

Lehigh County DA noted that he was reserving the right to reopen the investigation. The state police inquiry also ended without turning up evidence of criminal wrongdoing.

The dour male nurse—with the lethal bedside manner and the sober, measured, businesslike approach to murder—had survived another close call. That was a dreadful development for patients in the coronary-care unit at the Somerset Medical Center.

While death was stalking the Somerset Medical CCU, Cullen's personal life had temporarily leveled off. He moved from his home of ten years in the basement apartment in Phillipsburg to a two-story, two-family wood-frame and red-brick house with a white picket fence on Fernwood Street in Bethlehem. He set up housekeeping there with another nurse, named Cathy, as a live-in girlfriend. She already had children of her own, and by May or June she was expecting again.

The father-to-be didn't make any significant impression on his new neighbors, and his outward demeanor didn't vary much, if at all, from his behavior in Phillipsburg. The newcomers didn't exchange visits with neighbors, kept the shades on their windows down, and about the only times they were seen outside was when they were traveling to or from work or checking the mailbox decorated with the big American flag.

Cullen had little to say to neighbors beyond an occasional hello, in response to their greetings. But he didn't cause trouble, and unlike his performance in Phillipsburg, he faithfully shoveled the snow off his walks.

His outward demeanor was misleading. Inside, his mind was filled with thoughts of destruction, and his passion for murder was out of control.

When Cullen decided to kill, he most often gave in to a sudden urge to take a patient's life. On other, fewer occasions, the murders were committed only after studied reasoning and painstaking preparation. The more carefully planned murders usually occurred after he had watched a patient's condition steadily worsen over a period of a few days.

In his twisted, diseased mind, patients were dehumanized. In almost every case his victims weren't people with names, faces, and personalities to remember, but notations and statistics written in patient files and charts that he could study and interpret, figuring out which ones he could kill while attracting the least suspicion of foul play.

Successful murders left him with a mixture of feelings, according to his own recollections, which he shared much later. The fear of being caught was always there, he said, but the emotions were tempered by satisfaction that he had ended the patient's suffering. There was also guilt, which he said was sometimes so overwhelming that he felt sick about it, and would tell himself "never again." He knew in his heart that he had no right to play God, and he knew that eventually he was almost certain to be caught—but that didn't stop him.

Jin Kyung Han wasn't elderly, but in other important ways she was just the kind of patient he was looking for. When he began carrying out plans for her murder, she wasn't one of his patients, but he had been assigned to her care the night before, and he knew she was critically ill with cancer and heart problems. Cullen prepared for her murder with the typically meticulous planning that had served him so well in the past.

He was working his regular graveyard shift, from 7:00 P.M. to 7:00 A.M. on June 15 to 16, when he accessed medication through a wheeled drug-dispensing device with a locking cabinet and drawers, which is operated through a built-in computer. Cullen ordered digoxin from the machine, which is known by its brand name, Pyxis. The Pyxis device was a key element in one of two methods for storing and dispensing medications to patients at Somerset.

The least complex system called for the pharmacy to provide a twenty-four-hour supply of the medication needed by a specific patient to the nursing station. The drug container was clearly labeled with the name of the patient and with the dosage to be administered, then locked in a file cabinet.

Pyxis was used to keep additional supplies of prescribed medications for patients at the nursing station, so that it would be easily available in emergencies. Cullen used the drug supply to create emergencies.

Accessing the medication through the Pyxis device, Cullen entered his nurse's ID number on the touch screen, made a selection from a list of patient names, selected the name of an ordering doctor, then designated which drug and dosage he wished to withdraw. In moments a drawer containing digoxin slid open, and Cullen withdrew the medication. Then, in an effort to muddy the trail, he canceled the order on the computer. The next step was concentrated on his chosen victim. Cullen tapped into another computerized system called Cerner to bring up Han's medical records.

At some time in the late-evening or early-morning hours, while the hallway lights on the wards were dim and the hospital was quiet, the night-shift nurse injected the digoxin into a port on the woman's drip bag. The forty-year-old homemaker, and mother of two, reacted rapidly to the unprescribed medication. Her heart began acting up, and she lapsed into cardiac malfunction after showing classic symptoms of digoxin poisoning. Nurses responding to the emergency stabilized her and administered an antidote after recognizing the side effects of the drug. A drug called digibind is commonly used to treat digoxin overdoses, but it wasn't publicly revealed if that was the antidote administered to Han.

A blood sample from Han, which was rushed to the laboratory for analysis, turned up an alarmingly elevated level of digoxin. The drug was prescribed for her when she was admitted to the hospital on June 12, but it was discontinued after two days because she developed an irregular heartbeat. Nurses knew that and her medical chart showed that digoxin had clearly been off-limits as a medication for two days before she had her near brush with death.

The patient was critically ill when she was admitted to the hospital, and doctors, nurses, and other caregivers were already fighting tooth and nail to keep her alive. Knowledge that the battle was almost lost because an un-prescribed medication somehow found its way into her bloodstream was deeply disturbing. The mystery deep-ened on June 18, two days after the Han emergency, when an inventory of the hospital's medication-dispensing sys-tems disclosed that two bottles of digoxin were missing. No one could figure out what happened to them.

As troubling as the recent developments were, it didn't necessarily mean that the presence of digoxin in her system was evidence of a blunder of some sort or of a criminal act. There seemed to be a possibility that the digoxin could have found its way into her system in a completely innocent manner. The ethnic Korean woman from Basking Ridge had been drinking an herbal mushroom-based tea, and med-ical staffers wondered if ingredients in the drink might have been responsible for the high level of digoxin in her system. A sample of the tea was sent to the New Jersey Poison Information and Education System (PIES) at the University of Medicine and Dentistry of New Jersey in Newark for analysis.

There were other reasons for concern that something untoward was occurring on Somerset's critical-care wards, even before Han's close brush with death, but it would be a while before officials began connecting the dots. A series of problems involving the administration of apparently unauthorized medications had occurred. During the week between May 28 and June 4, two patients experienced sudden drops in blood sugar that were so precipitous that they had to have been caused by overdoses of insulin.

The mysterious difficulties with medication mishaps—or worse—wouldn't end with Han, and officials at Somerset

Medical were about to be forced by circumstances to sit up and take a hands-on role in straightening the matter out.

Jin Kyung Han was discharged from Somerset Medical Center on June 29 and returned home to her husband and two children after recovering from the toxic dose of digoxin. On September 5, she was readmitted to the hospital and died the same day. Her death was found not to be related to the potentially lethal dose of medication administered to her nearly three months earlier.

Chapter 10

Death of a Priest

While investigators were attempting to solve the baffling riddle of how the digoxin got into Han's blood, the Very Reverend Florian J. Gall suffered a fatal heart attack and died under disturbing circumstances.

The sixty-eight-year-old Catholic priest served as pastor at Our Lady of Lourdes Parish in the Whitehouse Station neighborhood in Readington, Hunterdon County, since 1984, and had experienced intermittent health-related difficulties after undergoing heart bypass surgery in March. He celebrated his first mass in months just a few days before he was returned to the hospital on June 13, with a high fever. The initial diagnosis was pneumonia, and he was admitted to the eight-bed ICU in critical condition. When his condition continued to deteriorate, he was placed in a drug-induced coma so that he could be hooked up to a ventilator to help him breathe.

Father Gall attended St. Charles College in Catonsville, Maryland, studied theology at St. Mary's Seminary and University in Baltimore, and earned his master's in theology from Princeton Theological Seminary. He served as a pastor at St. Joseph's Church in Bound Brook before moving to Our Lady of Lourdes.

He grew up in Perth Amboy, New Jersey, across the street from Holy Trinity, a Slovakian Catholic Church, where he and his parents and four siblings were parishioners. From early childhood his religion was a focal point of his life, and his closest friends were three other boys, who, like him, all wanted to become priests. When they weren't attending church or at a church-related affair, they were often in the Gall backyard, where they played games with a religious theme or sponsoring religious plays and festivals for other children in the neighborhood.

As an adult the taciturn priest was considered by many who didn't know him well to be a shy, even intimidating man, because he was so quiet and avoided displays of emotion. But his personality bloomed and he became more gregarious when talk turned to subjects he was familiar with and loved. One of those topics was his working-class Czechoslovakian background and growing up in a neighborhood of Czech immigrants, but his church was always first and foremost. As an adult he indulged his pride in his ancestry by twice visiting Slovakia. At other times he vacationed with a fellow priest, and the two old friends immersed themselves in reading and quiet conversation. Father Gall favored books on history and, of course, religion.

He had a special love for the liturgy, the ritual of the Catholic Mass. As a young priest he took an important hands-on role instituting reforms on a national level stemming from the Second Vatican Council in 1962, which included modernizing the language of the liturgy.

Father Gall's second love after the church was sacred music. He composed hymns and played the organ, piano, and several other instruments well. The fine acoustical features of the church's interior and the excellent quality of the pipe organ and piano were testaments to his hands-on love of music. Younger priests often looked to him for advice about music and the liturgy.

The Metuchen Diocese's first vicar for pastoral life, he founded the Diocesean Festival Choir, and belonged to several sacred music-related organizations. Despite his famous reserve, he was more popular with his flock than he may have believed and built up the parish at Our Lady of Lourdes to approximately 1,500 people during his nineteen years as vicar.

A few days after being placed on the ventilator, the priest's condition had improved so much that doctors recommended to his younger sister, Lucille Gall, that she cancel a DNR order. Ms. Gall was a nurse who took a leave of absence from her regular job to help look after her ailing brother during the two weeks he was hospitalized. Although he was seriously ill, he wasn't considered terminal, and Lucille, who was very close to her brother, was spending about twelve hours a day with him.

While she was visiting on the evening of June 27, an unobtrusive, frail-looking male nurse walked into the room to check on her brother's intravenous drip, but she didn't pay any special attention to him. He was quiet, avoided making eye contact, and it would be months before she learned of the little man's loathsome acts and how dangerous he was to her brother.

She expected Father Gall "to recover," she later recalled. His doctors told her that he was "doing better." Before declining and being placed in the coma, he was even talking optimistically about getting out of the hospital and celebrating mass.

On June 27, while his doctors slowly began to bring him out of the coma, she kept her daily vigil at his bedside until 9:00 P.M. Before leaving, she softly called his name, and he opened his eyes wide and looked at her. She believed he heard her voice.

Later that night Cullen repeated the same process with the priest that he carried out to administer the toxic dose of digoxin to Han. During his overnight shift of 7:00 P.M. to 7:00 A.M., the diabolical RN pulled up Father Gall's medical records on the Cerner system. The priest wasn't one of his patients, but he had easy access to his room and several hours of semiprivacy to work in while the wards were clear of visitors and only a handful of other health-care workers were around.

Just as he did with other victims, Cullen typed the name of one of his patients on the mobile Pyxis computer, and withdrew a dose of digoxin before canceling the order. As the final step in the process, he padded silently into the priest's room and administered a lethal overdose of the heart drug into his drip bag. Cullen checked out at the end of his shift before the patient died.

Like Han, who had been taken off the drug, at one time digoxin was prescribed for Father Gall to control a rapid heartbeat. But digoxin was discontinued as a medication on June 24, and doctors and nurses were closely monitoring the drug's levels in his system, with regular blood tests. Digoxin can remain in the system for as long as twenty days and drug levels are measured for up to two weeks after it has been administered to ensure that it has stabilized at acceptable therapeutic levels.

Blood tests conducted on June 24 and on June 27 showed acceptable levels of the drug. But when a routine blood scan was conducted at six o'clock on the morning of June 28, it disclosed a radical change in the digoxin level. It had surged to a perilous 9.61 nanograms per millimeter—even though he hadn't received any authorized doses of the drug for three days. Therapeutic levels of the drug range from 0.8 to 2.2.

Alarmed by the toxically abnormal readings, described in medical parlance as "panic values," the medical staff hurriedly intervened to change the course of the patient's treatment. But Father Gall's condition remained grave.

The frail, sick man was locked in a desperate battle for his life when his doctor, Ruby Halper-Erkkila, telephoned his sister at her home in the Fords neighborhood of Woodbridge, New Jersey, at about 9:00 A.M. Dr. Halper-

Erkkila advised Ms. Gall that her brother's condition had deteriorated. Lucille Gall later recalled that she was told he had an irregular heartbeat and high potassium levels and was going to be put on kidney dialysis.

The veteran health-care professional had been a hospital pediatrics nurse and was familiar with digoxin. Looking back months later on the morning her brother died, she said that if she had been informed that his digoxin level was so high, she would have asked that he be given an immediate antidote for the drug. With her experience she would have realized that digoxin caused him to go into ventricular tachycardia. No one told her about the alarmingly high level of digoxin in his system, either during the telephone call or later at the hospital.

Lucille Gall and her brother were very close, and she arrived at the Somerset Medical Center twenty to thirty minutes after she took the urgent call from the physician. Father Gall was in cardiac arrest, his complexion had turned blue, and the room was full of medical professionals struggling to keep him alive. A team of doctors and nurses were bending over the bed, administering cardiopulmonary resuscitation.

It was a ghastly scene, even for an experienced nurse, watching the medical team pounding on the frail chest of the gentle man who had lived his life for others and for his God. It seemed to Lucille Gall that it was her brother's time to die—that it was God's will—and she pleaded with the nurses and doctor working so desperately over his limp body to stop. When the medical workers said they wanted to give him a digoxin antidote, she replied: "Fine, but that's it."

Father Gall was pronounced dead at 10:15 A.M., slightly more than three hours after Cullen completed his shift. Early the same evening when the nurse began his new overnight shift, he called up the priest's medical records on the Cerner system once more to see if he had died.

Dr. Halper-Erkkila asked the priest's sister if she wanted an autopsy. It was a routine question. Unaware of the role digoxin played in his death, the heartbroken nurse said, "No, he's been through enough." A postmortem examination wouldn't bring him back to life.

The hospital also decided against requesting an autopsy, even though they are required by the state in cases of possible homicides, suspicious deaths, unattended deaths, such as suicides, or in other unusual circumstances. According to New Jersey state law at the time, hospitals, law enforcement authorities, physicians, and emergency medical workers were all authorized to request postmortems.

The death certificate signed by Dr. Halper-Erkkila two days after the priest lost his desperate struggle for life, listed pseudomonal sepsis (a bacterial infection), ventricular tachycardia (abnormal or irregular heart rhythm), and hyperkalemia (an excess potassium level) as causes of death. The conditions were all classic symptoms of digoxin poisoning, but there was no mention of the drug on the document. The death was described on the certificate as natural. But no one at the hospital told Father Gall's sister that his serum level of digoxin was almost quadruple what it should have been—or that he died of an overdose of the medication.

A few days after the appallingly violent scene in Father Gall's hospital room, he was laid to rest in a quiet, serene setting of Holy Trinity Cemetery in the Hopelawn section of Woodbridge near the church he attended as a boy.

There was still no public talk of digoxin poisoning on July 2, when one of Father Gall's closest and oldest friends, the Reverend William Mickiewicz, preached his funeral mass at Our Lady of Lourdes Church. The two priests met when they were teenagers attending St. Mary's Seminary in Baltimore almost a half century earlier and their longtime friendship grew even closer when they were assigned to neighboring parishes in Hunterdon County churches. Father Gall was pastor of Our Lady of Lourdes Church, and Father Mickiewicz was pastor of St. John Neumann Roman Catholic Church in nearby Califon. They went on vacation together, kept in close touch by telephone, and had celebrated the fiftieth anniversary of their ordinations only a short time earlier.

Every seat in the church was filled and people were standing in the back and outside for the funeral of the parish priest who used to worry because he thought people disliked him for being too standoffish. Mourners joined together singing old-world hymns that might have been selected for the funeral by the quiet, introspective priest himself if he had been around to ask.

Father Mickiewicz told stories about his old friend, and said he once gave him a license plate that read, TO KNOW ME IS TO LOVE ME. The St. John Neumann pastor got a big laugh out of that. So did the mourners at the mass.

The near death of Jin Kyung Han and the unexpected death of Father Gall, only twelve days later, were troubling enough, but there were other reasons for hospital authorities to be concerned. Three routine blood tests in June—the same month the Han and Gall emergencies occurred—indicated that somehow three patients were given "abnormal" doses of digoxin or insulin. Alarmed by the cluster of "abnormal" lab value findings, the medical center launched an internal investigation to get to the bottom of the mystery. On July 1 the puzzling enigma deepened when the hospital discovered that digoxin was missing from its medication-dispensing system.

While nasty suspicions were crystallizing into evidence of wrongdoing, technology, the times, and an alert medical expert—with an encyclopedic knowledge of poisons and the curiosity and deductive reasoning of a Sherlock Holmes—were catching up to the treacherous RN.

The medical expert was one of the nation's leading toxicologists, PIES executive director Dr. Steven M. Marcus. The agency was more commonly known around the state as the poison control center. On July 9, about two weeks after he was asked for help by Somerset authorities, Dr. Marcus told hospital officials during a conference call that the Han overdose could have resulted from "a malicious act." Hospital authorities chose not to tell him at that time about the high digoxin levels in Father Gall's system or about two other cases of critically low blood sugar levels, bellwether indications of insulin overdoses.

Digoxin was a sensitive drug to handle and accidents and other problems with it were far from unknown. The New Jersey poison control center recorded eighty-two overdoses from digoxin and related drugs the previous year, and 2003 would end with seventy-three reported. A report by the American Association of Poison Control Centers Toxic Exposure Surveillance System revealed 112 fatal digoxin overdoses in 2002, including two known suicides. The association report also noted 2,910 nonfatal overdoses from digoxin and related drugs. About half the overdoses occurred in hospitals. But the drug overdoses didn't usually come in clusters, and the flare-up at the Somerset Medical Center was alarming.

During the telephone conference hospital administrators tried to focus the conversation on the possibility that Han's mushroom-based herbal tea could have been responsible for her high digoxin level.

With growing exasperation Dr. Marcus insisted that Han's improper medication could have been malicious, and he was adamant about steering the talk back to the recent pattern of overdoses at the hospital. Somerset Medical Center chief medical officer Dr. William K. Cors later told reporters that Marcus was asked one simple question about the tea, and said it was felt that the toxicologist jumped to conclusions by suggesting a malicious act.

Marcus stubbornly insisted that it was time to notify other authorities about the suspicious deaths at Somerset. "If there is somebody out there that is purposely doing this to individuals at your hospital," he declared, "we have a legal obligation to report this."

Cors responded with an "okay," but later in the conversation seemed to backtrack and indicated hospital authorities were still unsure if outside authorities should be notified. "We have been trying to investigate this to get more information before we make any kind of rush to judgment," he said, according to recordings of the exchange.

Marcus responded by cautioning that in the past medical facilities faced with similar problems had made the mistake of waiting too long to notify other authorities.

"Physicians . . . are really infamously poor in doing a forensic investigation," the poison chief pointed out.

"Who does good forensic investigations?" Cors asked.

"Well, this is a police matter," Marcus replied. "Quite honestly, if you don't report it to the police and somebody else dies and then it comes up that you stonewalled it you're really going to look terrible."

Responding to a remark by Cors that he was more worried about protecting patients than he was about protecting himself, Marcus said he was concerned about patient safety as well. "I'm also very concerned that we'll all be caught with our pants down," the poison control chief added, "and we'll look like morons."

Dr. Marcus's dander was up, and frustrated by the attitude of hospital officials, he finally informed the medical center authorities that he was going to report the case to the New Jersey Department of Health and Senior Services (NJDHSS). Firing off a final shot over their bow, he disclosed that he taped the conversation.

As he had vowed to do, Marcus tapped out an e-mail to authorities at the state health department informing them about the trouble at Somerset. "I spoke to the risk manager of the hospital, the director of pharmacy, the chief operating officer and the chief medical officer and they told me that they were not planning on reporting these incidents to anyone, not the NJDHSS or the police until they mount a thorough investigation."

The toxicologist and poison control chief added that he told Somerset Medical authorities that he believed he was obligated by state regulations to make a report to the NJDHSS.

The fractious confrontation was distressing, and the next day the hospital contacted the New Jersey Department of Health and Senior Services and advised that "abnormal lab values" involving patients had turned up at Somerset Medical. That was hospital talk meaning that a measurement of a bodily function or state, such as cholesterol or blood sugar, was found to be outside the normal range. Four cases were identified in the initial report, and two more were added a short time later.

Federal privacy regulations prevented public disclosure of the names, but identifications of patients involved in the probe identified by number included:

Patient 1—A male with abnormally low blood sugar, who responded to treatment and was discharged with no additional problems.

Patient 2—A female with low blood sugar, who was immediately treated. She responded to treatment, but died several days later from an ailment unrelated to the blood sugar problem. She was elderly with multiple medical problems.

Patient 3—A female who was found with a high level of digoxin in her system. She was treated, responded well, and was discharged from the hospital.

Patient 4—A male found to have a high level of digoxin in his system. He died due to "multiple system failures," but hospital authorities indicated they couldn't determine if the high digoxin levels contributed to his death.

Patient 5—A female with low blood sugar, who was treated and responded well. She died a few days later from causes that were unrelated to the blood sugar level.

Patient 6—A male who died and was included in the group because he had low blood sugar. Hospital authorities indicated they believed his death was unrelated to the abnormal laboratory findings.

The health department responded to the alarms from the

hospital and from Dr. Marcus by sending a team of investigators to Somerset to determine if the medical center's laboratory had measured drug levels accurately. Faulty laboratory equipment and practices were quickly ruled out as possible factors in the abnormal results. A larger team of investigators dispatched to review the process for dispensing medication, and to confirm that the facility was complying with licensing standards, also failed to turn up anything that might account for the disturbing lab test results.

The medical center was allowed to continue its inquiry, and review of patient and employee records consistently turned up the name of the same nurse, Charles Cullen. But the hospital's mission was caring for the sick and injured, not detective work, and after deciding that it had exhausted its internal abilities to solve the mystery, outside experts were called in to take over and spearhead the rapidly expanding probe. The newcomers showed up in early August, interviewing physicians and staff members and conducting a thorough inspection of the medical center's processes. The investigation team was beefed up later in the month with additional experts. The expansive probe, nevertheless, ended with the same frustrating inconclusive results as the hospital's internal inquiry, but not until they uncovered strong confirmation of Cullen's links to patients with the abnormal lab results.

Somerset Medical Center may have been more tardy than timely when it finally got around to notifying the state health department about the disturbing lab test results. According to a directive from Health Commissioner Clifton R. Lacy, of New Jersey, issued the previous May to the CEOs of all hospitals in the Garden State, they were required to report any event "jeopardizing the health and safety of patients. . . ." Reportable events, including "patient death or serious disability associated with a medication error," were to be passed on to state authorities as soon as possible, but no later than three hours after discovery.

Discovery of the dangerously high levels of digoxin in

tests of blood taken from Father Gall and a female patient in mid and late June might seem to have been reportable events, but CEO Dennis C. Miller, of Somerset, later told reporters that no notification was passed on because other factors instead of medication error could have been responsible. Once, possible alternative factors such as faulty laboratory equipment, human error, defective medication, or other medical conditions were ruled out, the New Jersey Department of Health was contacted and asked to conduct an investigation.

There was no mention in the July 10 report about the computer records tying Cullen to the digoxin overdoses. Hospital officials also complained about the poison control chief to the state health department. They accused him of a rush to judgment and claimed he was unduly pressuring them, according to the Newark *Star-Ledger*. The medical center telephoned Dr. Marcus to let him know about the action taken—and continued to forge ahead with its own internal inquiry.

Months later a statement on the medical center's Web site described the poison center chief's warning as "an opinion that was based on limited facts and without having seen any patient files."

CEO Dennis C. Miller later told CBS-TV's *60 Minutes* that after the internal investigation failed to determine what was causing the digoxin overdoses tied to Reverend Gall's death and the other emergency (with Mrs. Han) that "certainly, it was—went through my mind, 'Could possibly someone be doing this maliciously.'"

Something that was very wrong was going on, and if Miller's suspicions were justified, it could mean the lives of patients were in deadly peril.

After two more overdoses occurred on the CCU, an alarmed state investigator tapped out an e-mail to her supervisor, Marilyn Dahl, the deputy health commissioner of health care quality. "In light of the 6th incident . . . where does our responsibility lie in terms of notification of, say, Legal Affairs?" the investigator asked.

Efforts by newspaper reporters to learn weeks later what the response to the query was were rebuffed by the department. Although investigators were unable to determine the cause of the high levels of digoxin of so many patients at the medical center, the health department did not bring the mystery to the attention of the state attorney general or notify any other law enforcement agencies.

Despite all the fuss and the fury, and the back-and-forth exchanges between Somerset Medical Center, Dr. Marcus and the state Department of Health and Senior Services about the "abnormal lab values" and alarming clusters of patient deaths, no one picked up the telephone at that time to inform Somerset County prosecutor Wayne J. Forrest's office about the problem. It would be almost three months before that would happen.

Serious trouble was shaping up on another front for the homicidal nurse. During the fifteen years Cullen was perfecting his techniques for committing homicide on hospital wards, sophisticated fail-safe systems were being developed and utilized that were making it more difficult for him to continue getting away with wholesale murder. At last, time was running out.

Some of the same sophisticated computer systems Cullen used to circumvent hospital safety systems and obtain information and drugs were called on to identify and pinpoint the nurse who was running amok on the wards and to pinpoint his operating techniques. The high-tech detective work tied Cullen directly to the digoxin used in the deadly attacks on Han and Father Gall.

The Cerner device that Cullen accessed to obtain patient records at Somerset was a cutting-edge computerized care system that permitted authorized health-care workers to use a terminal to punch up the medical and drug history of patients. A complete picture could be obtained in seconds.

Authorized employees also had access to the Pyxis

system, the computerized drug-dispensing machine that tracked and recorded the emergency medications disbursed from the locked drawers in a mobile cart. The automated machine, named for a small medicine box used by ancient Greeks, was devised to reduce human error and prevent patients from receiving the wrong medication.

Cullen may have believed his crafty manipulation of the Cerner and Pyxis systems were foolproof maneuvers, since anyone looking into suspicious deaths and code blues would be likely to look first at the nurses who were directly responsible for the patients involved. Bottles of digoxin were found to be missing from the dispenser's inventory after both the Han and Gall emergencies, but it seemed that by canceling the Pyxis orders he had covered up his link to the drugs. His crafty subterfuge may have worked in the past, but the slippery killer's multiple betrayals of patients and of his profession were at last catching up with him.

Before the end of the summer Dr. Marcus at the poison control center, the New Jersey Department of Health and Senior Services, and authorities at Somerset were all deeply involved in inquiries delving into the suspicious overmedication and deaths of patients at the hospital. Somerset County prosecutor Forrest still hadn't been notified about the turmoil at the medical center, but it wasn't long before the other investigators were focusing much of their attention on the same brooding male nurse.

Serious signs of monkey business linked to Cullen showed up when Cerner system records revealed that he had called up the medical files of Mrs. Han and Father Gall on the nights before their heart attacks. That was especially troubling because, although he had cared for both patients in the past, he wasn't their assigned nurse at the time. There appeared to be no legitimate reason for him to be poring over the medical records of either patient.

Then investigators looking into the Pyxis transactions also learned that Cullen had tapped into the medication-dispensing system at "an abnormally high rate" since he was hired by the medical center. Hospital officials still weren't ready to lower the boom on the suspicious nurse, but notified state officials that "four abnormal lab values" involving patients were experienced. There was no mention of the Pyxis evidence linking Cullen to two digoxin overdoses.

While the inquiries were slowly creaking into gear and attention was turning toward Cullen, he continued to move freely on the critical-care wards, and was keeping busy with murder. There was still no move to reassign, suspend, or fire him.

Three days after the nerve-jangling warning was received from Dr. Marcus, Cullen slipped quietly into the room of eighty-year-old Pasquale M. Napolitano and gave him an injection of dobutamine. The medication given to the elderly Peapack and Gladstone, New Jersey, man increases the heart rate, and Napolitano died on July 13, only three days after he was admitted to the hospital.

The bad blood already existing between Somerset Medical Center administrators and Dr. Marcus was exacerbated when hospital officials learned that the toxicologist had presented four cases of "unexplained overdoses at a single hospital" for discussion during a regular monthly gathering of medical and forensic professionals sponsored by the New York City Poison Center. Speaking before about seventy professionals at the Toxicology Consultants Conference on August 7, Marcus presented two cases involving digoxin serum levels over nine nanograms per milliliter and two cases of significant hypoglycemia related to an insulin overdose. When Dr. Marcus asked what others at the meeting thought about the cases, an anesthesiologist later recalled, they told him he had "a kook" on his hands. Dr. Marcus agreed, the doctor recalled.

Marcus didn't identify the patients or the hospital where the cases occurred, but when officials at Somerset learned about the discussion, they recognized the medical facility and the patients as theirs. They were outraged, and Dr. Cors branded the incident as "unethical and unprofessional," according to a news report. Marcus refused to comment because the case was still under investigation.

Meanwhile, as hospital authorities skirmished with the poison control chief and pressed their internal investigation, the renegade nurse stalking the hallways and critical-care wards continued to gather souls.

On August 11, Christopher B. Hardgrove, a thirty-eight-year-old Somerville father of two teenage daughters, Michelle and Melissa, died a few hours after being given an unprescribed injection of norepinephrine. A carpenter, he was hospitalized after suffering a heart attack, but he was expected to recover.

About two weeks later, on August 27, eighty-three-year-old Frances Agoada, who had been in the hospital less than two weeks, nearly died from an unprescribed injection of medication. Other hospital staff members reacting to the code blue emergency saved the Franklin Township woman's life. The hospital didn't bother to report the unauthorized drug injection to state authorities, and that got them into trouble a few weeks later when the Department of Health learned about the incident.

State Health Department authorities fined Somerset $5,000 for violating licensure standards by failing immediately to report an "unexplained, life-threatening laboratory result" that could have been tied to an insulin overdose, even though it was directed to do so. Despite the admonition, the hospital was allowed to continue with its internal inquiry.

The New Jersey Department of Health and Senior Services got into the action by mailing a disciplinary notice to the Somerset Medical Center for failing to notify Lucille Gall about the massive overdose of digoxin in her brother's blood. Somerset had failed to follow established procedures by notifying the family of the cause of death and the possibility an autopsy might be justified.

The NJDHSS accused the medical center of violating the

patient's rights section of hospital licensing standards by neglecting to tell Lucille Gall about her brother's overdose. According to Patient Right No. 77 in New Jersey's state standards handbook, a patient or next of kin has the right to an explanation of the complete medical condition, recommended treatment and recommended results.

"There is no evidence that she was informed that the patient had an unexplained, markedly elevated digoxin level on the day of his death . . . which would enable her to give an informed consent [for the autopsy]," the department wrote in the disciplinary note. The oversight was a serious violation of protocol and the hospital was ultimately fined $5,000, the same amount assessed for not reporting the alarming laboratory result in the Agoada case.

Cullen was working his regular overnight shift on September 19 through September 20 as the primary nurse caring for Krishnakant Upadhyay when he gave the seventy-year-old man an overdose of digoxin. The Bridgewater man died in the early-morning hours of September 20.

Three days after Upadhyay's death, the furtive killer padded quietly into the room of James R. Strickland and administered an overdose of digoxin to the eighty-three-year-old Bowie, Maryland, man. It was the second time since Strickland was admitted to the hospital on August 7, then transferred to critical care that the homicidal nurse tried to kill him. Strickland survived the first murder attempt on September 7, although it made him sick and he exhibited typical side effects of digoxin poisoning. More than two weeks later, after he was poisoned again, Strickland lost his struggle to live. The elderly widower was a big, tall man with a zest for life, but he was still grieving over the recent loss of his wife when he was killed. He had such a love for playing his harmonica that it was buried with him.

About one week after Strickland was murdered at the Somerset Medical Center with an injection of stolen digoxin, Pennsylvania health inspectors taking a routine look around Cullen's former killing grounds at St. Luke's Hospital discovered unlocked drug cabinets, drawers, and refrigerators. Digoxin and insulin, Cullen's favorite medications for murder, were among the drugs left improperly secured.

During the two-day inspection on September 29 and September 30, the examiners marked up six violations in the emergency department, and one in an operating room used by obstetricians and supporting staff. Insulin injections were discovered in unlocked refrigerators. Unlocked cabinets and drawers turned up supplies of digoxin, nitroglycerin, lidocaine (a pain killer), and heparin.

After inspectors cited St. Luke's for failure to provide locked storage for medicines, the hospital quickly took corrective measures, and no fines or other penalties were ordered. Health department employees routinely make on-site inspections of every one of the approximately 250 hospitals in Pennsylvania, looking for violations, including infractions of rules fashioned to prevent employees, patients, visitors, or others from stealing drugs for their own use or for sale in the underground narcotics trade.

Discovery of breaches of rules and regulations, similar to those found at St. Luke's, weren't uncommon. Lehigh Valley Hospital had already been cited twice in the new millennium for similar violations; once about four months after Cullen left his job in the burn unit in April 2000; and again in July 2003 while authorities at Somerset Medical Center were scrambling to figure out why so many "abnormal lab values" were showing up.

At LVH, where Cullen used stolen medications to murder Matthew Mattern and Stella Danielczyk, examiners discovered an unlocked anesthesia cart in three operating rooms. During the second inspection more than three years later, unsecured syringes were discovered in a perinatal unit, a pediatric ICU, and in various supply and storage rooms. Lehigh Valley also avoided penalties by quickly correcting the deficiencies uncovered during both inspections.

Authorities with the state health department's Bureau of Facility Licensure and Certification were aware that as part of the frenetic realities of dealing with code blues or other medical emergencies, the priority of health-care professionals was looking out for the patient and providing doctors with necessary medications as rapidly as possible. Refrigerators, cabinets, or drawers used to store medications could be inadvertently or temporarily left unlocked. Administrators and supervisors at hospitals usually did everything they could to comply with the rules, and penalties were usually assessed only if authorities at a medical facility were dragging their feet or showing outright reluctance to correct violations.

By the summer of 2003, when LVH was cited the second time by Pennsylvania state health inspectors for violating regulations, a few miles across the state line in New Jersey, stolen medications were still being used by Cullen to kill patients at Somerset Medical Center.

The hospital had hired its own private investigator to look into the suspicious code blues and deaths among some of its most seriously ill patients. But the string of suspicious deaths continued unabated, and when another patient experienced a mysterious drop in blood sugar and died less than an hour later, hospital authorities finally had enough.

On October 3, three months after Dr. Marcus's prescient warning that a patient may have been killed by a deliberate overdose of medication, hospital officials at last took the findings from their inquiry to Forrest, the prosecutor. They reported "a number of potentially suspicious deaths" at the facility. Forrest was a skilled professional, who was thoroughly schooled in criminal law, and was quickly restoring public faith in an office with a reputation soiled by his predecessor, who was convicted of a multitude of federal charges and ultimately committed suicide.

He responded to the alert from Somerset Medical by opening his own investigation, and later recalled that he stayed in "constant communication" with the hospital. Cullen was quickly identified as a person of interest in the rapidly mushrooming inquiry.

The hospital turned over the medical records of six patients to Forrest, but that was just the beginning of what
quickly was to become a flood of documents provided by
Somerset to help out in the investigation. The hospital also
made their employees available for interviews and to provide any other assistance that might be required. After what
some observers may have described as a slow start, Somerset was suddenly bending over backwards to cooperate
with law enforcement and move the inquiry forward. Ironically, doctors said they didn't believe the death of the patient whose blood sugar so precipitously plunged was
related to the earlier cases.

On October 21, nearly three weeks after he became a
person of interest in the suspicious hospital deaths, the
predatory nurse turned his lethal attention to another
patient. Cullen injected a fatal dose of digoxin into the drip
bag of seventy-three-year-old Edward P. Zizik. The retiree
was an electrical engineer with the Automatic Switch Company in Edison for thirty years before he retired in 1997.
He was married to his wife, Helen Joan, for forty-eight-years.
Ironically, after retirement he became a volunteer worker
at the medical center.

The death in critical care, five days after the Three
Bridges, New Jersey, man was admitted to the Somerset
Medical Center, was Cullen's last medical murder.

Still, no one had said a word to Lucille Gall or her surviving brothers about the internal investigation at the hospital or the real cause of the priest's death. And the moody,
menacing male nurse who killed Father Gall and so many
other patients was still stalking the hallways and wards at
the Somerset Medical Center.

The Somerset County Sheriff's Department and state
police were soon brought in to join investigators from the
hospital and the prosecutor's office in a wide-ranging probe
into the improper medication of patients and suspicious
deaths at Somerset. The New Jersey State Health Department also remained involved in the inquiry, although its

recommendations after the study of the medication-dispensing system at Somerset had already led to tighter controls over digoxin.

Several teams of detectives were assigned to the investigations, including a pair of skilled sleuths attached to the Major Crimes Unit of the Somerset County Prosecutor's Office. Between them, Detective Sergeant Timothy Braun and Detective Daniel Baldwin had more than thirty-five years of experience in law enforcement, all of it in Somerset County.

The son of a detective lieutenant, Braun had worked in law enforcement for twenty-four years, and received numerous awards, including fifty departmental citations. He was a member of the International Homicide Investigation Association and other professional organizations.

Braun's partner shared first and last names with a member of a famous Hollywood acting clan, but Daniel Baldwin, the real-life detective, was nothing like the boozy fictional cop played by his namesake in the 1993 NBC-TV series *Homicide: Life on the Street.* The Somerset County detective was a big, burly man with a neatly trimmed mustache, and while working approximately 150 homicide cases, he had stared down and discombobulated more than one criminal with little more than an intimidating glance.

Braun and Baldwin were a good team. Both men were thoroughly familiar with each other's investigative and interrogation styles. As soon as they were assigned to the challenging case, they swung into action. They knew, as all homicide detectives do, that they couldn't restore the lives of the dead and give treasured family members back to the people who loved them. But if they were able to ferret out the information they were looking for, and did their job right, they could bring the killer to justice.

One of their first steps was taking a long, hard look at circumstances surrounding the toxic digoxin overdose administered to Mrs. Han, and the lethal overdose of the same drug that took the life of Father Gall.

Somerset hospital authorities had pretty much accepted the fact that a staff member was administering overdoses of medications, usually digoxin, to patients, but it hadn't been able to collect sufficient proof to identify a solid suspect.

Braun and Baldwin weren't on the job long before they began to zero in on Cullen. Administrators, supervisors, and nurses were questioned; medical records, charts, and printouts of Pyxis and Cerner tracking statements were pored over. The Pyxis records showed how Cullen accessed the computer around the time Han was fed an overdose of digoxin to obtain the medication under the name of another patient, then canceled the order in an obvious attempt to conceal the theft. His nurse's ID number stuck out on a printout from the computer like a sore thumb, and he may as well have signed his name and added the word "thief" after it. In documents eventually filed in the Han case, Baldwin observed that the hospital never tried to account for the missing digoxin. "These medications are simply replaced, without requiring any explanation or accountability," he wrote in an affidavit.

Cullen's work schedule was also compared with code blues and patient deaths by the sleuths. Then they talked to health-care workers and took a close look at records in other hospitals in New Jersey and Pennsylvania where the suspicious RN had worked.

An inordinate number of questionable deaths occurred at several of the hospitals during the periods when he was an employee, they discovered. Sixty-seven percent of the suspicious deaths occurred on wards where the sickest patients were being treated while he was working graveyard shifts.

Braun and Baldwin also learned about the strange death of Ottomar Schramm at Easton Hospital nearly five years earlier and about the eight-month-long inquiry it set off; about the earlier inquiry into the death of Helen Dean at a nursing home after treatment at Warren Hospital; and the nasty fracas over Francis Henry's death, including the firing of Nurse Pepe, her lawsuit, and Cullen's eventual firing from his job at the Liberty Nursing and Rehabilitation Center. Nurse Pepe's wrongful firing lawsuit was settled in 2002, but terms of the agreement were not publicly disclosed.

Cullen's lifelong depression, treatment at psychiatric hospitals, hospital emergency rooms and outpatient clinics, repeated suicide attempts and other bizarre behavior, including the break-in of Michelle Tomlinson's home, were all uncovered and examined in detail. Most of all, the homicide detectives were impressed by the staggering number of unexpected and suspicious deaths that occurred on Cullen's watch at one hospital after another, while he bounced around from job to job and crisis to crisis.

Forrest wasn't sitting on his hands while his detective team was beating the bushes for answers and evidence. He was busy, among other things, telephoning prosecutors and police in other jurisdictions around the country who had previously worked cases of serial medical murder. Forrest accumulated all the information he could gather about how they put together successful investigations, and about what they did right and what they believed they did wrong or could have done better. One of the main lessons they passed on was the necessity to avoid making a premature arrest by obtaining all the facts that could be gathered before moving in.

October was rapidly drawing to a close when investigators obtained a court order and Father Gall's remains were exhumed at the cemetery in Woodbridge. An autopsy was conducted by the New Jersey Regional Medical Examiner's Office in Newark. Authorities were closemouthed about details of the proceeding, but Father Gall's sister was quoted in the press as saying investigators were seeking to confirm that the lethal level of digoxin found in his system prior to his death wasn't a laboratory error. It was expected to be months before a report on the results was available.

By the end of the month detectives had identified Cullen as the prime suspect in the suspected homicides and murder attempts. Forrest, the DA, later observed that he was "caught red-handed" by his nurse's ID number, which he entered into the Pyxis system to steal medication. The nurse who manipulated machines to kill was betrayed ultimately by a machine.

He was fired on October 31. Falsifying his employment history on his job application was cited as the reason for the termination. During the thirteen months he worked on the critical-care wards at Somerset Medical Center, at least thirteen patients died at his hand—an average of one every month.

The same day Cullen was fired, New Jersey police contacted St. Luke's Hospital in Pennsylvania and requested his employment records. The steady, dogged investigation by Braun and Baldwin, along with the work of their colleagues from various law enforcement agencies and state authorities, had taken on a new urgency not experienced in previous probes. A Death Angel was killing hospital patients, and he had to be stopped.

Cullen had too many responsibilities and too many bills waiting to be paid to depend for very long for a living on unemployment compensation. In November, a few days after his termination at Somerset, he applied for a job at the Muhlenberg Regional Medical Center Hospice in Plainfield. Established as a hospital in 1877, the facility had grown into a 396-bed teaching medical center with a service area focused on Somerset, Union, and Middlesex Counties. The medical center was within commuting distance of Cullen's home in Bethlehem. He told hospital authorities that he was fired from Somerset for lying on his nursing-license application. Muhlenberg began checking out the new job applicant.

At Somerset Medical the hallways and wards were brimming over with suspicions and rumors, and by early December, newspapers were beginning to publish the first cautious stories about an investigation into mysterious deaths at the healing center. Mary Strenko read one of the stories and telephoned the Somerset County Prosecutor's Office to tell them about the unexpected death of her son. Investigators suggested they get together with the family for a talk. At the meeting the detectives asked if there was a period shortly before Michael died when he was left alone. They also asked the couple for a description of the hospital room and a photograph of their son.

While Cullen was angling for a new job at Muhlenberg, and the Strenkos were contemplating the unthinkable, Braun and Baldwin were presenting their information to Somerset County authorities and obtaining a warrant for the nurse's arrest. Among the reasons spelled out in a probable-cause affidavit, Baldwin declared that Cullen "accessed the medication dispensing system for digoxin at an abnormally high rate during his employment, according to a review of the records. There was no medical reason or authorization for the high number of entries."

The order was issued, naming Cullen as a suspect in one murder and of one attempted murder. Muhlenberg never offered him a job.

Manhattan radio personality Zach T. Martin is the son of Eleanor Stoecker, the first known victim of nurse Charles Cullen at Somerset Medical Center. *(Photo by Emily Stoecker)*

Eleanor Sova Stoecker *(left)* with her sisters Helen Magaro *(seated)* and Regina Taworoski *(standing)*. *(Photo by Zach T. Martin)*

Emily Stoecker emerged as a strong victims' rights advocate after the murder of her mother-in-law. *(Photo by Zach T. Martin)*

Home of William and Eleanor Stoecker in Bedminster, New Jersey. *(Photo by Zach T. Martin)*

Sova family tombstone at the old St. Peter's church cemetery in Lodi, New Jersey, where Eleanor Stoecker was laid to rest beside her beloved father, Peter Sova. *(Photo by Zach T. Martin)*

Marker erected in memory Eleanor Stoecker.
(Photo by Zach T. Martin)

The Liberty Nursing and Rehabilitation Center in Allentown, Pennsylvania, where Charles Cullen worked from June 2000 to June 2002 and attempted to murder a patient with an unprescribed dose of insulin. *(AP Photo/Bradely C. Bower)*

Easton Hospital in Easton, Pennsylvania, where Cullen worked in the intensive care unit from late 1998 to early 1999. He murdered retired steelworker Ottomar A. Schramm and may have killed others there. *(AP Photo/Bradely C. Bower)*

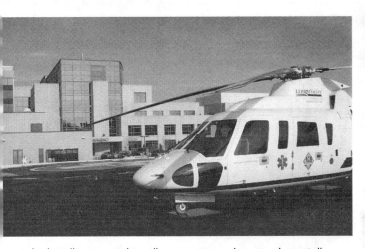

Lehigh Valley Hospital in Allentown, Pennsylvania, where Cullen murdered at least one patient and attempted to kill three others. He worked in intensive care units at the hospital from December 1998 to April 2000. *(AP Photo/Bradely C. Bower)*

St. Luke's Hospital in Bethlehem, Pennsylvania, where Charles Cullen later confessed to murdering five patients while working the night shift from June 2000 to June 2002. *(AP Photo/Bradely C. Bower)*

Sacred Heart Hospital in Allentown, Pennsylvania, where Cullen worked for eighteen days in 2002. He was still in orientation when other nurses issued an ultimatum that either he leave or they would. He was fired for what his employers described as "interpersonal problems." *(AP Photo/Bradely C. Bower)*

Somerset Medical Center in Somerville, New Jersey. During the nearly thirteen months in 2002 and 2003 that Cullen worked here, at least thirteen patients died at his hands, and two others survived murder attempts. *(Photo by Zach T. Martin)*

While awaiting adjudication of murder charges filed against him
in New Jersey and Pennsylvania, Charles Cullen was locked up
at Somerset County Jail in the center of Somerville.
(Photo by Zach T. Martin)

Somerset County Courthouse in Somerville, where Charles Cullen
pleaded guilty to the murder of fourteen patients and the
attempted murder of two others. *(Photo by Zach T. Martin)*

Relatives of Cullen's victims were mobbed by the press as they walked through this tunnel to the judicial center where the Death Angel pleaded guilty to serial murders. *(Photo by Zach T. Martin)*

The remains of Helen C. Dean are exhumed for a second autopsy after the arrest of her killer. *(AP Photo/Rich Schultz)*

A box containing the cremated remains of Larry Dean, whose ashes were buried in his mother's grave, is removed during her court-ordered exhumation. *(AP Photo/Rich Schultz)*

The Somerset County judicial building houses the office of Prosecutor Wayne J. Forrest, who spearheaded the investigation into the mysterious deaths at the local medical center. *(Photo by Zach T. Martin)*

Northampton County District Attorney James Morganelli *(right)* and Northampton county Coroner Zachary Lysek *(left)*. *(AP Photo/Bradely C. Bower)*

Lorraine Schramm *(left)* and her daughter, Kristina Toth *(right)*, at a news conference in Bethlehem, Pennsylvania, after prosecutors ruled the death of their husband and father, Ottomar A. Schramm, at Easton Hospital, was a homicide. *(AP Photo/The Morning Call, Michael Kubel)*

On March 29, 2004, Pennsylvania law enforcement authorities announced they would charge Cullen with the first-degree murder of Ottomar Schramm. Seated from left to right are: Captain Scott Snyder of the Pennsylvania State Police Troop M in Bethlehem; Northampton County DA John Morganelli; and Pennsylvania State Police Lt. William Teper, Jr., Troop M criminal investigations section commander. *(AP Photo/The Express-Times, Bruce Winter)*

New Jersey Attorney General Peter C. Harvey, at lectern, is joined by Vaughn McKoy, director of the New Jersey State Division of Criminal Justice *(left)*, at a press conference after Cullen pleaded guilty to fourteen murders and two attempted murders.
(AP Photo/Christopher Barth)

Somerset County Prosecutor Wayne J. Forrest fields questions from reporters at a news conference in his office on April 29, 2004.
(AP Photo/Christopher Barth)

Christopher Hardgrove's daughter, Melissa *(left)*, and his mother, Claire, listen during a plea hearing for his killer, Charles Cullen.
(AP Photo/Don Fisher, POOL)

With his lawyer, Johnnie Mask, at his side and his manacled hands on a Bible, Cullen is sworn in at a plea hearing before Somerset County State Superior Court Judge Paul Armstrong.
(Photo/Tony Kurdzuk, POOL)

On April 29, 2004, Public Defender Johnnie Mask read portions of an agreement between the prosecution and Charles Cullen, which spared Cullen the possibility of a death penalty in return for his cooperation with police and prosecutors.
(AP Photo/
Tony Kurdzuk, POOL)

Janece Strickland *(right)* of Dunellen, New Jersey talks with the news media at the Somerset County Courthouse. Her father, James Robert Strickland, was one of Cullen's victims.
(AP Photo/Daniel Hulshizer)

Phillip Mugavero talks with news reporters outside the Warren County Courthouse in Belvidere, New Jersey. A few minutes earlier, Cullen pleaded guilty to murdering Mugavero's grandmother, Lucy Mugavero, and two other patients at Warren Hospital in Phillipsburg, New Jersey.
(AP Photo/The Express-Times, Joe Gill)

Pennsylvania State Police Troopers Robert Glad *(left)*, and William Books *(right)*, escort Death Angel Charles Cullen through the Northampton County District Attorney's office to the Northampton County Court in Easton, Pennsylvania. *(AP Photo/The Morning Call, Pete Shaheen)*

On October 14, 2004, Lehigh County District Attorney James B. Martin announced the filing of six charges of murder and three charges of attempted murder against Charles Cullen at a press conference in the Lehigh County Government Center in Allentown, Pennsylvania. *(AP Photo/Douglas Benedict)*

Suzy Rose Yengo, daughter of former Jersey City Municipal Court Judge John W. Yengo, Sr., speaks at a press conference at the Essex County Prosecutor's office in Newark, N.J. Charles Cullen had just pleaded guilty to killing the former judge.
(AP Photo/Mike Derer)

Chapter 11

A Ghastly Confession

On December 12, most people dining at the Office Beer Bar & Grill, a popular restaurant on US Route 22, at the edge of Bridgewater, New Jersey, were too busy with their food or chatting to pay much attention to the little man with the close-cropped, prematurely gray hair sharing an early dinner at one of the tables with an attractive, statuesque blond companion. A diner in a business suit who was sitting at one of the other tables was an exception. He was keeping a close eye on the man with the blonde.

Drinking Coronas, picking at a chicken fajita and a spring roll, and casually chatting with his friend, Cullen was unaware of the attention he was attracting. He and his companion were being closely watched by a plainclothes detective with an arrest warrant tucked securely in his inside jacket pocket.

The gumshoe kept his eye on the couple while Cullen paid the bill, then hurried outside behind them as they drove away. Their observer and several colleagues tailed along behind, until Cullen stopped at a traffic light about a quarter of a mile from the restaurant.

In moments a fleet of police cars with their bar lights flashing overtook the stopped vehicle, and plainclothes and uniform officers leaped out, shouting, "Police!" As the lawmen swarmed around the stopped vehicle, it looked like a scene from the popular real-life television series, *Cops.*

Cullen was dragged, unprotesting, from his car, and his wrists were cuffed securely behind his back. A burly officer with his hand protectively cupped over the prisoner's head helped him slide into the back of one of the police cars. Cullen's companion was left behind, while he was driven to the Somerset County Jail at the corner of Grove and High Streets in the center of Somerville.

At the jail the handcuffed prisoner was helped out of the car, then led inside and run through the same booking process as anyone else preparing to be locked up there, whether for misdemeanor crimes, like failure to pay child support and drunk driving, to major felonies, like narcotics trafficking—or murder. For most prisoners, being booked into jail is a humiliating experience that is magnified by the realization that it is a first step in the loss of freedom. Aware that they are about to be left alone with their new keepers, it is a time when prisoners are at their most psychologically vulnerable. Some are so apprehensive, frightened, and miserable that they break down and cry. Others curse, struggle, or try to pick quarrels with the corrections employees whose job it is to book them into jail. Cullen did none of that.

The nurse was as unemotional as one of the shuffling zombies in director George A. Romero's cult classic *Night of the Living Dead.* He had been through the procedure at least once before when he was arrested and booked at the Palmer Police Department after breaking into the Tomlinson home.

He was quietly submissive while he was patted down and searched for possible weapons or other contraband, then moved through the routine by corrections officers who had performed it hundreds of times before. When he was directed to stand with his back to a measuring stick and face the camera, he stared unblinking into the lens while his mug shots were snapped. He was equally emotionless when he was directed to extend his thumbs and fingers for images of his fingerprints.

Finally the forty-three-year-old prisoner was ordered to strip down to his underwear and issued a simple tan jail-house uniform that looked a bit like a hospital scrub suit, along with a pair of blue athletic shoes for his feet. There were no belts, suspenders, or shoelaces. Wardens and corrections officers learned long ago to put such things on the list of prohibited items inside the institution because of the possibility they could be used by a prisoner to strangle or hang himself.

At last he was led to a cell and locked inside. The space was his new home, and he had no idea how long he would be there. There was no cellmate and there wouldn't be any. He was in an isolation cell and had the cold stone and steel-enclosed space all to himself. Isolation was routine for new inmates, pending completion of the classification process, which took into account the crimes they were accused of, their possible danger to other inmates or to themselves, and other factors. Information about the inmate's dismal record of suicide attempts was passed on to jailers and he was kept under constant surveillance.

Compared to the cramped jail cell, the limited living spaces aboard the *Woodrow Wilson* could have been accommodations in a luxury hotel. And there was no shore leave or oyster roasts to look forward to. In jail three meals of food, which were sufficiently nutritious but predictably uninspiring, were delivered to his cell every day.

Two days later, early Sunday morning, December 14, the quiet, dejected prisoner was led out of his cell and taken across the street to the Somerset County Prosecutor's Office for interrogation. An interrogation was exactly what the process was—although in these days of political correctness, many law enforcement agencies prefer to use the word "interview." An interview was what Cullen was submitted to when he applied for a job. An interrogation was the process that he and the homicide investigators were involved in at the prosecutor's office. It was meticulous and exhausting.

Detectives Braun and Baldwin talked briefly with the prisoner shortly after his arrest and the possibility of Cullen taking a polygraph test came up. Cullen said he didn't want to be hooked up to the device. He took a lie detector before when he was questioned about Helen Dean and managed to avoid incriminating himself when the results were found to be inconclusive. He had enough of polygraphs.

There were no polygraphs at the Sunday interrogation, but it was no brief talk. The homicide detectives were closeted with the prisoner for nearly seven hours. The videotaped marathon question-and-answer session in the Major Crimes Unit interview room pitting the puny nurse against the experienced homicide investigators was no contest.

After listening to the obligatory recitation of the Miranda warning, advising him that he had the right to have an attorney present to represent him and that he could refuse to cooperate if he wished, Cullen agreed to talk.

While the detectives and the murder suspect took occasional bathroom breaks and snacked on take-out food, Braun and Baldwin eased him through details of a wretched life that was filled with feelings of worthlessness, guilt, and misery. He talked about his navy service, lifelong depression, marriage troubles, alcohol abuse, and more than twenty suicide attempts. He told about swallowing chemicals from his chemistry set as a child, the stunt with the hibachi in Phillipsburg, drinking cleaning fluid, slashing his arm with a razor, and other halfhearted and failed efforts to kill himself.

He retraced his outpatient treatment by mental-health professionals, commitment to the Carrier Clinic, his two months at Greystone Park, several days in the behavioral unit of the Muhlenberg Regional Medical Center—and a five-week stay at Fair Oaks Hospital in Summit, after one of his attempts at suicide. A private psychiatric institution, Fair Oaks was operated by National Medical Enterprises, one of the nation's biggest psychiatric hospital chains, and offered drug and alcohol rehabilitation programs, along with other services.

When the homicide detectives moved on to the meat and potatoes of the interrogation, Cullen behaved as if he were anxious to share the sordid secrets he bottled up for so long and get things off his chest. For someone who was known among acquaintances for being closemouthed and aloof, there were times during the occasionally rambling confrontation when he seemed to be almost bubbling over with a desire to talk about himself.

Cullen described himself as someone whose desire to die was frustrated because he was afraid of death. Instead of summoning up the courage to destroy himself, he turned his frustrating death wish onto others, slipping quietly into the rooms of gravely ill men and women at night to kill them by directly injecting them with toxic medications, or by sneaking overdoses of drugs into their IV lines.

The dreadful elements of the confession couldn't have come as a surprise, but even for a pair of hardened homicide detectives, who may have thought they had seen or heard it all, it had to have been a sobering experience.

The wimpy, little string bean of a man owned up to the murder of an estimated thirty to forty "very sick patients" at hospitals and a nursing home in two states during a brutal fifteen or sixteen-year career as a medical serial killer. He broke down the estimated number of victims in each county for the detective duo, but he claimed that he took a hiatus from murder and didn't kill for more than three years while working at the Hunterdon Medical Center and the Morristown Memorial Hospital.

Responding to a question from Braun asking for "the why" behind all the deaths, Cullen described himself as a mercy killer. "My—my intent was to decrease suffering in people I saw throughout my career," he claimed. "I didn't intend for these patients, these people to suffer, to go through unusual things, you know. I know codes [blue] aren't pretty, but believed that my actions would not cause them pain and suffering. That I would just cause them to pass away and not to suffer or linger and, the terminal, or a high pain situation, or in the case of a couple of burn patients . . . just slowly being chopped away and so it was a very dehumanizing process."

Cullen said he sometimes hung around at the bedside of his victims, then watched and listened to the reaction of family and friends when the patient died. Most of the time when he killed, other people who were around were thankful for the patient's relief from suffering. "'Oh, my God, at least he's dead now,'" he quoted the unnamed onlookers as saying. "I mean, that happened most of the time," he said. "That was the consensus of the people around me, that the person is better off dead than alive."

The concept of mercy killings was a common defense by medical serial killers, but it was a hard story to swallow for law enforcement and most responsible health-care professionals. Some medical murderers who claimed to be mercy killers were flat-out liars. Some others actually managed to convince themselves they were doing something that was necessary and was best for the patient and his family.

Efren Saldivar, a respiratory therapist in California, who pleaded guilty the previous year to the murder of six patients by injecting them with a muscle relaxant or by withholding oxygen, used that excuse. The night-shift nurse described himself as an Angel of Mercy, but so many patients died on his watch at the Glendale Adventist Medical Center that other employees began joking about his "magic syringe."

The crusty homicide detectives knew that was faulty reasoning, whether it was used as an excuse by the California killer or by the little man, with skin the color of old cream just before it begins to thicken and curdle, who was sitting there telling them stories. They even may have known that Saldivar eventually gave another reason for murdering his patients. He claimed he and other nurses were overworked, so when he became exhausted with the demands of his job, he checked the patient board to figure out: "Who do we gotta get rid of?"

Braun and Baldwin had other questions to be answered about patients who died at Somerset Medical Center, and they eased their subject through the interrogation with the practiced skill that they had developed over years of investigating homicides.

He "felt very compelled to kill," even though he knew it was wrong, Cullen said, and wished he had been stopped years earlier.

While confessing to the murder of Reverend Gall and the attempted murder of Mrs. Han, Cullen admitted giving drug overdoses to a total of at least twelve to fifteen patients during the period he was employed at Somerset Medical Center.

Cullen began his lengthy murder spree on his first job, soon after graduating from nursing school, and recalled that he killed one or two patients at St. Barnabas, although he couldn't remember names. One of the patients was given a fatal overdose of medication while Cullen was assigned full-time to the burn unit. Cullen said he thought the man was a judge. The other was an AIDS patient who died after Cullen transferred to Livingston Services in 1989 and became a "floater," he said.

Cullen confirmed that St. Barnabas was on target when he was dumped for tampering with IV bags kept in a storage closet by contaminating them with potentially lethal doses of insulin. He told the investigators that he didn't think anyone died because of his meddling with the bags. Hospital authorities knew what he did, he said. "They had narrowed it down to me. It's a place where I believe they knew it was me."

At times during the interview he lapsed into rationalization, and attempted to shift the blame from himself to others. Former employers were criticized for lax security or for ignoring harmful behavior that led to the injury or death of patients. Officials of at least four hospitals knew what he was doing but ignored it, apparently because they didn't want to deal with the consequences, he claimed.

Turning to his catastrophic sojourn at St. Luke's, Cullen blamed lax security by the hospital for making it easy to steal medicine. He told Braun and Baldwin the hospital "had an open med room." Although the room had a lock, it was never locked, he said. All he had to do was walk inside and help himself.

Cullen claimed he stole thousands of dollars' worth of drugs from the medical storage room and threw them away. "I mean, you know they would stock thirty Pronestyl, which they never used; the next day it would be gone. They would replace it with thirty; it would be gone the next day," he said. "I mean, I mean, you know, maybe seventy, eighty bottles of a drug that was never used. . . . I mean, large, large quantities of drugs I threw away." Pronestyl is a brand name for a medication used to slow rapid heartbeat.

Other medications were stashed in the sharps boxes, according to the treacherous RN. Authorities at St. Luke's twice found the boxes empty before his shift, and filled with drugs after he ended his shift and checked out, he said.

Cullen claimed St. Luke's suspected him of worse things than stealing drugs, and claimed an unnamed individual he described as the "legal officer" suggested he had harmed patients. "I mean, they didn't come out and say one hundred percent, but they implied, when he was taking notes, he implied that they thought there were deaths associated with me." Hospital authorities gave him a choice of being fired or resigning with neutral references, he said of his termination. "I chose neutral references."

As the interrogation droned on, Cullen showed flashes of enthusiasm when the talk turned to hospital procedures, rules of conduct, and the everyday responsibilities of caring for gravely ill patients. His demeanor changed and his memory appeared to have deteriorated when the talk turned to specific victims, why they were marked for death, and the nitty-gritty details of how the murders were carried out. He lived much of his life in a fog that blurred his memory and made recalling such details impossible, he explained.

"I can't even remember all these people. It's like a fog, maybe that's how I've gotten to this point," he declared. "I'm thinking, how could I do that and not remember? But I can't."

The family court system came in for a backhanded slap, when he suggested he would have ditched his nursing career in 1993, if he wasn't left so financially tangled up and broke because of the devastating quarrel over his divorce and custody matters involving the girls.

After leaving Warren Hospital in the wake of Mrs. Dean's death, he wanted to quit nursing, and his psychiatric counselor recommended that it would be a good move because he wasn't dealing well with his depression and the stress in his life, Cullen told the detectives.

"I think that I would have gladly walked away from nursing at that point in my life, just because I had done these things and did not want to do these things anymore," he said in carefully veiled references to the patient murders he had already committed. He knew that if he continued to "be placed in these situations" that he would "feel the need . . . to end suffering," Cullen explained.

Referring to the family court, he said he was being told that he was a deadbeat dad, and had to support his children, even though he was unemployed because of depression. It was made clear to him that he had to pay the same amount of child support money, and he couldn't figure where else he could earn the same pay—$22 to $25 an hour—that he was receiving as a nurse.

"I went back into nursing—totally, totally depressed— totally not wanting to do this job anymore." He said he felt "totally depressed" and "very trapped." It was impossible for him to be able to say, "I can't do this job."

Both he and his ex-wife were going through difficult

times, Cullen told his interrogators, and his attempts to avoid her by spending as much time as possible on the job rebounded on him when court authorities looked at all the overtime hours and figured his potential earnings in 1991 were very high. So his child support payments were set at $13,000, at a time when he recalled that he was probably earning an annual salary with overtime of about $50,000. Since that time, he said, there were years when he earned over $40,000 and other years when he took in almost $70,000.

"I—I felt very trapped," he ruefully recalled. "I felt even with me working extra hours, which I tried to do for the most part, I—I felt very trapped in—in my social situation which I—I—I—I lived in a basement apartment. I did without things you know, I tried to provide for my kids, I tried to, I tried to get them what they wanted, what they needed."

The repetition of words and phrases, the stops and starts and run-on sentences in Cullen's speech, were typical of suspects being interrogated by police about serious crimes. In real life, criminal suspects don't speak like they do on television cop shows or in many novels. Their words don't flow smoothly in an uninterrupted rhythm. They stutter, gasp, fight to retrieve an elusive word or thought, and often stop talking and start all over again. Telling his story was a struggle.

The suspect complained that during the divorce his ex-wife accused him of not caring about his family, and of trying to wiggle out of his child support obligations. The children would repeat that at times, he said.

"I—I—I didn't, I didn't want to be this nurse. I didn't want to continue, but it was the only thing I thought I could do, and felt that I was competent enough to do and earn the type of money . . . in order to not continually to fall behind because every time I fell behind or, or there were times I would miss payments because of depression or suicide attempts you know, I—I was painted as the father who didn't care about his kids not only from my ex-wife to my kids, but from the court system to me. And I, and again, I was told several times that I would go to jail, and you know I would be this deadbeat dad and I decided I had to continue working as a nurse. I would rather not have been."

The skilled homicide detectives allowed the miserable prisoner to run off at the mouth and keep talking, even when he was repeating himself, interrupting only occasionally to ask for clarification of a particular point, to redirect gently the interrogation to another area of thought or subject, or to interject a question. When they did ask a question, it was usually brief and to the point. Cullen was the talker; they were the listeners.

"Why is that?" Braun asked when Cullen said he would rather not have continued his nursing duties.

"Because I felt guilty for what I had done, even though I was trying to reduce people's sufferings," he replied. Cullen said he sometimes went for long periods before the old feelings of being overwhelmed with the suffering returned. ". . . feeling like I couldn't watch people hurt and die and be treated like nonhumans, and at times the only thing that I could feel like I could do was to try and end their suffering, and I don't believe I had that right, but I did it anyway."

It went unsaid during the interrogation, but the two years when he worked at the Hunterdon Medical Center, and possibly the approximately ten months at Morristown Memorial that immediately followed, may have been one of those periods when his life was less chaotic and he took a hiatus from murder. His messy divorce had become final; he had left the debilitating turmoil at Warren Hospital behind him and for the time being sidestepped any criminal action stemming from Mrs. Dean's death. He even had four months between jobs to cool his heels and catch his breath before landing a position at Hunterdon.

Throughout much of the interview Cullen blamed others, indulged in self-pity, and commiserated with the victims' families because of the lives he had snuffed out before their time, the anguish and emotional pain caused for those left behind, and for hurting the people that he personally loved the most. He was overwhelmed with guilt for failing to be a better father to his girls, and for drawing his girlfriend, who was also a nurse, into the mess his life had become. During a conversation his girlfriend began crying after asking him if he really did the things that were being said about him, he told his interrogators. "I think even to the very last second she still wants to believe I didn't do this." He didn't want her and their unborn child to suffer for his behavior, he said.

The skinny serial killer, who ruthlessly snuffed out the lives of his patients with hardly a second thought, worried because his girlfriend was pregnant, might lose her job, might have to move from her home, and wouldn't have him around to support her. She didn't have the slightest idea about the terrible things he was doing, he said. He ruefully acknowledged that he "screwed a lot of lives up a lot."

Cullen worried that his notoriety would stalk his daughters throughout their lives, and said he was fearful that someone who was angered over his behavior would look for revenge by hurting the girls. He didn't want to think of them being afraid to walk home from school someday because someone might sneer that "those are Cullen's kids, and he was a murderer. . . ." So far as he himself was concerned, he said, he didn't see any advantage in his being alive.

Cullen told the detective duo that he didn't share anything about his terrible secret with his colleagues, his ex-wife, his girlfriend, or other women he had dated. "This is something that I kept inside of me, something that I kept on telling myself that I could stop if I had someone in my life," he said.

At times the dismal recitation of his life and problems took on an aura of a therapy session. He was the emotionally messed-up patient, and Braun and Baldwin were the shrinks who looked serious and patiently listened, occasionally clucking a tongue or scratching a nose, while he rambled on and on about anything that was troubling him. That wasn't surprising. He had been through numerous counseling sessions with mental-health professionals many times in the past, following breakdowns and suicide attempts.

Cullen talked about the problems that cropped up early in his marriage, his failings as a father—and his efforts to commit suicide.

"And I tried to kill myself throughout my life because I never really liked being who I was, because I didn't think I was worthy of anything," he explained. The world would have been a better place if he had only shown the courage to carry through with his wish to commit suicide, he miserably conceded.

"I wish I would have taken my own life a long time ago so I wouldn't—would have—what I did," Cullen stuttered in a typical example of his grossly tortured syntax. "You know, maybe if I was nine years old and would have had to die that day, all these lives, including my family, wouldn't be affected in this way."

The old inconsistency and contradictions that plagued the disgraced nurse throughout his adult life reared its ugly head throughout the interview when he interrupted his recitation of self-loathing by repeatedly attempting to excuse his contemptible behavior with claims that he was motivated by a desire to spare patients from pain and from continuing to suffer. By intervening to end the lives of patients, he said, he moved them out of reach of other health-care workers who treated them as "nonhumans," while ignoring the pain and suffering he inflicted on his victims—and the people who loved them.

He showed similarly curiously flawed reasoning about his role in causing pain and anguish when he claimed to have given drug overdoses to some patients to spare them from the resuscitation attempts when they coded, or went into cardiac or respiratory arrest.

"I really did not enjoy the codes, especially ones that were the result of what I had done because I saw stuff go on, you know, the chest compressions, the intubation, the shocking. I didn't want them to go through that." He said his "intent was to decrease suffering in people," and he didn't intend for the patients to suffer or "to go through unusual things, you know. I know codes aren't pretty," he added, "but I believed that my actions would not cause them pain and suffering."

But patients—and their family members—were caused "pain and suffering." And the detectives already knew that bedridden, critically ill men and women repeatedly experienced code blues precisely because they were poisoned by the spindly little man who was claiming to be a compassionate nurse who was acutely attentive to their distress.

Administering fatal drug overdoses was his way of ending "a high-pain situation" or the "dehumanizing" of patients whose burns were so severe that their limbs had to be amputated, Cullen explained. The prisoner singled out the young burn patient Matthew Mattern, who was given a fatal injection of digoxin at Lehigh Valley Hospital, as an example.

"He constantly had infections. He constantly was coming back for surgeries," Cullen told his interrogators. "They were amputating him piecemeal. I just wanted to end his suffering." Death by lethal injection was a faster, more humane way to accomplish that, he said.

The existence Cullen retraced for the detectives was composed of self-hatred, betrayal, and secrecy. His life and the murders he committed were described as his "dirty, dark secret."

Late in the evening, near the end of the arduous confession, he told the detectives: "I did not want [people] to see me as this, what I am."

"What are you, Charles?" Sergeant Braun asked.

"A man, person, who was trusted and had responsibility for a lot of people dying," he replied. "And whether or not they had a couple of days, or weeks, or whether even they sometimes had months, whether that was with pain or without pain, I had no right to do this. I had no right! I just couldn't stop! I couldn't stop it!"

The pathetic response didn't seem to satisfy even the puny prisoner himself, and he struggled to provide a better explanation.

"I—I hate myself for it 'cause I don't believe I had the right, but I couldn't stop," he said of the murders. "I couldn't."

Cullen theorized that he might have been able to stop the slaughter if he had found someone to love, who would love him back. His compulsion to kill waxed and waned, depending on what was going on in his personal life, he said. "There were long periods of time where I did nothing and I thought—I thought I was working through it, but . . . I kept on going into these deep depressions and I would say that this was part of it."

Cullen's energy appeared to be fading fast when Braun finally asked if he had attempted to take the lives of many more patients than he actually succeeded in killing.

The reply from the apostate nurse was chilling, and bluntly to the point: "No," he said, "I think it's pretty close to the same, that most of the attempts were completions."

For the time being, when the exhausting interrogation session ended, Detectives Braun and Baldwin were through with the self-appointed Grim Reaper. But a long relationship between Cullen and the criminal justice system in two states was just getting off the ground.

While Braun and Baldwin were moving into their question-and-answer session with the malignant RN, a few miles away in Whitehouse Station, Bishop Paul G. Bootkoski, of Metuchen, was serving mass in the Roman Catholic church where one of Cullen's victims served as vicar for Hunterdon County.

Bootkoski told the packed assemblage at Our lady of Lourdes that he chose to celebrate mass at the church so he could be with them at that troubled time, and urged them not to seek execution of the man who was believed to have murdered their priest.

"Is that the Gospel's message?" the bishop asked. "You took Florian's life, we're going to take your life? Who has the right to take a life? Only God!" The bishop said they were a faithful community, and they had to wonder if they were people seeking revenge. "Tit for tat doesn't work," he declared. "Maybe life with no parole is the answer."

Bootkoski said that although the priest's death was a tragedy, there was reason to be proud of the manner in which he died. "People take it upon themselves to do things to each other that are not of God, and this is painful. Be thankful that we can see that Florian even in death had a ministry to fulfill. As his life ended, in that instance, he made known his suspicions and then the domino effect took over," the bishop said in his homily. "Even in death, Florian did something for the people of God. God used him as an instrument to bring about justice, to stop this nurse from doing it again and again."

On the Monday morning after Cullen's arrest, December 15, 2003, a flurry of newspaper, radio, and television reporters converged on the judicial building in the center of Somerville to watch and listen to the accused killer as he appeared at a hearing in the state superior court, where he was to be informed formally of the charges against him.

Cullen had already requested a public defender, but was not yet accompanied by an attorney when he appeared before state superior court judge Paul Armstrong, presiding in Somerset County. Somerset County prosecutor Forrest represented the people.

Unshaven, haggard-looking, and dressed in a rumpled jailhouse uniform with his hands securely cuffed behind his back, Cullen leaned over the wooden jury railing, staring at his feet with his classic hangdog expression. When he was formally advised of the charges against him, he sprang a surprise on the judge and a courtroom that was filled with news reporters from New Jersey, Pennsylvania, and New York.

"I don't want to contest the charges. I plead guilty," the

exhausted-appearing defendant blurted out. "I don't want to be represented. I don't intend to fight this."

Armstrong quickly interrupted and explained that the arraignment wasn't set up to enter or accept pleas, but Cullen was persistent. Speaking clearly and with conviction, he repeatedly attempted to plead guilty to the charges.

Suddenly the nonentity—who was kicked out of the navy, divorced by his wife, filed bankruptcy because he couldn't pay his bills no matter how hard he worked, was fired or forced to quit numerous jobs, repeatedly tried to commit suicide, and was shuttled in and out of psychiatric hospitals—was someone important. A crush of news reporters and camera crews were recording his every word.

When Judge Armstrong asked Cullen about the application he filed requesting a public defender, the defendant replied: "I wish to rescind that. I don't plan to fight this."

While the judge repeatedly advised him to remain silent, and to get himself a lawyer or accept appointment of a public defender before making any further statements, Cullen stubbornly stuck to his guns. He respectfully insisted he wanted to plead guilty, didn't want a trial, and didn't want a lawyer.

The brief hearing ended after Armstrong ordered the suspected serial killer held on $1 million cash bail on charges of murder in the death of Father Gall and of attempted murder for his effort to take the life of Mrs. Han. The next step in the legal proceedings would be submitting the case to a grand jury, Armstrong said. The hearing had barely lasted ten minutes.

Moments later the prisoner was led out of the courtroom, returned to the jail, and locked up again in his single cell.

At the conclusion of the hearing Detective Sergeant Braun approached Zach Martin and gave him an envelope with a letter inside. Signed by Braun, the letter expressed condolences for the loss of Zach's mother, and advised him about services available through the local victims' assistance program. The veteran detective also offered to provide any help that he could in the future. A photo of Eleanor that was borrowed from Zach Martin was also returned with the letter. Similar letters were distributed to other survivors of victims, along with any photos loaned to investigators. Every family in court that day got one.

Forrest followed up the brief hearing with a news conference. Cullen's arrest in Bridgewater, and his claim to detectives of being a serial medical murderer, were retraced for the reporters. The prosecutor commended Somerset Medical Center for its role in exposing the suspected medical serial killer. "If they had not done that, this gentleman may have not been stopped," he declared. Forrest also told the crush of reporters to look for a protracted investigation that would include drugs used, and the possible further exhumation of bodies for toxicological and other tests. One body had already been dug up, he disclosed.

"As you can imagine, this is by far the biggest homicide investigation undertaken by the Somerset County Prosecutor's Office, and maybe by any law enforcement agency in New Jersey," he told the crush of reporters. "There's still a lot of work to do to investigate thirty or forty homicides and maybe others."

Underscoring the remark about more homicides, Forrest said the records of four other patients at Somerset Medical Center—who experienced critically low blood sugar levels that may have been caused by "an external administration of insulin" and contributed to their deaths—were being examined by investigators. All the patients were elderly and had multiple serious medical problems, he said.

Charges in a third case were already being considered, depending on the results of an autopsy. The prosecutor said he didn't know if Cullen might have had accomplices, or acted at the request of patients or their kinfolk when he killed, but indicated that the male nurse more likely acted solely on his own. There was no evidence any of the deaths were assisted suicide, he said.

Cullen was no Dr. Kevorkian, the Michigan doctor who

became America's best-known advocate for physician-assisted suicide in the 1990s. Dr. Kevorkian made international headlines when a videotape he made showing him giving a lethal injection to a terminally ill man was aired on CBS's *60 Minutes*.

Prosecutors subsequently won a second-degree murder conviction against the sickly and elderly euthanasia crusader, who had boasted of ushering more than 130 sick people to their graves. He was sent to the Thumb Correctional Facility in rural Lapeer, Michigan, to serve a sentence of from ten to twenty-five years.

Unlike Cullen, however, Kevorkian, dubbed "Dr. Death" by the press, gave patients the final say in whether or not they wished to live or die. Cullen, the Death Angel, made the life-and-death choice himself. The patient had nothing to say about it.

Forrest talked about the attempted murder case involving Mrs. Han, but like other authorities up to that time, used only her initials, JKH. He explained that her name was being withheld from the public and the press pending further discussions with family members.

Recalling that Cullen likely began his criminal behavior years earlier at St. Barnabas, the prosecutor said he would consider seeking the death penalty for any Somerset County murders.

While the admitted Death Angel was formally informed of the charges against him in New Jersey, authorities at Somerset Medical Center were preparing to turn over more patient files to investigators.

After notification of Cullen's alarming claims to have begun his murder campaign years earlier at St. Barnabas, hospital authorities and the Essex County Prosecutor's Homicide Squad launched their own investigations. The prosecutor and his sleuths ultimately subpoenaed the medical records of 150 patients who died on the St. Barnabas burn unit while he was employed there.

The hospital struggled to comply with the subpoena as

quickly as possible, but digging into fifteen or sixteen-year-old records and coming up with the information wasn't an easy task. In the late 1980s, computerized filing wasn't as common as it was later, and for most medical facilities and private businesses, it was still a few years in the future. Patient records were initially compiled on paper, sometimes running thousands of pages each, then transferred to microfilm or microfiche for permanent storage. Retrieving the files for the prosecutor meant employees had to search through the microfilm and microfiche by hand and eye, then photocopy those that were needed for the investigation.

Once the files were delivered, the prosecutor's office needed to find a means of translating complicated medical terms and other health-care jargon into simpler layman's language. A forensic nurse was hired to review the medical files and work with homicide detectives and assistant prosecutors assigned to the case.

Authorities in Pennsylvania were also busy working to uncover murders the confessed Death Angel may have been responsible for while working at hospitals there. In some cases prosecutors began issuing subpoenas for medical files, and in other cases hospitals contacted authorities and turned over records on their own. Lehigh County DA Martin told reporters that the hospitals involved in his investigation were so cooperative he didn't need to prepare subpoenas.

Pennsylvania state police resurrected the abandoned probe into the sixty-seven deaths in the coronary care unit at St. Luke's Hospital during the last six months Cullen worked there.

Investigators in Northampton County, began taking a close new look at the controversial death of Ottomar Schramm at Easton Hospital. Cullen was behind bars only six days when Northampton County coroner Lysek changed the cause of Ottomar Schramm's death from undetermined to homicide. Northampton County DA Morganelli announced in Bethlehem that the retired steelworker's death had been ruled a homicide and the former RN was the primary suspect.

On January 5, police executed a search warrant at the hospital seeking Schramm's medical records and documentation of the hospital's internal investigation into his death. In March, state police joined Morganelli at a press conference in the Northampton Courthouse in Easton and announced that Cullen would be charged with the elderly retiree's murder.

When it came to matters of life and death, Cullen had always been maddeningly inconsistent. Time and again he stole medications from the hospitals he worked at and used them to kill patients, but although he tried suicide at least twenty times, he never resorted to the same drugs in his own efforts at self-destruction. And his suicide attempts always failed. Sometimes he selected his victims after careful study of their medical files and condition, but at other times he killed on impulse. Most of his murders were committed with digoxin or insulin, but there were times when he turned to other drugs.

He demonstrated that old inconsistency when he backtracked on his courtroom claim that he didn't want legal representation, and the day after the hearing he accepted legal help in New Jersey. A short time later he also accepted help from a lawyer in Pennsylvania.

Johnnie Mask, a deputy public defender with the state public defender's regional office in Somerset County, stepped in to represent him in New Jersey. A graduate of the Duke University School of Law, Mask was a lawyer who was deeply committed to holding up the rights of his clients. A survivor of one of Cullen's victims later suggested that the public defender with the salt-and-pepper hair and full white beard and mustache looked almost like a double for the Civil War–era abolitionist firebrand, Frederick Douglass.

Cullen was represented in Pennsylvania by Gary N.

Asteak, a coal-mine-country lawyer who was known for his ponytail, cowboy boots, and such a flair for the outrageous that he could have been a transplant from the Texas bar, where flamboyancy among the stars of the trade is almost a given. Unlike colleagues from the "Lone Star State," Asteak had a fascination with international Communism and Communist leaders. He had visited Lenin's tomb, the mausoleums of Mao Tse-tung and Ho Chi Minh, trekked through Castro's Cuba, and even crawled through some of the notorious tunnels of Cu Chi ringing Saigon, where Viet cong guerrillas fought an underground war against Americans and the Army of the Republic of Vietnam.

Aside from Asteak's eccentricities, he was a skillful, experienced lawyer with private law firm offices in Easton and Nazareth, and a résumé that included malpractice, divorce, and zoning cases—and the criminal defense of clients ranging from accused killers to reputed flashers and child pornographers. Cullen was well represented in both states.

The prospects for confirming Cullen's claims and linking individual hospital deaths to him were suddenly made more difficult when Mask notified police that he was forbidding any further questioning of his client.

Mask told reporters he didn't know exactly what his client told police, but didn't think Cullen had provided a detailed list of victims. "My job is to persuade prosecutors not to kill the guy. My job is to save his life," the attorney was quoted by the *New York Daily News* as saying. "His bottom line is to get it over with. I think he understands he has to spend the rest of his life in a box."

The job facing Braun, Baldwin, and other detectives involved in the investigation had just become more daunting than ever. Furthermore, Forrest wasn't far off the mark when he suggested that the Cullen case might be the biggest homicide investigation in the history of the state, although crime historians would be likely to compare it with the kidnapping and death of the twenty-month-old

Lindbergh baby. The abduction of curly-haired Charles A. Lindbergh Jr. from his second-floor bedroom in the tiny Somerset County village of Hopewell, on the night of March 1, 1932, captured headlines around the world and launched an investigation leading to an arrest and execution that are still being debated. The baby's father, Charles A. Lindbergh Sr., vaulted to a position as one of the world's most celebrated heroes in May 1927 when he became the first man to fly nonstop across the Atlantic Ocean.

The investigation of the kidnapping was headed by Colonel H. N. Schwarzkopf, head of the New Jersey State Police Department, and the father of U.S. Army General H. Norman Schwarzkopf. General Schwarzkopf led Operation Desert Storm, the First Gulf War, that brought Iraqi dictator Saddam Hussein to his knees in 1991.

The badly decomposed remains of the Lindbergh baby were recovered from a farm field ten weeks after the kidnapping, and Americans throughout the country were outraged at the ghastly crime. Notorious Chicago Mob leader Al Capone offered to help run down the kidnapper/killer of the son of "Lucky Lindy," before a German immigrant named Bruno Hauptmann was arrested and convicted of the crime. Hauptmann died in New Jersey's electric chair in 1935.

When the suspected Death Angel was arrested, it wasn't Bruno Hauptmann who was on the hot seat. It was Cullen who found himself mired solidly in the middle of the mess, and it shouldn't have been a surprise to anyone who knew much about him that he began to wilt from the stress and talk about doing away with himself.

By Wednesday, less than a week after his arrest, Cullen's self-destructive ramblings coupled with his history of suicide attempts led to his examination at the jail by medical and psychiatric professionals. Jailers requested a psychiatric evaluation after the inmate "mentioned suicide," Somerset County sheriff Frank Provenzano told reporters.

After the examination Cullen was stripped naked in order to remove any foreign object he might possibly use to kill himself and was locked in a padded cell. The Death Angel, who admitted to murdering thirty to forty helpless men and women during his blood-soaked career as a nurse, was reduced to a pitiful, naked wretch who was more dangerous to himself than to anyone else.

Cullen remained in the lit cell, safely isolated from other inmates and under close observation until he was helped by corrections officers to dress, led outside, and driven to the 150-bed Anne Klein Forensic Center at the maximum-security Trenton State Psychiatric Hospital for the criminally insane in the West Trenton suburb of Ewing. Patients admitted to Anne Klein were typically so deranged that they needed constant supervision, were found to be criminally insane, or too incompetent to be put on trial. Patients were watched over by highly trained medical security officers, and movement from one room or space to another was controlled by automated sliding doors. Commenting to the press about his client's transfer to Anne Klein, Mask suggested that once Cullen was locked in the psychiatric hospital, he might "never get out."

Cullen was still languishing in the padded cell when the previously arranged voluntary surrender of his New Jersey nursing license was accepted by state authorities on December 17. The license had been valid until 2005.

Somerset Medical Center had notified the state nursing board about Cullen's troubles after learning that he had applied for a job at Muhlenberg, and the story of the Death Angel was just coming to the attention of the print and broadcast media when the agency temporarily suspended his license.

Cullen lost his license in Pennsylvania a few days later when the state nursing board announced it was being suspended for six months as the first step before permanent revocation. Three weeks later chief hearing examiner John F. Alcorn conducted a hearing in Harrisburg and determined that prosecutors had gathered enough evidence to uphold the temporary license suspension of the confessed killer. In January, Pennsylvania Bureau of Professional and Occupational Affairs acted to make the suspension permanent. The license had been good until October 2004.

While Cullen was cooling his heels in the padded jail cell, then at Anne Klein, the investigation into his crimes was rapidly mushrooming. New Jersey State attorney general Peter C. Harvey assumed responsibility for coordinating the widespread probe. Ironically, the state's chief legal eagle, who was spearheading the investigation into what was shaping up as one of the nation's worst-ever cases of serial medical murder, was the son of a nurse.

Harvey was in his first year in the job, and although he was selected in 2003 by the *New Jersey Law Journal* as its first "Lawyer of the Year," it had already been a rocky ride. He reorganized the five-hundred-lawyer Division of Law, wrote a new law requiring all felons to provide DNA samples, ordered videotaping of all confessions, and weathered a wave of negative publicity accusing him of being too friendly with boxing interests in Atlantic City.

Then the Cullen case showed up on the radar, and the attorney general was faced with the herculean task of assisting local prosecutors from five counties exchange information and coordinate their strategy, instead of tangling in a futile turf war over jurisdiction or who would get first crack at the defendant. On top of all that, everything had to be worked out in concert with authorities in Pennsylvania.

While Harvey was busy planning overall strategy, pathologists conducting tests on Father's Gall's remains finally confirmed what most everyone involved already suspected: the parish priest was killed by an overdose of digoxin.

In Pennsylvania, Lehigh County DA Martin requested that the Pennsylvania police reopen the inquiry into Cullen's activities at St. Luke's Hospital. Administrators at LVH were already moving on their own to take a new look at the records of patients who died on the burn unit while Cullen was one of the nurses there.

Northampton County DA John M. Morganelli named Cullen as a suspect in the death of Ottomar Schramm, which occurred almost exactly five years earlier at Easton Hospital.

In New Jersey, Morris County prosecutor Michael M. Rubbinaccio asked the state attorney general to relieve him of responsibility for investigating possible deaths at Morristown Memorial Hospital because of a potential conflict of interest. An individual who was employed at the hospital who might have relevant information had a relationship with members of his office, he explained. Rubbinaccio asked that either the attorney general take over the investigation or give him permission to hand responsibilities over to the Somerset County prosecutor.

Acting Essex County prosecutor Paula T. Dow disclosed that her office was contacted by six families that suspected the deaths of family members may have been caused by Cullen while he worked at the St. Barnabas Medical Center.

In Warren County the investigation into the death of Helen Dean was reopened and preparations were begun to exhume the body for another look at the forensic evidence. Permission for the exhumation was obtained from Sharon Jones, Mrs. Dean's niece, in order to satisfy a state law that required approval from a family member of the deceased. Larry Dean died of esophageal cancer in October 2001, and according to his wishes, his body was cremated and buried in a box in the grave of his beloved mother. Shortly before his death, he took her tissue samples out of the home freezer and discarded them. Sharon Jones figured that her cousin Larry would have approved of the exhumation. A court order was obtained to carry out the dismal process.

On a chilly, overcast Thursday morning in late January, under orders of acting Warren County prosecutor Frank Bucsi, the body of Mrs. Dean was exhumed from her grave at Fairmount Cemetery. Even though the spunky old woman was in her grave for more than a decade, chances were good that the body would be well preserved, although no one could be sure until the casket was opened. Temperature, soil conditions, the quality of the embalming, and how airtight and watertight the casket was could all work to keep the body preserved—or to speed up the rate of decomposition.

Mrs. Dean's granite tombstone had already been moved away from the snow-covered grave the day before, and grave diggers chopped through the snow, then began chipping away with jackhammers at the frozen earth beneath, until a backhoe was brought in to begin removing the exposed soil. Even with the machinery, it was a daunting job and it was about ninety minutes before the exhumation team reached the concrete vault holding the coffin.

A hydraulic crane mounted on the back of a flatbed truck owned by the vault company was finally driven up to the grave and used to help cemetery workers lift the heavy concrete cover of the vault. About 10:00 A.M. approximately two hours after workers began the process by clearing the snow from the grave, Mrs. Dean's bluish gray casket was lifted out and put aside, along with the box containing her son's cremated remains.

The old vault was loaded onto the truck to be taken away and discarded and a new vault was lowered into the grave. The casket containing her remains and those of her son would be lowered back into the new vault later that same day after the autopsy, to again lie next to the grave of their husband and father. Mark Dean's grave was undisturbed.

About a dozen people were present when the men removed their hats and everyone bowed their heads while Jeffrey Finegan, director of the Finegan Funeral Home in Phillipsburg, led a brief prayer. Finegan was a longtime friend of the Dean family and was asked to attend the exhumation by Ms. Jones. State law required the presence of a funeral director. At last Mrs. Dean's casket was loaded into a van and driven to Warren Hospital for a second autopsy.

Dr. Mihalakis assumed personal charge of the second examination, and he took samples of tissue, organs, and body fluid to be tested for the approximately one hundred compounds scanned for as part of the initial autopsy. This time—the ME armed with knowledge of Cullen's preference for the drug as a killing tool—the dead woman's remains were also examined for digoxin. Fortunately, considering the lengthy period since Mrs. Dean's death, digoxin is a fairly stable compound. Even after ten years, if she was given an unauthorized dose of the drug at Warren Hospital, it could still be present in her tissue. If traces of digoxin were found, it would most likely be in muscle tissue.

The tissue samples were sent to a Newark laboratory for processing, and Mihalakis told news reporters that it could take up to six months before all the analysis was completed. When toxicologists returned their report on the tests, they confirmed the suspicions: traces of the drug were found in her tissues. Larry Dean wouldn't have been surprised.

Chapter 12

A Dreadful Foreboding

Police, prosecutors, and hospital authorities began informing families in two states that their fathers, mothers, brothers, sisters, and sons were victims of the killer nurse.

Many families didn't wait for the knock on the door, but contacted police, prosecutors, or hospital authorities on their own to ask if their relatives might have been among the victims of the homicidal nurse.

Authorities in Somerset County, where the admitted serial killer worked most recently, were probably kept the busiest by concerned relatives. The hospital and chief medical officer, William K. Cors, moved swiftly to initiate damage control measures.

"It causes us a blemish today, but we're confident the actions we took were the proper ones," he said in a public statement. "The systems and processes we have in place were critical to our ability to quickly uncover the current problem."

Cullen was more than a problem for the medical center, he was a catastrophe. Cors, however, would do his best to shine the best possible light on the hospital. He would point out that after the killer nurse had worked at nine other patient-care facilities during the lengthy murder spree, it was Somerset that finally helped develop evidence that stopped the decade-and-a-half slaughter. It was an explanation that was less than satisfactory to most of the relatives of patients who were murdered.

Cors was persistent in his efforts to repair the public relations disaster and the hospital announced that he was planning to meet with relatives of the six patients already identified as having been given overdoses of either digoxin or insulin. Office employees were kept busy fielding a flurry of calls from concerned families whose loved ones had died on Cullen's watch. Other concerned relatives placed calls directly to the office of the Somerset county prosecutor to express fears that family members may have been murdered by Cullen.

As soon as Tom and Mary Strenko heard about suspicious deaths at the medical center, they thought back to the weirdo nurse who confronted them while doctors were trying in vain to resuscitate their son. Mary Strenko telephoned the prosecutor's office to pass on their fears that their son was one of the Death Angel's victims.

Carey Fedorczyk and other relatives of eighty-five-year-old Nicholas Senko Jr. were also among worried family members who arranged a meeting with the prosecutor to look for answers. Fedorczyk said that three days before her grandfather's death at the medical center on June 3, he clutched a pencil in his crippled hand and wrote in laboriously formed large letters that a strange doctor had come into his room and he was being drugged. The thirty-year-old woman observed that the retired Manville letter carrier, like many elderly people, would expect a nurse to be female and may have thought a male nurse was a doctor, according to a *Star-Ledger* story.

That suggestion led to even more awful speculation that the killer nurse may have told what he was doing to her grandfather or other patients who were unable to talk. "Maybe he told them he was going to put them out of their misery or help comfort them," she speculated. "I think something had to be said for my grandfather to be suspicious."

When Mary Ann Jones contacted the prosecutor's office to pass on fears that her mother may have been one of the serial killer's victims, a detective told her he had already taken thirty calls. After laboratory tests showed unusually high levels of digoxin in her system, seventy-six-year-old Charlotte Klimko was in and out of Somerset's critical-care unit during much of the summer. She was called back to the hospital twice after test results turned up excessive amounts of digoxin in her system; she died eventually at home from congestive heart disease, on October 26.

The daughter said that when her mother was given a heart examination shortly after leaving the critical-care unit in September, she was found to have high levels of digoxin. The family assumed Klimko had taken too much of the medication accidentally, but after learning about Cullen and his use of digoxin to kill patients, they wanted her file looked into. By late July 2005, more than eighteen months after Cullen's arrest, he had not identified Klimko or Senko as being among his victims.

At the Liberty Nursing Center, authorities began telephoning family members of residents and patients who died there while Cullen was an employee, to let them know ahead of time that they would be reading or hearing about the admitted medical serial killer in the media. HCR Manor Care, the Ohio-based owner/operator of the nursing home, disclosed that the company already had begun to review records and had received a request for documents from the Pennsylvania nursing board.

The Hunterdon Medical Center established a hot line with a publicized telephone number for people to call for information about family members who were hospitalized there while Cullen was an employee. Hunterdon County prosecutor J. Patrick Barnes said his office was inspecting records at the medical center covering the period Cullen worked there. Both the prosecutor and the hospital launched inquiries into possible suspicious deaths at the facility before Cullen's arrest and before it became publicly known he was suspected of turning on patients at Somerset. The Hunterdon Medical Center's internal investigation was focused on all patients who were on the ICU while Cullen worked there from April 1994 to October 1996.

In Pennsylvania, Lehigh Valley Hospital spokesmen issued a cautious statement disclosing that it was reviewing all areas of the accused killer nurse's employment there.

At Sacred Heart Hospital a spokesman pointed out to the media that the murder suspect was still in orientation when he was terminated, and during the sixteen days he worked there he wasn't allowed unsupervised contact with patients.

During the first three weeks after Cullen's arrest, more than a dozen telephone calls were fielded at the office of acting Warren County prosecutor Frank Bucsi from relatives of patients who died at Warren Hospital between early 1992 and late 1993. The prosecutor quickly eliminated a handful of the cases after determining that the deaths occurred either a few days or weeks before Cullen was employed at the hospital, or shortly after he left. Investigators were assigned to take a close look at the other deaths.

The death of Mary Natoli was one of the cases getting an especially close look. That was due in part to her sister, a receptionist at Warren Hospital when Natoli died. After learning of Cullen's arrest the receptionist requested her sister's medical records. She and her nieces looked over the files for clues that might reveal whether or not Natoli was one of the Death Angel's victims. The homicidal RN had signed several of the documents, so they notified the Warren County prosecutor about suspicions that their family member may have been murdered. Within a few days after the story broke, the prosecutor's office had subpoenaed the files of nearly two dozen patients who died at the hospital while Cullen worked on the ICU. The records of

Mrs. Natoli, Mrs. Mugavero, and Mrs. Dean were among those subpoenaed.

The Two Rivers Hospital Corporation notified the Pennsylvania state police and the Northampton County Coroner's Office of another suspicious death at Easton Hospital that the medical facility's former owner/operator had uncovered. Ottomar Schramm's death was already under investigation when the new case at Warren Hospital came to light.

The patient wasn't publicly identified, but a company spokesman told reporters it was an elderly man who had an extremely low glucose level just prior to his death. Abnormally low glucose levels are a bellwether symptom of an insulin overdose.

Morris County prosecutor Michael Rubbinaccio announced that his office had launched an investigation with Morristown police and Alan Robinson, Morristown Memorial Hospital's director of corporate security.

Reaction from families of St. Barnabas patients who died while Cullen was working there, at the beginning of his career, was slower to develop, and almost a week after his arrest, only one telephone call had been fielded by hospital employees from a concerned relative.

Throughout the two-state area, relatives of former patients reacted with shock and grief. Some were torn by rage, but the tears in the eyes of others washed away any hatred, leaving only pain and regret as they contemplated a rapidly unfolding story of almost gothic horror. Immediately the terrible question arose: was their own loved one a victim of an Angel of Death who lurked in the semidarkened hospital hallways poisoning vulnerable patients he was sworn to help?

Relatives who thought they were done with the grieving, months or years ago, were devastated and left emotionally drained by the reopening of old wounds. Some were hurt but forgiving, and in many cases those who did allow anger to surface directed their bitterness toward the medical establishments whose slack hiring practices and flawed security permitted the slaughter to continue.

Sharon Jones, Helen Dean's niece, was watching a television newscast when she heard that a male nurse had been charged with murder, according to a *Star-Ledger* report. She knew who the nurse was even before the newscaster announced his name. If she needed any further confirmation, it came moments later when maps were shown locating the hospitals where he worked. "I knew this was no other Charles Cullen," she said. "There couldn't be any other Charles Cullen."

While the Catholic Diocese of Metuchen was deeply distressed by the news that their priest was murdered, Bishop Bootkoski released a statement declaring: "His life was one of service and devotion, and his death was a tremendous loss not only to his parish but also to the entire diocese. As Father Gall would have done, we also pray that God grant forgiveness to the individual who caused his death."

Lucille Gall's brother was dead almost four months when a police detective knocked at her front door and said he had a few questions he needed to ask. He wanted to know what she could tell him about the priest's medications, especially about the heart drug digoxin. She had been aware that digoxin was prescribed for him at one time. But she hadn't known that Father Gall's lab work for digoxin was normal the day before he went into cardiac arrest—when the amount of the drug in his system was tripled. Somerset Medical Center still hadn't shared information with her about the real cause of her brother's death. Nor were she and her surviving brothers aware of the internal investigation conducted by the hospital.

Lucille had been a nurse too long not to recognize what the detective was getting at. "Well," she said, "somebody gave him something."

For a woman who knew a lot about hospitals, the news that her brother was murdered in one must have been like a fist to the stomach. She had worked in hospital administration and in risk management, so she had an insider's knowledge of much of the good and the bad that can occur there.

A spiritual person, like her brother, she told a reporter she believed the elderly priest's death left behind positive meaning. It was his death that finally led police to the serial killer who was preying on patients, and ultimately stopped the slaughter. The newfound knowledge that Cullen sidestepped safeguards set up to protect patients was already leading to the tightening of security measures.

The experienced nurse and loving sister was nevertheless left with questions that were unlikely ever to be answered completely. Did nurses on the ward see other things going on that didn't look right and tell their supervisor? Do hospital administrators always take steps to correct such things when they learn something is wrong? She didn't know. Lucille Gall admittedly was bothered also by the notoriety of the case that was keeping the Death Angel in the limelight, because she believed killers like Cullen enjoyed the notoriety. "What about those poor people who are buried?" she asked.

If her questions were ever to be addressed, the answers would most likely come from police and prosecutors, who were touching all the bases to retrace the malignant steps of the recently confessed Death Angel. Other survivors of Cullen's victims were already asking similar questions, and looking to law enforcement to come up with answers.

John Michael Shanagher was a schoolteacher and he was sitting at his computer putting together a study plan when he noticed something on a ribbon at the bottom of his screen headlining a news story about a nurse charged with murders at Somerset Medical Center. *That's weird, that's our hospital,* he thought. It was still a few days before Christmas and the story had been on the news for a while, but the Shanagher family had been experiencing a series of deaths since his father died, and he was busy juggling his teaching duties with the task of regularly driving his mother back and forth to another hospital, where her brother was dying. He hadn't been paying much attention to the news.

But he was intrigued by the mention of Somerset Medical Center and he clicked on the story. When he got home, he began catching up on local newspaper articles about the man who was being touted in the press as a Death Angel. He realized that he knew who the nurse was. He wasn't sure if it was the same man who offered to help out with the bathroom chores, but he definitely had seen him around while Jack Shanagher was in critical care.

The younger Shanagher was driving his mother home from his uncle's funeral when he decided to call the hospital. He said he wanted to know if his father was one of the six victims Cullen had already identified and admitted killing at Somerset. After a few transfers of the call, he reached someone who told him: "Well, he is not one of the people we have referred to the prosecutor's office." The hospital source also suggested he might wish to call the prosecutor.

Families all over Somerset County were contacting police, prosecutors, and hospital administrators, wanting to know if parents or other kin who died at Somerset or at other hospitals in New Jersey and Pennsylvania expired while Cullen was working as a night nurse in critical care, where they were being treated. The calls started as soon as the media began flashing the news of Cullen's arrest and the suspected murders at the Somerset Medical Center.

Two people answering telephones at the Somerset County Prosecutor's Office fielded fifty calls from concerned families in a single day. Shanagher wasn't even among the first wave of callers, but when he telephoned a few days before Christmas, he wound up leaving a message for a callback. No one called back, but he wasn't too surprised.

"Obviously, at that point that was when everybody on the planet was calling the prosecutor's office," he later recalled. So a couple of days after Christmas, he telephoned again and left another message. This time Detective Braun returned the call, asked a few questions, and said he would get back to him. It took a while.

The realization that Irene Krapf might have been murdered in her hospital bed dawned on Carolyn Henne, her daughter, when she first started to read newspaper stories about Cullen. She realized that he was her mother's nurse at St. Luke's.

Several survivors recalled seeing Cullen around their loved ones before the patients died.

Chapter 13

A Life-and-Death Decision

Emily Stoecker was listening to WCBS-AM 880 on the car radio while driving with her mother and three-year-old daughter, Sophie, to buy Christmas gifts when she heard something about the Somerset Medical Center on the newscast.

A wave of nausea swept over her as the story of a series of suspected murders of patients unfolded, and she realized that was the hospital where Ma had died. As the shock settled in, she felt like the newscaster's words were echoing in the car. Turning to her puzzled mother, she said: "This is where Richard's mom died."

Emily knew then that her mother-in-law was murdered, but she didn't want to believe it. Even when her mother broke her stunned silence and tried to reassure her, telling her that something like that simply couldn't happen to them, Emily was shaking and felt like she was going to vomit. She struggled to hold on to her composure because her daughter was staring curiously at her, and she didn't want to scare the child.

As soon as Emily got home, she walked down to the

basement for privacy and telephoned the Somerset County Prosecutor's Office. She was still upset and had some difficulty explaining what she wanted to the woman who answered the telephone, but was finally transferred to a police officer who worked with Detective Braun. As he began writing down information, he asked, "What was the name again?"

Emily spelled it out: *"S-t-o-e-c-k-e-r!"*

As she finished spelling out the last name, she heard the officer say half under his breath to himself or to someone else nearby, "Okay! There she is."

That was when any last possible doubts that her mother-in-law was murdered evaporated. She knew the police officer knew something that he couldn't tell her just then. And whatever it was, it had to be bad.

The officer told her that he could only talk with one of Eleanor's blood relatives and the dead woman's kin would have to provide proof of their relationship.

Zach had also heard of Cullen's arrest and wondered if the male nurse could have had something to do with Eleanor's death. He considered calling the prosecutor, but decided against it. He was at work when Emily telephoned him at the radio station and told him about her talk with the prosecutor's homicide investigator.

Zach put in a direct call to Detective Braun and told him he suspected Cullen may have had something to do with his mother's death. The probe was still in its infancy, and Braun had been an investigator too long to make any rash assumptions or needlessly upset someone whose family member might have been a murder victim. His reply was cautious and judiciously noncommittal. He said her case was under review, but he couldn't provide any more information at that time because the suspected hospital murders were part of an ongoing investigation.

Braun also asked for a photo of Zach's mother. Most of the family photos were lost in a flood, so Zach telephoned his mother's chum, Janet Sonic. Sonic said her niece had a photo of Eleanor on her desk and would send it to him. Zach e-mailed the picture to Braun.

Communication between Zach and Braun slowed after that, but the DJ kept in touch with the detective with occasional telephone calls to ask how the investigation was proceeding. Braun, like other major players in the investigation, understood the emotional strain on relatives who suspected their loved ones were murdered at the Somerset Medical Center; he was good about accepting the calls. Like a good detective, he let the caller do most of the talking.

Zach told Braun about a fleeting recollection of the gloomy male nurse with skin that was so sallow it looked like cracked parchment, who was hanging around his mother's hospital room while she was fighting for her life. The detective still didn't have much to say in response—but he was a good listener. Braun didn't say anything to confirm directly the suspicions that Eleanor was one of Cullen's victims, but Zach figured he had taken a correct reading on the vibes that were being sent out: his mother was murdered by the medical center's resident Death Angel.

It was almost four months before Braun telephoned Zach at home one morning near the middle of April. The detective said they needed to talk right away.

"Okay," Zach replied. "How about sometime next week?"

"I was thinking sometime this evening," the detective replied.

Whatever Braun had to say to him, Zach realized, he wasn't going to drive to Oradell to tell the family that police had cleared Cullen of any responsibility for Eleanor's death.

Zach telephoned his sister, Diane, and his father, and asked them to come to Oradell because a detective wanted to talk with the family about Eleanor's death. William Stoecker said he couldn't take time off from work, so Zach promised to telephone him later and bring him up to date on the meeting. Diane and her husband drove to

Oradell from their home in the central part of the state. Fearing the worst, Emily arranged for her parents to take Sophie out for the night to spare the three-year-old from possible trauma.

It was a Thursday, a warm spring evening in the quiet suburb, when Detective Braun and a woman from a Somerset County victim's advocacy unit drove up in a plain car and rang the doorbell. Braun was carrying a huge blue folder under his arm. Their faces were sober.

A few minutes later everyone was seated on sofas and chairs in Zach and Emily's front room listening in growing horror while Detective Braun confirmed that Eleanor was one of Cullen's murder victims. After looking at Eleanor's photo and examining medical records, Cullen had admitted in February to the murder, the husky lawman said. Braun apologized because he couldn't tell them sooner. Eleanor was probably the first to die at Cullen's hands at the Somerset Medical Center.

Although the news wasn't unexpected, it was devastating. Zach's sister was in tears. Emily was nauseous again, but she asked what would happen to Cullen.

That was when Braun dropped another bombshell. A plea agreement had been worked out between prosecutors and Cullen's public defenders that would keep him out of the execution chamber in Trenton in return for cooperating with investigators in efforts to identify all the victims of the near sixteen-year murder spree, the detective explained. The compact was hammered out without any input from relatives of known victims, and without their knowledge that it even was being considered. It was a done deal.

As soon as Braun disclosed that Cullen's lawyers had worked out a deal to spare him from the death chamber, Emily's mind flashed back to the terrible night that she watched Ma die. She realized she was a witness to the murder of her mother-in-law, and hadn't even known it. She watched helplessly while the dying woman's skin seemed to smooth out, her face turned blue, her lips blackened, and a growling or rattling sound escaped from her throat. Two doctors finally walked into the room and one of them said: "She's gone. We're sorry."

No one was present from Amnesty International or from any other well-funded organization opposing the death penalty to plead with the executioner for Eleanor's life. Her killer decided that it was time for Emily's mother-in-law to die, and he took her life with a lethal injection, just as surely as if she were strapped to a gurney in the death chamber at Trenton State Prison.

Although Emily didn't notice Cullen inside the room while Ma was dying, she had read in news accounts that he sometimes hung around to watch the lives of his victims slip away—and to witness the grief of the families. She wanted to see Cullen executed! Someday she had hoped to watch while poison dripped into his arm through an IV, and doctors checked his heart to confirm his death—just like he had made her and everyone else who loved her mother-in-law witness Eleanor's appalling death.

Emily didn't want to believe that the man who ruthlessly snuffed out the lives of her mother-in-law, and who knew how many other helpless patients in their hospital beds, was going to be allowed to squirm out of the mess with his life intact. She repeatedly asked if there wasn't some chance that Cullen would be executed.

The replies from the detective and the victim's advocate were firmly consistent: Cullen's execution wasn't going to happen. If he was honest and stuck to the terms of the agreement expected to be signed by the prosecution and the defense, as soon as a few rough edges were ironed out, he would be allowed to live out the remainder of his miserable life in a prison or a secure psychiatric institution. There was no execution in his future. Although there were still a few *t*'s to cross and *i*'s to dot, the compact was expected to be signed by both sides in less than a week

There wasn't much the detective or his colleague could say to ease the emotional trauma, except to reassure the family that they and other relatives of victims would have a chance to face the killer at his sentencing. They were unaware of it at the time, but that was a promise that would be difficult to keep.

Zach accepted the inevitable—and in fairness to the other families who were still waiting to learn whether or not their loved ones were murdered—he respected the decision that was made by the authorities. He and his wife agreed that they could understand the importance of obtaining Cullen's cooperation to pinpoint exactly which patients who died on his wards were victims of the murder spree, and which ones died natural deaths. As hurtful as it was to know that Eleanor was murdered, at least the wondering and the doubt could now be laid to rest by her loved ones. Other families also deserved to know the truth.

Zach earned a bachelor's degree in criminology at St. John's, and he was aware that New Jersey had a miserable record for carrying out the death penalty, no matter how heinous the crimes someone might be convicted of. He also knew that the violent men that Cullen would eventually be locked up with observed a different system of criminal justice than the system that was followed by the state's higher courts and the federal judicial system. He thought especially about the late cannibal Jeffrey Dahmer.

Dahmer escaped the death penalty when he was sentenced in Milwaukee after murdering at least seventeen young men and boys, then butchering and eating several of them. Three years after Dahmer was locked in prison, another inmate imposed the death sentence on his own, beating the cannibalistic sex criminal and another killer to death with a lead pipe. Zach knew that when all the fuss and the fury in the courts finally ended for Cullen—a small, physically weak, middle-aged man—he would be locked up with the same kind of savage neighbors with whom Dahmer was imprisoned. The Death Angel's story wouldn't be over when he was sentenced in the courts, or when he was processed into a maximum-security prison or psychiatric hospital. Zach figured he could live with a life sentence for his mother's killer.

With Braun's approval, Zach called his baby brother in Wisconsin and activated the speaker phone so that William could listen while the detective brought everyone up to date on the investigation and the scheduled court proceedings. William was stunned by the dreadful news, and hardly said a word.

It was especially painful for Zach to deal with the knowledge that the gentle, loving woman, who studied to be a nurse before finances and other circumstances interfered, was killed by someone practicing the profession she so admired. He especially worried that his mother may have known she was being murdered, but was so frightened and so helpless she couldn't let anyone else know what was going on. If that was so, she was tortured, and the whole death experience was not as antiseptic as Cullen and some of his apologists would like others to believe.

Zach remembered going to his parents' house after the funeral and looking through the belongings his mother left behind. These items offered solid affirmation that she expected to return home from the hospital. She loved to order things from television shopping channels, and put in a store of weight-loss products that she planned to try out. She wasn't much of a cook, but she was still trying, and had just unpacked a new spaghetti cooker and strainer combination before leaving for the hospital. It was still sitting in the kitchen, unused. Eleanor didn't go to the hospital expecting to die.

While the serial murderer cooled his heels at the psychiatric hospital, events continued to move rapidly.

Cullen was willing to cooperate—in large part because he wanted to protect his daughters and his seven months pregnant girlfriend the embarrassment of a prolonged trial that threatened to become another sleazy media event like the judicial circuses that surrounded the O. J. Simpson and Scott Peterson cases. That was fine with Mask, just so long as he could make sure that sparing his client the death penalty was also part of the deal.

Mask told the press that authorities from both states had to agree, and if the Somerset prosecutor could get them on board, he would do his best to get Cullen to identify his murder victims. Families wanted to know if their loved ones were victims, he pointed out, while making it clear that his client was the only one with the answers. Mask was a competent, experienced professional and he was playing hardball. It had to be all or nothing: no deal, no cooperation!

Although not totally unexpected, the public defender and his client were offering a devil's deal that was speckled with thorny practical problems, and could become a public relations disaster if it wasn't handled right. Mask had tossed down the gauntlet, and law enforcement authorities in the two states were faced with a dilemma.

If they agreed to spare Cullen the death penalty, he would provide the names of all the patients he could remember killing, meet with prosecutors and state officials to pinpoint hospital security flaws that permitted him to remain undetected during his decade-and-a-half murder spree, and help investigators in other ways, according to his attorney.

That was an attractive option because forensic specialists had a daunting task ahead of them to pinpoint victims and produce hard evidence and other information to document the murders. The job wouldn't necessarily be impossible, but it would be much more complicated and difficult without Cullen's cooperation. The task of digging through mountains of hospital patient and medication records, interviewing witnesses about occurrences that might be anywhere from a few months to more than a decade old, exhuming bodies and conducting necropsies on ancient remains, would also be prohibitively expensive.

The exhumation and two autopsies conducted in the Helen Dean case cost more than $1 million.

In Lehigh County, where it was believed Cullen may have killed as many as twelve patients, the attitude of DA Martin seemed to capture the thinking of at least some of his colleagues about their ability to solve all their hospital murder cases on their own when he told the press that it was unlikely investigators would be able to "get them all."

Gaining a confession to thirty to forty murders—especially in the absence of names of all but a victim or two—didn't mean that prosecutors could swagger into court and obtain slam dunk convictions. If cases against Cullen ever came to trial, prosecutors had to be ready with a combination of medical testimony and mounds of first-class forensic and circumstantial evidence.

Confessions had to be backed up with solid evidence produced by toxicologists and other medical and scientific experts, as well as information from other avenues such as patient and medication files. Homicide detectives and other law enforcement professionals investigating Cullen's crimes or suspected crimes in the two states had to be prepared to use all the appropriate investigative tools normally at their disposal. That included, if necessary, grand jury subpoenas, search warrants, exhumations of the remains of former patients, and the expertise of a host of forensic scientists ranging from pathologists to toxicologists and assorted laboratory technicians.

Hospital colleagues of the accused man and families of victims also needed to be questioned to produce witnesses to some of the events in certain cases, but it appeared most likely that the only real eyewitnesses to the actual murders—besides the killer himself—were dead. Authorities didn't want Cullen to confess, to any death he wasn't really sure he had a hand in, and when he did confess they wanted to be certain that they could back it up with other evidence. No one wanted Charles Cullen to become an Efren Saldivar.

Cases like that of the California respiratory therapist were exactly the kind of long, drawn-out investigations Forrest hoped to avoid and to learn from when he made his round of telephone calls to other law enforcement agencies that had dealt earlier with instances of medical murder.

When police and prosecutors in the Los Angeles suburb of Glendale collared Saldivar, they quickly got a confession to hospital murders, but gathered little or no reliable physical or other evidence to back up his statements. Police and prosecutors found themselves in a bind when Saldivar recanted his confession, and was freed from jail while detectives and medical sleuths scrambled to put together enough hard evidence for the prosecutor to take a successful case to trial.

That took six full-time investigators four years to accomplish, including one year just studying medical records. A medical professional was flown in from Texas to work with the detectives on the documents. The sleuths rented a house across the street from the hospital, converted the bedrooms into offices, and filled another room with massive stacks of records. Other rooms were used for interviews.

Focusing on the most recent deaths thought to have been caused by the suspect, the detectives looked into 170 patient deaths, which they finally reduced to twenty. The mass of documents was trimmed to about three hundred thousand pages that were considered pertinent and eventually shared with defense attorneys. When exhumation of bodies for toxicological tests was begun, about one set of remains was dug up every week for almost six months. Saldivar was finally sent to prison for life, but the task that looked so promising after he confessed turned into a massive nightmare undertaking that ate up thousands of man-hours and was a tremendous burden on taxpayers.

It could be years before the cases against Cullen would come to trial, and when that happened, prosecutors would have to be ready with the proper blend of medical testimony, circumstantial and other evidence, to convince juries beyond all reasonable doubt that it wasn't the frail health of patients that caused their death—but the criminal interference of the defendant.

With or without Cullen's cooperation, the process would be tedious, time-consuming, and expensive. The drain on law enforcement agencies from police to prosecutors and the judiciary in both manpower and financial costs could be staggering, especially for less populated counties with small tax bases. Everything would be more difficult and more costly without Cullen's cooperation.

A few years before Cullen's arrest, Death Angel Kristen Gilbert was suspected of killing up to fifty patients at the Northampton, Massachusetts Veterans Affairs Medical Center by injecting them with overdoses of the heart stimulant epiniphrine. Prosecutors were able to bring charges against her in seven of the cases. Five years after investigators first began looking into the string of fatal cardiac arrests on her shifts, prosecutors convicted her in four deaths and two attempted murders.

Prosecutors said the mother of two sons abandoned her family and went on a killing rampage during 1995 and 1996 in a bizarre attempt to impress her lover, who was a security guard at the VA hospital. The woman, who was exposed when colleagues at the hospital tipped off authorities, is serving life in a federal prison for the murders.

Investigators in New Jersey and Pennsylvania were already exhuming bodies and preparing to dig up more to examine the remains for traces of digoxin and other medications that were not prescribed at the time of death. But Cullen was believed to have begun killing shortly after beginning his first job as a nurse sixteen years earlier, and the length of time his former patients were in the grave and the drugs used would be important factors. The usefulness of any toxicological evidence obtained from tests on exhumed bodies could vary significantly.

Even the most skilled forensic pathologists may have difficulty gauging the levels of digoxin found in tissues from exhumed bodies. The condition of the tissue found to contain digoxin can make a big difference. If it is shriveled or condensed, that can lead to abnormally high levels of the drug. But abnormally low levels can result if the digoxin has broken down, or if it has been diluted somehow. Embalming fluid or water filtering into the casket and the remains can produce that result.

The best-case scenario for concluding that a digoxin overdose occurred would be finding exceptionally high levels of the drug in a body with tissue that was well preserved. That could apply even if digoxin was prescribed for the patient, but even that scenario carried with it the possibility of seriously intimidating pitfalls. Cullen's guile in overdosing some of his victims with drugs known to have been prescribed for them could make it difficult for prosecutors to prove before a jury that a patient died from anything but the natural cause listed on his death certificate.

Remains that were more decomposed, with more tissue damage, would be naturally more difficult to work with, but they could still be made to yield up their secrets to skilled pathologists, toxicologists, and other medical sleuths.

In most situations muscle tissue is the last to decompose, and that includes the heart muscle, which is attacked by digoxin and is where the drug accumulates. So even some badly decomposed bodies could have sufficient heart tissue in good enough condition to disclose the presence of the drug in measurable levels.

Even remains that had so wasted away that there was no tissue left on the skeleton could sometimes provide evidence of digoxin in some cases, by testing for the presence of the drug in the hair. But it did depend on the circumstances.

It takes about twenty-four hours from the time of the drug overdose for digoxin to make its way into the hair. Unfortunately, in the cases of someone who has not been taking the drug under medical supervision, fatal digoxin overdoses can cause death within an hour. Intravenous injections, especially, speed up the lethal results.

Despite all the difficulties tracking it down through laboratory tests after exhumation of a body, if digoxin was not prescribed for a patient, any amount that showed up during an autopsy would be evidence that somehow he or she was given an unauthorized dose of the drug.

Exhuming a body and finding evidence of criminal intent or a medical blunder was accompanied by other special difficulties, if digoxin was already prescribed for a patient who died of an overdose. It was already known that digoxin was prescribed at one time for Father Gall, and Mrs. Han was also on the drug early in her hospital stay, although it was ordered discontinued before her overdose. Making conclusive deductions based on the levels of digoxin found in their tissues would be extremely difficult. That would apply to any other patients for whom digoxin had been prescribed, if that was the drug believed to have been the cause of death. It was a delicate business. Using digoxin to kill patients for whom the drug was already prescribed, was as cunning as it was ruthless.

Clinical records were certain to play a key role in piecing together the puzzle, but like exhumations, the time factor also had to be considered. Some of the records went back more than a decade to a period before everything was computerized, and documentation of early murders could be spotty or nonexistent.

Putting together death penalty cases could tie up valuable manpower of law enforcement agencies in two states and seven counties for years, with financial costs reaching into the millions of dollars. It was a dizzying prospect, but justice can be expensive.

There was another problem. Cullen was a nut, and he had a track record to prove it. His lifelong depression, suicide attempts, and treatment in psychiatric hospitals could all be cited in capital murder trials, if it came to that, to plead for a lesser penalty than death because he suffered from mental illness or insanity. If a defense lawyer ever had a client on whom to base a strong argument that he shouldn't be executed because of his mental state, it was Cullen. Obtaining a murder conviction (or multiple convictions) and seating a jury that would vote for the death penalty wouldn't be a piece of cake for the prosecution, despite the enormity of the Death Angel's crimes.

Officially, New Jersey was a death penalty state, and if the killer nurse wasn't sentenced to execution, it didn't require much imagination to perceive sometime in the near future when a defense attorney would plead that his client shouldn't go to the gas chamber because he only murdered one, two, or three people. How could that be fair and equitable, he might ask, when the courts approved a deal that spared the life of Cullen, who admitted killing ten times that many or more?

Although polls consistently show that approximately three-quarters of the state's adult citizens favor the death penalty as a means of preventing criminals convicted of committing its most heinous crimes from killing again, New Jersey has a miserable reputation for carrying out their will. No one has been executed by the state since Ralph Hudson, an Atlantic City man who murdered his wife, was strapped into the electric chair in 1963.

New Jersey executed its most vicious criminals in the electric chair until the disastrous 1972 U.S. Supreme Court ruling in *Furman* v. *Georgia* that the death penalty was unconstitutional because application was too random and arbitrary. Some of the most vile hated killers in New Jersey, and elsewhere in the country, were moved permanently off death row in the wake of the ruling.

Some were eventually released from prison altogether. A surprising number, like New Jersey sex slayer Richard Biegenwald, killed again. After escaping the electric chair for the murder of a storekeeper in 1958, the stickup artist and sexual predator was freed from the New Jersey State Prison in Trenton and launched a murder spree in the

1980s targeting teenage girls. The ex-convict, who sought out girls with long, dark hair, lured some of his victims into his car with promises of marijuana, then drove them to isolated locations before stabbing or shooting them to death.

When he was finally tracked down, Biegenwald played Henry Lee Lucas and claimed to have murdered three hundred females in New Jersey, New York, and Pennsylvania. Lucas was the one-eyed moronic drifter who once confessed to six hundred murders, then recanted every one except for the murder of his mother, which he had already done prison time for. Homicide investigators who were clearing cold cases all over the country with his fanciful and convenient confessions wound up with egg on their faces.

Lucas was finally sentenced to death after confessing four times to the murder of a young woman known only as "Orange Socks," because that was the only clothing on her body when it was dumped along a rural Texas road. He escaped execution in 1998 when then Texas governor George W. Bush commuted his sentence to life in prison. Lucas died a natural death behind bars in 2001, but police and prosecutors didn't forget the painful lesson he taught about trying to clear up murder cases with unsupported confessions from suspects.

Lucas may or may not have been a serial killer, but there was no doubt about Biegenwald's status as a multiple murderer. He was eventually convicted of four slayings and sent back to death row. State supreme court reversals saved him from the death chamber twice before his sentence to die in New Jersey's gas chamber was wiped out and he was ordered to serve life in prison.

After another U.S. Supreme Court ruling in *Georgia* v. *Gregg* in 1976 ended the ban on capital punishment, legislatures around the country began drafting and adopting capital punishment laws designed to meet the new standards. Death rows started filling up again.

In the summer of 1982, while Cullen was serving aboard the submarine tender *Canopus*, Garden State legislators responded to widespread discontent by citizens over run-away crime and wrist-slap punishments by voting to rein-state the death penalty. New Jersey became the thirty-seventh state to bring back capital punishment. Once again New Jersey courts began sentencing some of the state's most abhorrent criminals to die in the death chamber, but the new law stipulated lethal injection as the manner of execution.

After some reworking of the statute by the legislature and the courts, authorities agreed that the supreme penalty would be restricted to criminals who committed: "Purpose-ful or knowing murder by your own conduct; contract murder; solicitation by command or threat in furtherance of a narcotics conspiracy." It was left to the jury to deter-mine the sentence.

Thomas Ramseur, who stabbed his girlfriend to death while her grandchildren watched, was the first person sent to death row after the new law was enacted. Biegenwald was another. At one time twenty-nine men and women were on death row, but not one of them or anyone later ordered to be executed have had the sentence carried out. Most were moved into general population or released altogether after decisions on appeals by higher courts. A few died natural deaths, and some—like Marko Bey, who was sentenced to death while Cullen was in the navy—are still there.

In early 2004, while lawyers for the defense and prose-cution were working to hammer out a plea agreement for Cullen, thirteen men were locked up on New Jersey's death row, which is referred to by corrections authorities with the more politically correct title of Capital Sentence Unit. The last to arrive was the notorious Jesse K. Timmend-equas. The longtime pedophile and prison parolee was thirty-three when he lured apple-cheeked seven-year-old Megan Kanka into his home supposedly to look at a puppy, then sodomized her and strangled her with a belt. A cam-paign led by the child's mother, Maureen, led to Megan's

Law, requiring that neighbors be notified when a known sex criminal moves into the community.

Bringing a death penalty prosecution and obtaining a conviction of someone like Timmendequas—or Cullen— is a painfully expensive process that can cost anywhere from $2.3 to $3.2 million in New Jersey. That doesn't even take into account the cost of seemingly endless appeals. The staggering costs would likely be considered money well spent to relatives of the young women and girls murdered by Biegenwald after the New Jersey Supreme Court enabled him to sidestep execution for his first-known murder. But the backbreaking expense can be a terrible burden on taxpayers in small counties with numerous bills to pay. Costs of possible multiple death penalty prosecutions had to be carefully considered when pondering Cullen's fate.

The old electric chair used in the days when Judge Yengo campaigned for Jersey City mayor with a mock-up of the device didn't survive the shake-up of the capital punishment laws. The chair used to end the lives of notorious New Jersey felons, such as Bruno Hauptmann, was no longer designated as the means of execution.

Ironically, if the demented RN who killed the judge and a still-to-be-determined number of other desperately ill hospital and nursing home patients was ultimately sentenced to die, the penalty would be carried out by lethal injection. That was Cullen's favorite method for taking a life.

The execution chamber at the New Jersey State Prison at Trenton was set up neat, clean, and sterile, just like the hospital wards that the killer stalked for a decade-and-a-half in his ruthless search for prey. The death chamber is in the middle, separated by a two-way mirror from a witness room with several straight-back chairs on one side, and on the other side by a blank wall shielding the executioner's room from the view of the condemned.

The executioners' room is set up with a couple of straight-back chairs and a table holding a TV monitor. A square box on the table holds one end of an IV tube, which extends through the wall into the death chamber. The death chamber is empty except for a TV camera mounted on the ceiling at the side above the mirror.

The carefully worked-out process calls for the condemned to be given a sedative to calm his nerves, while leaving him conscious and able to cooperate with the proceedings. Then he is helped onto a gurney, securely strapped down, and wheeled into the execution chamber to be hooked up to the IV tube. Two executioners are waiting in the next room, where they pour fluid into a machine. The fluid handled by one of the executioners is a toxic cocktail of three deadly drugs, one to render the prisoner unconscious, one to stop his breathing, and the other to stop his heart. Only the drugs would pass through the IV, and neither of the executioners would know which one of them actually delivered the poison. Four minutes after the drugs are administered, two physicians present at the execution are required to examine the body and confirm the death, then issue a death certificate.

Everything is carefully organized to keep fear to a minimum and to make the execution painless, or as near free of pain as possible. Of course, no one except the condemned really knows if the process is as painless as it is supposed to be. Death row historians are quick to tell the story of Barbara Graham, the tough prostitute and gun moll who was executed in California in 1955 for fatally pistol-whipping a crippled old woman during a home invasion robbery. As the pretty killer was being led into the gas chamber, a sympathetic guard assured her that it wouldn't hurt. Emotionally drained by last-minute telephone calls from the governor's office stopping, then giving the final all-clear for the execution, she showed some of her old spirit when she turned to the guard and snapped: "How the hell would you know?"

Ironically, if Cullen died in the state prison's spanking clean execution chamber, he would know more than most of the condemned about how his death was accomplished. He had used deadly drugs and IVs many times to kill, but he didn't exercise the same meticulous care to avoid fear, distress, and pain while carrying out his atrocious acts. Grandma Natoli and Mrs. Dean vomited; William Park fought desperately and rallied four times before the repeated assaults claimed his life; and Francis Henry, who was given an insulin overdose, inhaled his own vomit, his blood sugar plunged, and he was shuttled back and forth between a nursing home and a hospital before he finally lost his tenacious struggle for life. They died nasty, needlessly miserable deaths.

Legislators fashioning New Jersey's new death penalty law stipulated that witnesses to the execution should include the commissioner of corrections, two physicians, six adult witnesses, one or two members of the clergy, and eight journalists. When Cullen killed, he carried out his evil work secretly in a darkened hospital room, and the only witnesses were himself and his victims.

Pennsylvania was also a death penalty state, and had only a slightly better record for carrying out executions. Most of the condemned camped on death row for decades, while they avoided paying the ultimate penalty by waiting out endless appeals or died of old age and other ailments.

Pennsylvania legislators restored the death penalty on March 26, 1974, but it was 1995 before the first killer was led into the execution chamber at the State Correctional Institution (SCI) Rockview. Only two other executions had been carried out after that. The last to die was Gary Heidnik, who kidnapped six women and kept them as sex slaves in a torture chamber/house of horrors in the North Philadelphia slums. He was convicted of killing two, including one he cooked and fed to the others, before he was executed by lethal injection in July 1999. Like Cullen, the disabled army veteran had a history of mental instability. He was repeatedly treated in mental hospitals and clinics, and had attempted suicide seventeen times.

The "Quaker State" has the unusual distinction of having three death rows—two for men and one for women—that held more than 230 condemned prisoners at the time of Cullen's arrest. It has the fourth-largest death row population in the country. A separate execution complex was set up next to SCI Rockview near State College and Penn State University, with a spartanly furnished air-conditioned death chamber, where the condemned die by lethal injection. The complex is conveniently isolated from the major metropolitan areas of Philadelphia and Pittsburgh.

Condemned men are currently held at the SCI Graterford in suburban Philadelphia, and at SCI Greene, a super-maximum-security prison near Waynesburg, a few miles from Pittsburgh in southwestern Pennsylvania. Opened in the mid-1990s and one of Pennsylvania's most modern prisons, SCI Greene was designed to house troublemakers and security risks who are considered to be the state's worst of the worst. Condemned females are housed at the women's prison at SCI Muncy, just off Interstate Highway 180, near Williamsport in central Pennsylvania.

First-degree murder committed with any one of seventeen aggravating circumstances is the only capital offense. Like New Jersey and most other states with capital punishment today, Pennsylvania executions are carried out by lethal injection.

Families of Cullen's victims were already suffering dreadfully from the knowledge that the people they loved were murdered in their hospital beds by a health-care professional trusted to nurse them back to health, or at the very worst, to help them die with as much comfort and dignity as possible.

If their killer was sentenced to die by lethal injection, relatives of the dead could expect to endure decades of legal wrangling that would leave them exhausted and emotionally drained. In the end, if past experience was any measurement, Cullen was far more likely to be murdered by another inmate, die a natural death, be moved off death row into the general population of a prison, or spend the rest of his life in a psychiatric hospital than he was to be executed by the state.

The prospect for many survivors of never knowing for sure if their family member was murdered or died naturally—because Cullen was expected to take many of his secrets to the grave with him if he wasn't spared the death penalty—would only add to the misery. Investigators had uncovered solid evidence pointing to the murder of Helen Dean and Father Gall. But families of Francis Henry, Irene Krapf, Stella Danielczyk, and other patients who died in hospitals on Cullen's watch would be left to live with the uncertainty of never knowing if their loved ones were among his victims.

For the present Cullen wasn't doing much talking with anyone except psychiatrists and other hospital workers in West Trenton.

He remained at the Anne Klein Forensic Center for twenty days before he was returned to the Somerset County Jail in Somerville. The streets were dark and there was little movement on the chill midwinter Tuesday night when the serial killer arrived back in Somerville. There was no advance notice to the media and no sign of journalists or television news trucks hanging around when he was led inside and processed back into the lockup at about 9:45 P.M.

Because of Cullen's recent commitment to the Anne Klein center and his history of psychiatric problems, he was placed under continuous watch. Provenzano declined to describe the special security measures as technically a suicide watch, but for all intents and purposes, that was exactly what it was. The notorious inmate with the record of suicide attempts and the fragile mental health was placed in a cell near the intake area of the jail, where four or five officers could check him every few minutes to confirm that he wasn't harming himself or in any kind of physical distress that might lead to his death.

Soon after Cullen's return to the jail, he was submitted to another evaluation by a team of forensic psychologists. Frank Dattilio, a prominent Allentown area forensic psychologist, was hired by Cullen's New Jersey public defender as one of the shrinks. A veteran student of the criminal mind, during twenty-five years of practice, Dattilio provided professional services by evaluating some of the most notorious killers in the Lehigh Valley and Allentown area. Skinhead brothers Bryan and David Freeman, who murdered their parents and eleven-year-old brother, teenager, Jeffrey Howorth, who fatally shot his parents, and Matthew Duch, who slit the throats of his two daughters and mother-in-law, all had previously come under his professional scrutiny.

Dattilio spent a day screening the former nurse for neurological disorders, administering standard psychological tests, and bombarding him with questions. The widely known Rorschach inkblot test was included in the package. Information collected during the daylong face-to-face session was supplemented by meticulous review of documents from police, hospital, and other sources. Dattilio ultimately produced a fourteen-page, single-spaced report for Mask on the accused Death Angel.

The psychologist concluded that the inmate was sane and capable of understanding the charges against him and the court processes. Cullen was not psychotic, and he had the ability to work with his attorneys in his own defense. Based on evaluations by Dattilio and the other forensic psychologists, Mask concluded that his client wasn't a good candidate for an insanity defense.

The confessed serial killer was back in jail, just across the street from the courthouse, for almost two days when law enforcement authorities, including prosecutors from five counties in New Jersey and two counties in eastern Pennsylvania, met at the office of Somerset County prosecutor Wayne J. Forrest. They were there to share information about the case, the possibility of using some of the same forensic experts, and to discuss the devil's deal fashioned by Cullen's defense. The January 7 meeting was organized by the New Jersey State Division of Criminal Justice, with help from the New Jersey State Attorney General's Office, and was the first gathering to bring together investigators from all the jurisdictions involved since Cullen's arrest.

Nearly forty law officers, including prosecutors from Somerset, Hunterdon, Essex, Morris, and Warren Counties in New Jersey, and the Northampton and Lehigh County district attorneys, jammed into the offices to talk behind closed doors. Representatives of the New Jersey Division of Criminal Justice and Pennsylvania police were also present.

Emerging hours later, they responded to pleas for information from a horde of news reporters with brusque "no comments." From the viewpoint of reporters, although no witnesses were called to testify at the coordinating session, in some respects the meeting resembled a grand jury proceeding. Reporters could watch and try to identify the police and public officials who went inside and emerged from the skull session, but they couldn't listen in on the proceedings or question the participants.

John R. Hagerty, director of communications for the New Jersey Division of Criminal Justice, which oversaw the activities of New Jersey's prosecutors, did what little talking to the press there was.

"The seven prosecutor's offices are taking this investigation very seriously and are sparing no resources in the largest investigation ever undertaken to get to the bottom of any and all deaths Charles Cullen may have been responsible for," he told reporters. Describing the inquiries as "unprecedented in scope," he said they would involve grand jury subpoenas, search warrants, and forensics.

Individual investigations would be conducted by each prosecutor's office, and the New Jersey Division of Criminal Justice would continue to coordinate the exchange of information. "For instance, they've done a lot with forensics on the two cases here in Somerset County," he said. With the Division of Criminal Justice coordinating the exchange of information, the job of obtaining background data from Somerset would be made easier. "This is what Somerset did, this is what you need to do to move forward."

The agency could also be helpful expediting the inquiries by making statewide law enforcement resources available, he said. Those resources included the New Jersey Medical Examiner's Office, the New Jersey State Police DNA and Forensic Laboratory, and the investigative resources of the New Jersey state toxicologist, along with other specialized investigative resources of the Division of Criminal Justice and the state police.

State attorney generals from New Jersey and Pennsylvania huddled with the prosecutors, Mask and others, trying to work out a deal that would be most acceptable to everyone involved, including survivors of the dead. Cullen had voluntarily waived his right to have a Pennsylvania attorney appointed to help negotiate terms of the plea agreement. In the absence of another defender, Mask agreed to comply with statutes and rules of the commonwealth.

Hagerty acknowledged that Mask's demand for immunity from the death penalty for his client in return for helping out in the investigations was discussed at the meeting, but firmly declined to provide any details.

Cullen was still cooling his heels at the jail on February 22, 2004, a Sunday, when he observed his forty-fourth birthday there. There was no cake, no candles, no special meal, and no reported visits by members of his family to wish him well. There was only the austere surroundings of a cell, five feet by seven, with a metal sink, toilet, and a bunk, and the institutional surroundings of a typical jail. His birthday passed amid the acrid smell of antiseptics, uniformed guards, and the moans, cries and sweat of hundreds of men locked up together in a tightly enclosed brick and concrete box.

While shielded from contact with other inmates during the weeks of isolation, Cullen had a few visits from family members, and was also seen by social workers, mental-health professionals, and, of course, by his legal counsel.

He spent much of his time reading, writing letters, or jotting down notes related to his predicament.

In March, he was transferred to general population and placed in a cell with another inmate. There had been no more talk of suicide, there were no known threats against him, and doctors and jailers had decided that he could be moved safely out of isolation.

The transfer of Inmate No. 71533 to a two-man cell was a big improvement over his previous stay in isolation while on suicide watch, although over time his accommodations alternated between cell blocks on the second and third floors of the jail. Constructed in 1991 to hold about 345 inmates, modern, cutting-edge security features were given precedence over inmate comfort. The cell blocks were solid and secure, and designed to house prisoners charged with the most serious felonies, who were considered to be the most dangerous—or who were in the most potential danger from other inmates.

The layout of the cell blocks were the same, each with twenty-four cells on two floors overlooking a five-hundred-square-foot common room. The common room was outfitted with a television set, two telephones, and several heavy metal tables and metal benches bolted securely to the floor. Corrections officers were separated from the common room and the cells by bulletproof glass, and had additional help keeping their collective eyes on activities in the common room and the cells by more than one hundred surveillance cameras.

The second-floor cell block housed maximum-security prisoners; the toughest and meanest, most serious-accused felons and inmates with a history of escapes or those who were considered to be escape risks. The third floor held protective-custody prisoners, usually in order to shield them from other inmates. Protective-custody prisoners typically were accused of sexual offenses, were effeminate homosexuals, known snitches, or belonged to gangs in prison and outside that might lead to their being attacked by other inmates in general population.

Celebrity prisoners are also often isolated in jails and prisons around the country to keep them away from inmates looking to make a name for themselves by attacking or killing someone who has achieved status for accomplishments on the outside or notoriety for especially heinous crimes.

A man of few accomplishments, but plenty of notoriety, Cullen kept his nose clean inside the jail and had no trouble with other prisoners, so he was permitted to share in the limited but prized freedom accorded to inmates in general population. Except for the devilishness of his crimes, Cullen didn't stand out in any obvious way from other inmates he was locked up with.

This meant that he and his cellmate, along with well-behaved neighbors, could roam around the cell block, watch whatever was on TV, talk, or stare aimlessly into space. Inmates also played lots of videotapes obtained from the jail library, but Cullen rarely paid any attention to them. Most of the videos featured martial arts, and that was never something that had much appeal to the malignant nurse.

The alternative to roaming the common room was camping for hours in his cell, which was spartanly furnished with a double bunk, a steel toilet connected to a steel sink, an unbreakable mirror, and a steel desk bolted to the walls. Activities available in the cell were almost as limited as they were in the common room. Inside the cramped space Cullen could nap or read one of the books selected from the limited fare in the jail library. He had always liked to read, and he checked out novels and nonfiction books.

Thursday, April 29, 2004, was the most memorable day in the history of the Somerset County Courthouse. The courthouse, in the center of the historic town, had been the scene before of other big civil and criminal matters that drew national or international attention. Never before, however, was it the scene of such tight security, or the center of such media frenzy.

Former heavyweight-boxing champion Mike Tyson appeared in court there in 1988 to divorce his actress wife, Robin Givens. Tyson returned in 1995 to give court-ordered depositions in a civil action after his ex-wife's publicist claimed he roughed her up and sexually assaulted her.

Nearly a decade later scores of news reporters from the print and electronic media gathered outside the courthouse, then jostled each other for space inside for a double-feature event. Significant developments were anticipated in two high-profile criminal cases that had drawn national attention.

A jury was expected to end three days of deliberation and report a verdict on the third day of the three-month-long trial of former Philadelphia 76ers and New Jersey Nets basketball player Jayson Williams. The one time six-foot ten-inch NBA star was accused of aggravated manslaughter, reckless manslaughter, and other charges in the fatal shotgun shooting of limousine driver Costas "Gus" Christofi at Williams's mansion in rural New Jersey. His trial was moved to Somerset County after a judge ruled that the extensive publicity made it impossible for the retired athlete to receive a fair trial in Hunterdon County, where the shooting occurred.

Williams eventually was acquitted of aggravated manslaughter, of aggravated assault, and of possession of a weapon for unlawful purposes. The jury was unable to reach a verdict on a charge of reckless manslaughter, and guilty verdicts were returned on four other charges related to efforts to cover up his role in the driver's death. Sentencing was withheld until after retrial for the charge of reckless manslaughter, scheduled for early the next year.

But most of the stepped-up security arranged by Sheriff Provenzano was for the other defendant, Charles Cullen, the Death Angel. The finishing touches had been applied to the global plea agreement demanded by Mask, and

Cullen was scheduled to make it official by entering guilty pleas to fourteen murders and two attempted murders. (This agreement is printed with some editing by the authors at the end of the book.)

In its final form the pact called for "full and complete disclosure" by Cullen about an unknown number of murders and attempted murders he may have committed from 1984 through 2003 when he was a nursing student or licensed nurse in New Jersey and Pennsylvania.

The agreement also called for Cullen to provide information to investigators and others about his motivations and the methods he used to carry out the murder spree. One of the major aims of the stipulation was providing hospitals and other health-care facilities with information that could be used to improve security and operating procedures relating to patient access and the dispensing of medications.

County prosecutors or deputies in New Jersey who helped hammer out the agreement and were signatories to the agreement included Forrest in Somerset County, Thomas S. Ferguson in Warren County, Rubbinaccio in Morris County, Dow in Essex County, and Steven Lember, Hunterdon County first assistant prosecutor. Northampton County DA Morganelli and Lehigh County DA Martin were Pennsylvania signatories to the pact.

Provenzano was well prepared to deal with the beefed-up security needs, and had drafted a plan for just such eventualities shortly after he took office in 2001. Although no outside help from other counties, cities, or state police departments were called on for assistance, extra sheriff's officers, in uniform and in plain clothes, worked crowd control and kept their eyes peeled for trouble when Cullen was loaded into a white armored van at the county jail and driven around the corner to a parking lot behind the courthouse.

His hands were cuffed, his head was lowered, and his eyes were focused on his shoes while he was escorted by two sheriff's deputies. The prisoner was dressed in light trousers and a yellow-and-green patterned short-sleeved Hawaiian shirt over a bulletproof vest. Metal detectors were set up at the entrances to the courthouse long ago, and even if an enraged assassin managed to sneak a handgun or other weapon inside, the vest and Cullen's armed escort would make it difficult to get to him.

A light jail-issued jacket was draped over his bony shoulders to protect him from the late spring chill, the sleeves hanging loosely at his sides, and extra officers were standing by when the notorious prisoner was escorted from the van into the courthouse. The emaciated, desolate-looking prisoner was dwarfed by the burly lawmen surrounding him, and he kept his head lowered while he walked into the fourth-floor courtroom, glancing up for only a moment at the gallery, before sitting down in a chair at the defendant's table next to his lawyer. His face was emotionless. Two huge sheriff's deputies stood behind him, their eyes tracing his every move.

More than sixty family members of patients Cullen murdered or attempted to murder at the Somerset Medical Center, and one patient who was killed in Pennsylvania, were waiting inside the Somerset County State Superior courtroom. Court employees made sure the relatives had seats by ushering them into the gallery a half hour early. Sheriff's deputies carried in extra chairs to accommodate latecomers. A court aide provided the families with a new box of tissues, in preparation for the emotional ordeal of the hearing.

Relatives of Michael Strenko, Christopher Hardgrove, Jack Shanagher, James Strickland, and Helen Dean found seats alongside Zach and Emily and other survivors of victims. Then they waited, occasionally turning to whisper or talk in muted voices to each other as they prepared to watch and listen to the Death Angel admit in public for the first time that he murdered their loved ones.

Dressed in funereal black, Kristina Toth, the daughter

of Ottomar Schramm, sat a few rows almost directly behind the defendant. She was seated with her husband, and with Kelly Rambo, the lawyer who was representing the Schramm family in civil lawsuits against Easton Hospital and other defendants.

Toth agreed with the decision of prosecutors to accept the pact worked out by the defense and the prosecution, but she wanted to hear Cullen explain why he killed, and she wanted to talk with him. She wasn't buying into his claim that he killed to alleviate pain.

"He was supposedly some sort of angel of mercy, ending people's suffering," she told Allentown's *Morning Call.* "Well, he should look around the courtroom."

A horde of news reporters, lawyers, courthouse workers, and the simply curious hurriedly grabbed up the few remaining seats, or stood quietly in the back waiting for the plea by the notorious star of the judicial spectacle.

As the legal process got under way, it had some of the doleful aspects of a funeral, with mourners squirming uncomfortably, already rubbing at teary eyes and sobbing in their seats. There was an abundance of black dresses and suits, and a full measure of tears. But if anyone showed up expecting the Death Angel to apologize for his monstrous crimes, they would be disappointed.

After standing and placing his manacled hands on a Bible to be sworn in, the defendant spent most of his time staring blankly down at the wooden table in front of him, while Somerset County deputy first assistant prosecutor Robert C. Lang Jr. explained the terms of the plea agreement. Cullen studiously avoided turning to look at the relatives of his victims, seated behind him.

When it was his turn to talk, the string-bean-thin defendant was as closemouthed and stingy with words as he was before his arrest. In response to a question from the judge asking if he was "ready to address the court, the assembled families of victims present, and society as a whole concerning these charges," his reply was a typically brief "Yes, Your Honor."

He responded with the same terse reply to a long list of questions from the judge. When a response absolutely seemed to require a few more words, he made it as short as possible, but spoke audibly and with enough volume to be heard throughout the courtroom. His tone whenever he spoke was so distant and phlegmatic that he could have been a stockroom clerk discussing the purchase of pencils, or an office secretary ordering a dozen new printer ink cartridges.

The only time Cullen volunteered information he wasn't specifically asked for occurred when he broke in to correct his lawyer, who improperly attributed the death of Han to an injection of digoxin given to her by his client on June 16, 2003. Cullen corrected him by pointing out that she was given an antidote and survived the drug overdose, but she died later from cancer.

When he was asked what his intentions were when he injected a patient with medication, he responded with an answer that sounded as flatly unconcerned as it was shocking. "To cause death," he replied.

It was already publicly known that he used digoxin and insulin on patients, but relatives and others in the packed courtroom learned for the first time that they were just two medications among several in an evil cornucopia of drugs that he used to kill. Cullen admitted giving patients unprescribed dosages of nitroprusside, norepinephrine, dobutamine, and Pavulon, as well as digoxin and insulin.

He pleaded guilty to the murder of thirteen patients and attempted murder of two others at the Somerset Medical Center, and committed himself to a later guilty plea to the first-degree murder of Ottomar Schramm at Easton Hospital in Pennsylvania. Plans called for him to enter the guilty plea formally in Northampton County Court, where he would eventually be sentenced in the Schramm case.

Murder victims at Somerset named in the guilty plea before Judge Armstrong were:

> *Eleanor Stoecker*
> *Joyce E. Mangini*
> *Giacomino J. Toto*
> *John J. Shanagher*
> *Dorothea K. Hoagland*
> *Melvin T. Simcoe*
> *Michael T. Strenko*
> *Reverend Florian J. Gall*
> *Pasquale M. Napolitano*
> *Christopher B. Hardgrove*
> *Krishnakant Upadhyay*
> *James R. Strickland*
> *Edward P. Zizik*

After each name was read off and Cullen was asked if he killed the patient intentionally, the stone-faced RN replied with an unemotional "Yes." The hearing marked the first time that more than half the patients he had just admitted murdering were publicly revealed as his victims.

Cullen admitted unsuccessful attempts to murder Jin Kyung Han and Frances Agoada. As part of the agreement he also admitted committing "a number of murders or attempted murders in medical facilities in Lehigh County and Northampton County," Pennsylvania.

Except for correcting his defense lawyer about Han, there was no other volunteered elaboration about anything from the defendant, and he expressed no apologies during the approximate hour-long hearing inside the courtroom. When Cullen repeated his previous claim that he was a mercy killer who snuffed out the lives of his victims to spare them further pain, angry murmurings in the courtroom made it plain that families considered the excuse to be an insult rather than an explanation.

Many relatives were clearly stung by his seeming indifference, and testimony from the confessed murderer about the particular drugs used to poison each patient was particularly difficult to endure. At times their tenuous hold on fragile emotions snapped, and anguished wails echoed through the courtroom. Men and women passed around the box of tissues and wiped at teary eyes.

John Michael Shanagher, who attended the hearing with a sister and two daughters, had become inured to seeing his father referred to in newspaper articles or on television newscasts as a "murder victim." But he cringed when the name of John J. Shanagher was read into the record. He and other family members didn't want the gentle old man remembered that way, because there was so much more to Papop's life than the ghastly manner in which he died. Theresa Shanagher didn't attend the hearing, because the family feared it would be too emotionally devastating for the eighty-year-old widow.

When the grueling proceeding finally ended, Cullen had agreed to thirteen consecutive life sentences in prison for the murders at the hospital in Somerville. He wouldn't be eligible for parole until he had served two back-to-back life sentences—a total of 127 years—in 2131. He would have to live to be a staggering 167 years old before he could even be considered for release. As long as he honored the agreement to cooperate with law enforcement agencies to identify his victims, he would be spared death in the execution chamber at the state prison in Trenton. But the meek and brittle little man who told homicide detectives during the grueling interrogation that produced his confession that he didn't want to live, and hoped "they don't just decide to lock me in jail," had just made sure that was exactly what his fate would be. By pleading guilty to the murders, he had ensured that he would live out the rest of his life behind bars.

It was agreed that Cullen would serve his prison time in New Jersey, and sentences in Pennsylvania would be ordered to run consecutive to the terms in the Garden State.

Although not on death row, he was likely to spend the rest of his life at the maximum-security state prison at Trenton.

If that occurred, he would be joining a monstrous rogues' gallery of nefarious criminals and miscellaneous cutthroats who were either still serving time or were previously in residence inside the walls of the ancient fortress. Inmates who served time or ended their lives there included such archfiends as Charlie "the Bug" Workman, the Mafia hit man who gunned down "Dutch Schultz" (Arthur Flegenheimer); "Duck Island Killer" Clarence Hill, convicted of six lover's-lane slayings in the pre–World War II years; John List, the meek accountant who got into a financial bind and slaughtered his wife, mother, and three children in order to "send them to heaven"; and Richard "the Iceman" Kuklinski, a freelance hit man who claimed more than one hundred successful assassinations.

But formal sentencing for Cullen was still months, perhaps as much as a year or more, in the future. Sentencing was withheld until investigations were completed in all seven counties in the two states, according to the pact. Even after sentencing, he would be evaluated by corrections officials before determining if the state prison at Trenton or some other maximum-security institution would become his new home.

Once all the pleas were entered in every jurisdiction, prosecutors would get together to decide if he had fulfilled his promise of "full cooperation." If they were satisfied that he had complied and all the pleas were correctly entered, then the case of the Death Angel would move on to the sentencing phase. Sentencing would first be carried out for crimes that occurred in New Jersey, then followed up with sentencing for crimes committed in Pennsylvania. But no timetable was established for bringing an end to the judicial processes that Cullen and legal and law enforcement authorities in two states were entangled in.

The tension and exhaustion of the past hour was clearly visible in the faces and behavior of many of the relatives of victims when the skinny, hollow-cheeked runt at the center of the storm was finally escorted outside and driven back to the jail. They looked haggard and drained by the ordeal, most were disappointed by the absence of apologies, and others were outraged at Cullen's earlier claims to be a mercy killer.

They were admittedly bothered by the inconsistency between what he said and what he did. Although all the victims at one time were gravely ill and under treatment in ICUs, several of them seemed to be well on the road to recovery and weren't in pain when they were targeted for death. Michael Strenko's heart and blood pressure were normal, and his parents didn't believe his life was in danger. Jack Shanagher was expected to return to the nursing home in a couple of days. Helen Dean's anticipated move to a nursing home actually occurred shortly before her death from a drug overdose administered by her nurse.

"How could such an insignificant little man have caused so much pain to so many people?" one of Jack Shanagher's granddaughters asked her father as they left the hearing.

"Because he is an insignificant little man who tried to find significance in a way that was horribly, horribly destructive," her father replied.

Cullen couldn't even logically plead that he was merely putting the elderly infirm out of their misery, because Strenko was twenty-one, Christopher Hardgrove was thirty-eight, and Eleanor Stoecker was only sixty—not even old enough to draw Social Security.

The real reasons Cullen selected a particular patient to murder instead of another were as elusive as butterflies, and grief-stricken relatives were left to wonder if even he knew exactly how and why he made the deadly choices.

Law enforcement authorities and several family members held impromptu news conferences outside the courtroom or talked individually with the press. Kristina Toth said she wanted to ask Cullen why he did what he did. She and her family were suffering, and she wanted him to suffer for what he did to them and to other families, the woman said.

Claire Hardgrove, whose son died at the hands of the bloodthirsty nurse, described Cullen as "an evil person," and said he had to pay for his actions. Mrs. Hardgrove attended the hearing with her son's two daughters. The anguished mother added that the guilty pleas did nothing to relieve her hurt. The plea didn't bring her son back, and she told a reporter she was devastated because no one at Somerset acted in time to save her son's life. Christopher Hardgrove was the first of the five people who were killed after Dr. Marcus warned the hospital that someone may have been deliberately harming patients.

Most of the gathered reporters, still photographers, and television camera crews quickly headed for the Somerset County Prosecutor's Office, where New Jersey state attorney general Harvey and other law enforcement officials held a formal postplea news conference.

"This is just the beginning. What is important is that we bring certainty to the families," Harvey declared as the eager newshounds scribbled furiously on notepads, photographers snapped pictures, and television camera operators jockeyed for the best position. "Hospitals are a place where people should go to get well, not a place where people should go to get killed." The attorney general described Cullen as an "egregious serial murderer of innocent and helpless victims."

Recalling the serial killer's accounts to detectives about the stolen medications he used to carry out his decade-and-a-half murder rampage, Harvey said it was critical that investigators learn exactly how the killer sidestepped security measures set up to protect patients. Cullen used six different drugs to harm or kill patients at the Somerset Medical Center.

It still wasn't known what drugs were used to kill in other medical facilities except the hospital in Somerville, and investigators needed to debrief Cullen to learn how he was able to get away with his crimes for so long, Harvey said. "We need to find the flaws in the system."

Other law enforcement figures added their own observations about the case during the official press conference and in other discussions with the press.

Mask told reporters that the plea agreement was an all-or-nothing deal, and a piecemeal effort to save his client from the death penalty wouldn't have been acceptable. All the law enforcement agencies involved in the case in both states had to agree to sign off on the pact.

Prosecutors said Cullen would be charged and enter guilty pleas in other counties, as additional murders and attempted murders were admitted, then confirmed by investigators. Lehigh County DA Martin followed up by disclosing that Cullen attempted to kill several residents at the Liberty Nursing and Rehabilitation Center in Allentown, and evidence indicated he may have killed other patients at St. Luke's and at the Lehigh Valley Hospital.

Vaughn L. McKoy, director of the New Jersey Division of Criminal Justice, said that although Cullen would escape the death penalty, he would pay with his life for his crimes. "Our intention with this agreement was to make sure Mr. Cullen would never see the light of day again," he declared.

Lang pointed out that if sometime down the line Cullen tried to fudge on his vow to provide truthful, full, and complete cooperation, the plea agreement could be scrapped and prosecutors would be free to seek the death penalty for murders where the Death Angel had already admitted his guilt.

About a week before the plea agreement was sealed with Cullen's court appearance before Judge Armstrong, the New Jersey State Prison's Capital Sentence Unit had swelled by one. Brian P. Wakefield, a vicious young thug from Absecon, was sentenced to death for fatally stabbing, beating, and setting an elderly couple on fire during a robbery. Cullen might well land in the same prison, no matter what he did, but unless he really wanted to end his life and didn't mind waiting ten or twenty years for the judicial processes to creak slowly into gear, he wasn't expected to cheat on the agreement and become the fifteenth current resident on the Capital Sentence Unit.

In the wake of the hearing the local hospital—where the Death Angel had just pleaded guilty to having committed murder—issued a prepared statement expressing condolences to the families and regret over the "heinous crimes" by their former employee. "That Cullen chose a place of healing to commit these acts makes them all the more tragic and despicable," the statement read. "He struck at the heart of our most basic mission of caring and compassion."

The Strenko family released their own memorial statement to the media describing their son: "You were caring and thoughtful, always remembering special occasions, and always lent a helping hand to your family and friends."

There was less fanfare and only a smattering of news reporters present a week after the hearing when the heavily shackled prisoner was once more led from the jail and driven across the street to the courthouse in the backseat of a black sedan. He was dressed in his usual mustard-colored jail uniform and laceless blue athletic shoes. He was flanked by a pair of uniformed law enforcement officers when he shuffled clumsily inside the prosecutor's office.

Members of a task force of Pennsylvania investigators were the first to show up in Somerville looking for information after the plea agreement was sealed by Cullen's court appearance. When the lawmen settled in for new rounds of interrogation aimed at unraveling the sordid secrets of the prisoner's destructive life, they were prepared with cardboard boxes and stacks of accordion files loaded with medical history and medication records of patients who died on Cullen's watch at Pennsylvania hospitals.

Four homicide investigators from the Pennsylvania State Police Department, Dr. Mihalakis, and Lehigh County DA Martin had driven from the Quaker State. Forrest hosted the meeting, but stuck around only briefly before leaving the prisoner with the authorities from Pennsylvania.

The exhausting session lasted six-and-a-half hours as Cullen peered through the files and answered questions about suspicious patient deaths at St. Luke's, the Lehigh Valley Hospital, and the Liberty Nursing and Rehabilitation Center. The homicide detectives took turns, with first one, then another, assailing him with questions.

As he began to unburden himself, the investigators were treated to unsettling glimpses into a disordered, chaotic mind that was a place where evil lurked. Even without the murders, Cullen's medical career was filled with incidents of deviation from standard nursing practices that he referred to as oversights and mistakes, to random and deliberate acts of mischief, like slipping potentially lethal doses of insulin into the stored IV bags at St. Barnabas.

Cullen's memory for names was as spotty as it was the first time he was questioned, but with the help of the medical files, he was able to recall even some of the most minute details of patient murders that he could only vaguely remember earlier. Martin told reporters after the meeting that Cullen's memory was clear, although his recollection of events wasn't as good in some cases as it was in others. The files were used to help jog his memory in the cases that he didn't recall very well on his own. Martin said there would probably be several other meetings, and Cullen would most likely plead guilty to all the Lehigh County cases at one time.

Cullen was answering questions again the next day from Warren County prosecutor Thomas S. Ferguson and other law enforcement authorities about the deaths of Helen Dean and her sister, Anna Smith, at Warren Hospital. He didn't need the medical files to remember the name of the elderly woman whose murder a decade earlier entangled him in such a mess and led to his resignation at Warren Hospital. He not only remembered her name, but the time of day he injected her with an unauthorized dose of digoxin and exactly how much of the drug he used.

Ferguson's office had received inquiries from about twenty other families, but none of those were scheduled for discussion during his initial question-and-answer session with Cullen. The prosecutor was proceeding steadily but cautiously and arranged for Lois Magill, a forensic nurse, to help investigators comb through the files and pick out possible victims, while eliminating other patients who died natural deaths.

Other meetings with the confessed serial killer were being planned by DA Morganelli and investigators examining suspicious deaths at Northampton County hospitals. Additional files, some of them hundreds of pages long, were also being examined. Cullen was questioned at the jail, questioned at the Somerset Prosecutor's Office, and several times was driven to other cities in New Jersey or Pennsylvania for questioning by local authorities.

Curiously, while names often eluded him, he showed a remarkable ability to recall details about the personal belongings of patients, and, of course, their medications and medical conditions. In many of the cases where he was able to pinpoint a victim from his study of the files, his success was due to his ability to recognize some medical abnormality. He cared for so many thousands of patients during his trouble-speckled career that he didn't remember faces well, but he had a curious propensity for recalling other features of their physical appearance. Perhaps more curious yet, he sometimes remembered the names of relatives of patients whose names he had forgotten.

The prisoner spent hours seated at the desk in his cell poring over his "homework," studying the bulging volumes of medical files to refresh his memory, while attempting to pick out the cases of patients he murdered or tried to kill. When he finished with one thick stack of records, or found something especially significant, a meeting was set up with homicide detectives. At the debriefing session he told them what he discovered, answered questions as best he could about the details, then returned to his maximum security jail cell with another pile of homework.

Photographs of suspected victims, like the picture provided by Eleanor Stoecker's friend, were used to jog his memory. They helped some, especially when they were of more recent victims, but his difficulty remembering faces continued to intrude and short-circuit his powers of recall.

Another of the pictures the confessed serial killer examined was of Jack Shanagher. Detective Braun had gotten back to the former paratrooper's son weeks before Cullen entered his guilty plea to the Somerset Medical Center murders. The detective advised Shanagher that detectives had found sufficient reason to move his father's case up to the next level and continue the investigation. A week or two later, Braun asked for a photo of the elderly man.

Shanagher was off work that day driving his son from a doctor's appointment, so they drove together to the prosecutor's office and he dropped off the picture. Investigators assigned a victim's advocate to work with the family. The situation was already about as ominous as it could be, but if there was any doubt left that Jack Shanagher was one of Cullen's victims, it dissolved in March almost exactly one year after the death when authorities confirmed that the lethal RN had accessed his father's medical chart. Cullen was not Jack Shanagher's assigned nurse, and had no legitimate business snooping into the elderly man's medical history.

His son knew the truth at last, but if any confirmation was necessary, investigators provided it in April when he responded to a request for a meeting with investigators who telephoned him and said they needed to talk. Shanagher drove to the prosecutor's office, and investigators told him that Cullen confessed in January to the murder of his father.

So far, the former nurse was keeping his word and cooperating with the investigation, but authorities were aware of his fragile mental health and the danger of pressuring him so hard that he might be pushed into a breakdown that would land him back at the Anne Klein Forensic Center. Cullen had a sad history of not handling pressure well. After observing him at a court hearing, McKoy told reporters that he didn't know how much stress the prisoner could take on a daily, weekly, or monthly basis. The Division of Criminal Justice chief pointed out that everyone wanted to bring as much closure as possible, but in order to do so, they had to keep Cullen healthy and competent.

Early in the investigation, Hunterdon County prosecutor J. Patrick Barnes recused himself from the probe to avoid any possible suspicion of conflict of interest. His late mother-in-law, Joan Monsul, of Lebanon Borough, was a patient in Somerset's ICU while Cullen was employed there. Critically ill with cancer and emphysema, the seventy-five-year-old woman died on January 25, 2003, and Barnes said he didn't believe she was one of Cullen's victims. But he decided to recuse himself anyway after discussing the matter with authorities at the state attorney general's office, who recommended he step out of the case. Hunterdon County assistant prosecutor Marcia Crowe took his place to lead the local phase of the investigation.

Authorities in Essex county, at St. Barnabas Hospital, retrieved the medical records of scores of former patients and provided them to investigators who looked over them, then passed them on to Cullen to study in his jail cell. "Nope, not me," he said after inspecting some of the documents. He was unsure about others and asked investigators to help him out by looking into their own records and notes to figure out which wing or unit in the hospital he was working on when a particular patient died.

Murders at St. Barnabas were especially hard to recall and document, in large part because they were the oldest and the most difficult to reassemble. Some four hundred to five hundred patients died at the hospital while Cullen worked there, and most of their records were long ago converted to microfilm. Some, dating back to the earliest period of his employment, didn't even record viable work schedules that showed the days and hours he worked. That made the task extremely difficult of narrowing down the search through hundreds of files and weaning out those of patients who died or could have been poisoned with drug overdoses while the renegade RN was on duty.

The old, incomplete records added significantly to the difficulties of relying on them to back up Cullen's hazy recollections. Potential witnesses to events surrounding possible murders or murder attempts were also difficult to locate and interview after the passage of so much time. Even if they were still alive and located, being able to go back so far to recall events that may have seemed inconsequential at the time, could be difficult. Like anyone else, Cullen's memory faded with time. But he kept to his bargain, and apparently made sincere efforts to recognize and admit to patient deaths he was responsible for, while denying involvement in those he was not.

During an interview at the jail on May 14, 2004, Cullen chose the names of seven more people from the records of ninety patients who died while he worked on the St. Barnabas burn unit. Recalling victims killed later while he was a roving nurse was more complicated and difficult because he wasn't confined to a single contained area.

Cullen eventually revised his estimated death toll at St. Barnabas and told his interrogators that he may have caused four or five patient deaths there. Some, like the AIDS patient, he couldn't be sure about. He remembered that he interfered with the patient's treatment in an effort to kill him in 1991, but didn't know if he actually caused the death because the man didn't die right away. Even if he was eventually successful dredging up more details, investigators would have to develop evidence that the patient died at Cullen's hand so that he could be charged with murder. After so many years, that would be an extremely difficult medical call. A charge of attempted murder wouldn't be good enough, because the five-year statute of limitations had already expired.

Judge Yengo was a different story. After painstakingly studying the medical files and viewing a photograph of the former jurist, Cullen told Essex County prosecutors that he was sure about murdering Maximum John. He was the judge that Cullen had told Braun and Baldwin about when he was first interrogated after his arrest. Cullen said he wasn't sure if Yengo was his first victim, but at the time he admitted to the murder, he couldn't remember any others that were earlier.

His memory was better when it came to more recent slayings, like those at the Somerset Medical Center, at St. Luke's—and at Warren Hospital in Phillipsburg, where he first got into serious trouble over his penchant for murder. Early in May 2004, at a meeting in the office of Warren County prosecutor Thomas S. Ferguson, Cullen admitted giving a fatal injection of digoxin to Helen Dean. After inspecting medical records and photographs he also identified two other victims at Warren Hospital.

When law enforcement authorities contacted Phillip Mugavero to tell him that his grandmother was murdered, it was devastating news. He never suspected that her death wasn't from natural causes, not even after Cullen was arrested and news stories revealed that he worked in intensive care while Grandma Mugavero was a patient at Warren Hospital. Hospital authorities also expressed surprise over the identity of Mrs. Mugavero and Mrs. Natoli as victims. Medical files indicated both women died of natural causes, and there were no requests for autopsies.

A Warren Hospital spokeswoman told reporters that 217 patients died at the facility in 1993, and there was no reason to think that the Mugavero and Natoli deaths were any different than the others.

On the early afternoon of May 19, Cullen was led into the early-nineteenth-century Greek Revival courthouse on the Belvidere, New Jersey, town square to answer for the murders of three elderly women while he worked in critical-care units at Warren Hospital. Appearing before Warren County

Superior Court judge John H. Pursel in Belvidere, he pleaded guilty to killing Lucy Mugavero, Mary Natoli, and Helen Dean. Investigations in about twenty other Warren County cases, including the death of Mrs. Dean's sister, Anna Smith, remained open.

Shackled at hands and feet, and wearing a county-jail-issued uniform that drooped limply from his gaunt frame, Cullen was thinner than ever. The widow's peak in his closely trimmed hair seemed to have receded farther than before, and he appeared exhausted. That wasn't particularly out of character for him, because even when things were going well in his life, he looked drained and washed out.

Cullen's plea to the Warren County murders would eventually add another ninety years in prison without parole to sentences he had accumulated previously for other murders. But in accordance with the plea agreement worked out months earlier, formal sentencing was deferred until the investigation was completed in all jurisdictions.

The confessed killer was as seemingly emotionless in his Warren County Courthouse appearance as he was at earlier court hearings in other jurisdictions. He replied three times—with the same firmly audible but flat—"Yes, it was" in responding to questions by the judge asking if it was his intention to "cause death" when he administered digoxin to each of the patients.

It was justice at last, but it was a long time coming for the family of Helen Dean, who had suspected from the beginning that she was murdered. Vindication of Helen Dean's son, Larry, for his stubborn pursuit of his mother's killer came too late.

Grandma Natoli's family hadn't become suspicious about the cause of her death until they heard of Cullen's arrest. Mrs. Mugavero's family didn't learn the truth about her death until less than a week before the plea hearing. Deborah Yetter Medina, Mrs. Mugavero's granddaughter, described the renegade RN in the *Courier News* of Bridge-water as "Satan's son."

At a posthearing press conference while Cullen was being driven back to the Somerset County Jail, New Jersey attorney general Harvey and Warren County prosecutor Ferguson said Cullen would be sentenced eventually to three consecutive life terms. The sentences would be stacked on top of those already ordered for the murders at the Somerset Medical Center, and subsequent life sentences for other murders in the two-state area also would be ordered served consecutively. Each of the life sentences for the murders at the hospital in Phillipsburg would stipulate minimums of thirty years before becoming eligible for parole.

Harvey said prosecutors were continuing "to investigate every case, every allegation, every instance of murder, in order to identify Cullen's victims and to allow families to know now the truth." He pointed out that they had met with the disgraced nurse over the past several weeks and obtained information valuable to the overall investigation. It was expected that the information would lead to additional murder charges in the two states, he said. "It is tragic that patients seeking medical treatment to regain health," Harvey declared, "died instead of the hands of a self-proclaimed merchant of death." The New Jersey Division of Criminal Justice was to oversee information-sharing meetings between prosecutors in New Jersey and Pennsylvania.

The pleas brought Cullen's official murder toll in New Jersey to sixteen, and eclipsed the number of slayings by World War II army veteran Howard Unruh, who previously held the old record for the most murders in New Jersey by a single killer. With the pleas, Cullen also tightened his hold on a malefic record as the Garden State's most prolific serial killer in modern history.

Unruh set the old murder record in 1949 when he stalked through the streets of Camden on a previously quiet Saturday morning, fatally shooting thirteen people in a deadly twelve-minute-long killing spree because he thought neighbors were making fun of him behind his back.

During the war Unruh was hailed as a hero and decorated for his performance as a U. S. Army machine gunner who mowed down advancing German soldiers at the Battle of the Bulge, Adolph Hitler's doomed last-ditch effort to turn around the war on the Western Front. Other soldiers remembered their fellow GI for his dedicated Bible reading and the diary he kept to record the date and circumstances surrounding the death of every German soldier he shot.

Back home after the fighting ended, he was considered to be a recluse and a bit of a character, but likable enough until pranksters stole the gates from the wooden fence constructed around his house and he launched the murderous attack on his neighbors. Unruh was holed up in his house with an arsenal of guns when police used tear gas to flush him out and put an end to the morning violence.

In those days when capital punishment was ordered and carried out with far more frequency than today, Unruh was never put on trial or sentenced to death. Instead, he was adjudged to be incurably insane and was committed to a state mental hospital for life. While Cullen marked time in the Somerset County Jail, the white-haired octogenarian who electrified the country with his bloody shooting rampage, more than half-a-century earlier, was still in treatment at the four-hundred-bed Trenton Psychiatric Hospital in West Trenton.

But there are almost zero chances he would have been executed if he had slaughtered his fellow New Jersey citizens and been convicted of multiple murders fifty years later—even without an insanity plea.

Unless he committed some egregious violation of the plea agreement, Cullen had also successfully sidestepped the death penalty, but he was still caught firmly in the crosshairs of prosecutors and police working to identify victims and elicit guilty pleas to murders in the two-state area. They were keeping him busy keeping his word.

On the last day of November he was driven to the Essex County Prosecutor's Office in Newark for his second meeting with local law enforcement authorities and confirmed the murder of Judge Yengo. He also admitted during the four-hour meeting that he injected the AIDS patient with an unauthorized dose of insulin. About a dozen other patients who died on his units at St. Barnabas were also discussed, but Cullen either denied responsibility or requested more information to help him figure out if he was involved.

In mid-December, almost a year after his arrest in Bridgewater, Cullen appeared in Newark before New Jersey State Superior Court judge Donald Volkert Jr. and pleaded guilty to a single count of murder for causing Yengo's death. He was handcuffed and dressed in khaki prison scrubs, but in deference to the chill early-winter weather, he had added a blue-denim jacket. SCJ, the initials of the Somerset County Jail, was stenciled in big black block letters on the back.

In accordance with the plea agreement, Cullen would eventually be sentenced to serve life without parole for thirty years. The sentence would be piled on top of prison terms previously ordered for twenty-three other murders and five attempted homicides. The result was the same; he would still be required to serve a total of 127 years in prison before becoming eligible for parole.

About the time Cullen pleaded in the Yengo case, he suggested that he might have caused one or two patient deaths at Morristown Memorial Hospital during his abbreviated career there, but he couldn't remember names.

As police and prosecutors continued to provide the Death Angel with medical files to inspect, additional families in the two-state area were receiving phone calls and visits from investigators.

Pennsylvania state police drove to Somerville to question

Cullen at the jail and showed him photographs provided by relatives of other hospital patients suspected to have died at his hands to jog his memory. A police spokesman said investigators planned to conduct additional interviews before any charges were filed related to deaths at Easton Hospital.

Chapter 14

The Blame Game

The ink was barely dry on newspaper headlines carrying the chilling story of the Death Angel, who killed helpless victims in seven counties in New Jersey and Pennsylvania, before hospital and law enforcement authorities began ducking for cover, making excuses and blaming each other.

People were already beginning to understand how the rogue nurse managed to bounce around murdering patients in nine hospitals and a nursing home. It was more difficult for the people in charge to explain why he got away with it for so long, and why so many opportunities to stop him were bungled.

Relatives of victims were left reeling and woozy by what seemed to be a never-ending pattern of shocks and renewed grief. For some, just about the time they were beginning to deal with their bereavement over the loss of a loved one, the killer was arrested and they were besieged by nasty suspicions that their mother, father, son, or sister may have been murdered. Then they answered a knock on the door to find a police officer or prosecutor waiting to confirm their worst fears, and the grieving began over again.

Families were demanding to know how a nurse like Cullen—with his ominous reputation, appalling work record, and personal history of alcoholism, mental illness, and suicide attempts—could be fired from one hospital for irresponsible or suspected criminal behavior, then so easily move on to a job at another medical center, without being rejected because of a background check.

As information filtered into the news media from law enforcement and legal authorities, and from hospital administrators, it became increasingly clear that the diabolically toxic nurse's life and career were speckled with failure, disappointments, and trouble. His life had been in a death spiral almost since he was born, and he was a nightmare waiting to happen. So, why wasn't the danger from the darkly lethal Angel of Death recognized sooner by the string of employers he seduced and betrayed in seven counties in two states? families wanted to know.

A nationwide nursing shortage, and fear of slander suits over sharing employee background information, played major roles in the debacle. Lax oversight of nurses, medications, and missing or defective tracking systems set up to monitor patient mortality were other factors that at various times in various places seemed to have worked in his favor.

Finding the right people for the right job, especially when looking for an RN willing to work night shifts in critical-care units, can be a difficult task. But that's what nurse recruiters and others who work with them are supposed to do, and settling for second-best or someone who hasn't been sufficiently vetted isn't good enough. It's dangerous to patients and to the reputations of the facilities they're hired to work for. It's also dangerous when information about bad employees isn't passed on to other prospective employers checking out references.

At hospital after hospital where the killer nurse worked,

authorities acted as if they were scared to death of saying a single negative word to colleagues at other medical facilities about Cullen's dangerous, off-the-wall behavior. When they were contacted about the rogue RN by human resources personnel at another hospital, they had nothing to say about his ominous run-ins with colleagues, the theft or misplacing of medications on his shift, and suspicious connections to mysterious patient deaths that led to his being either fired or forced to resign. About the only thing they were willing to share was the former employee's job title and the dates of employment.

So they passed on the bad apple, and the new employer had little reason to believe that the RN they were hiring had anything less than a spotless employment record. The old employers did their best to wash their hands of the mess he had left behind. It was a dangerously flawed system, and hospitals knew it.

The handwriting was already on the wall several days before Cullen's arrest when Dennis C. Miller, Somerset's CEO, met with state legislators, then scheduled a session with area congressmen to talk about the pressing need to design laws governing disclosure of trouble with licensed caregivers to prospective employers.

The Somerset Medical Center, where the curtain was finally brought down on the serial killer, was caught firmly in the eye of the storm that blew up in his wake. Some of the finest medical facilities in the two-state area wound up with conspicuously painful black eyes as a result of the distressing development. Trouble was flying at hospitals from families, the media, legislators, and state agencies and departments with oversight responsibilities.

Although Cullen was never hired by Muhlenberg Regional, the medical center/hospice was even drawn into a mini-controversy in the press over whether or not Somerset responded to telephone calls seeking information about Cullen when he applied for a job at the Plainfield hospital. Somerset CEO Miller said employees not only called back, but the chief nursing officer also warned Muhlenberg not to hire Cullen. A spokesman for Muhlenberg's parent company, Solaris Health System, told reporters that Somerset never contacted them.

Responding to press queries, St. Luke's Hospital also denied that Somerset contacted them to check Cullen's record, and a spokeswoman said that if they were asked, they would have recommended against hiring him. It began to look like finding out exactly who was responsible for Cullen's atrocities depended on who was questioned last.

Somerset authorities took a slap at some of Cullen's previous employers during a press conference for failing to warn them about problems they had with him. Somerset had no plans to sue sister institutions for neglecting to pass on a warning, Miller said, but wanted changes in regulations and laws to require that hospitals be given access to the information. In other remarks Miller pointed out that when Somerset checked out Cullen's reference, the only information provided was his employment dates. Chief Medical Officer Cors, Miller's Somerset colleague, shared the CEO's concern over that.

"It's not acceptable that we can't pass along information of concern because we're afraid of getting sued," Cors, was quoted in London's *Daily Telegraph* as saying. The Cullen case was an international story.

Miller contacted state and federal lawmakers with requests to testify in Trenton and Washington, DC, about the Cullen case and the need to create a national data bank with information about hospital employees. The hospital was trying hard to get its story out and remind people that their facility was the one that provided information that helped put an end finally to Cullen's ghastly blood feast. "Without our staff, this guy wouldn't have been arrested," the CEO claimed at a December press conference.

Late in April 2004, the medical center issued an unsigned statement calling for tougher licensing and background checks on hospital employees. "For the past six months, we have supplied thousands of records to help the Somerset County Prosecutor's Office bring Cullen to justice," the statement read. "We will continue to work closely with law enforcement authorities to help them in their ongoing investigations of Cullen."

Fear of lawsuits and the culture of silence that it spawned was no secret to anyone closely involved with hospital administration or in upper levels of law enforcement, including New Jersey attorney general Harvey. Most employers today wouldn't say anything derogatory about a former employee, he told CBS in an interview. And that was because their lawyers would tell them not to, he said.

Hospitals and nursing homes weren't the only ones hobbled by fear of getting into legal troubles with trial lawyers, if they dared to share information about dangerous employees, he indicated. According to Harvey, the "see no evil, hear no evil, speak no evil" attitude spilled over and hampered state agencies that licensed nurses, as well as hospitals.

State nursing boards in New Jersey and Pennsylvania exercised an abundance of caution before courage, and refused to disclose complaints filed with the agencies unless they were followed up with disciplinary action.

New Jersey required criminal background checks on nurses, doctors, and other health-care professionals before they were licensed. But once they passed the initial scan, there was no requirement for repeating the criminal background checks, and only violations that were reported to the board were retained on file. So despite Cullen's long, miserable record of brushes with police, mental breakdowns, suicide attempts, and psychiatric commitments, there was nothing negative about him on file with the state nursing board.

Peter Biondi, a New Jersey state assemblyman from Hillsborough, called for the establishment of a national database containing information on the personal histories of health-care workers. Other members of the state assembly also began drafting legislation to allow the healthcare industry to take a closer look into the past and present activities of employees.

New Jersey state senator Thomas Kean Jr. introduced legislation to exempt former employers from civil liability if they disclosed information in good faith about a former worker's job performance or the reason for termination to a prospective new employer. Employers would also be granted a qualified immunity for cooperating with requests for information from a federal, state, or industry regulatory authority or law, under the Union County politician's proposal.

On a national level, Senator Jon S. Corzine, of New Jersey, also called for changes aimed at making it easier and safer for medical facilities to conduct meaningful background checks on employees and job applicants.

He suggested that rules governing the securities industry, which require companies to disclose if an employee was fired for malfeasance, might be used as a model for a new law applying to hospitals and other patient-care facilities. Medical institutions would be protected from legal repercussions stemming from negative reports, except in cases where they passed on false statements maliciously.

State statutory laws in both New Jersey and Pennsylvania were seriously flawed when it came to protecting patients from health-care providers, especially nurses and ancillary caregivers, such as nurse's aides. At the time Cullen was carrying out his bloody killing crusade, a state law mandated that health-care facilities report suspicious activity by doctors that might be negatively affecting patient care. There was no similar statute for nurses.

State medical boards were also hindered by a lack of manpower and authority to go into the workplace at doctors' offices, clinics, hospitals, and the many other venues where nurses were employed to monitor their behavior actively. They depended on hospitals, doctors, and the public to lodge complaints and provide them with the information and impetus to go after nurses who were suspected of criminal misbehavior.

The scant existing state and federal agencies that were set up to warn health-care providers about bad nurses and doctors were almost universally considered to be weak and ineffectual. Their authority and requirements for reporting errant employees and behavior were so full of holes and ambiguities that it was easy for people like Cullen to slip through the cracks and continue on virtually unnoticed.

No one was available to sound the warning and tell human resources employees at hospitals if job applicants had been the subject of filed complaints or of criminal investigations. Criminal background checks did not reveal investigations that ended without the filing of charges.

Although laws and regulations in both states required medical facilities to report drug-addicted nurses, and mistakes such as administering unauthorized medications to patients or other serious errors to nursing boards, people with special expertise in the field told reporters that hospitals often deal with the problem by firing the miscreant nurse.

There seemed to be every reason to believe that the Cullen case, and the mini-tornadoes it was already spawning in the civil courts, could drag on for years, while police, prosecutors, judges, and state authorities tangled over jurisdictional matters and other problems associated with meting out justice for a killer whose monstrous crimes were committed over a decade-and-a-half. The story wasn't even close to disappearing from front pages and nightly newscasts.

In the midst of the gloomy shower of negative news, early in April 2004, Cullen's former employers in Lehigh Valley hospitals got some good news when the State Health Department announced its conclusion that none of them failed to report information that could have stopped the killer. The state agency took the blame for what officials described as a new reporting system that was misunderstood and unevenly enforced.

Periodically, while authorities struggled to deal with the dreadful fallout from the disaster and to calm emotions, Cullen picked new names from the patient files or appeared in court to plead guilty to additional murders, and the public was reminded all over again in distressingly graphic terms of the slaughter.

On October 7, 2004, almost five months after admitting before a judge that he deliberately snuffed out the lives of three elderly women at Warren Hospital, Cullen appeared in the Northampton County Court in Easton to at last face justice for the 1998 murder of Ottomar Schramm. He was dressed in a light burnt-orange, short-sleeved jailhouse-issued shirt over a T-shirt, and his manacled hands were chained to his belt in front of him, when he was led into the courtroom past members of the victim's family.

Kristina Toth, her husband, Joseph, and the widow, Lorraine Schramm, were seated just two rows behind the defense table. About a dozen other relatives representing four generations of the family, including two brothers, were also in the courtroom.

The heavily shackled prisoner was flanked by a pair of stone-faced Pennsylvania troopers as he was ushered down the center aisle to a chair beside his defense attorneys. The lawmen were so tall and the prisoner was so small that the top of his head barely reached their shoulders.

A few minutes later he pleaded guilty before Judge Stephen G. Baratta to first-degree murder in the slaying of the retired steelworker with an overdose of digoxin. It was the seventeenth on-the-job slaying he had pleaded guilty to, and the first in Pennsylvania. In accordance with the plea agreement, Judge Baratta deferred imposing Pennsylvania's mandatory life term in prison for the charge until Cullen was sentenced for his crimes in New Jersey.

Significantly, for the first time, a family member of one of the patients whose lives he snuffed out was permitted to read a victim's statement in the presence of the serial killer in open court. Cullen watched and listened with his head slumped on his chest from only a few feet away as Kristina Toth stood face-to-face with the former nurse who murdered the gentle man who was her father.

"I want to know if you even remember who my father was?" she asked. Reading from a legal pad she used to finish jotting down the statement she completed the night before the hearing, she continued: "Did you know that no doctor ever told us that my father was terminal? You want to think of yourself as an Angel of Mercy, but you are no Angel of Mercy. You don't know what being merciful is."

Observing that a psychiatrist who spoke with Cullen claimed he wasn't the monster people believed him to be, Kristina Toth told the disgraced RN with the hangdog look that her family considered him to be "a monster of the worst kind. You used your nursing position to murder patients entrusted to your care, regardless of their age or their medical condition," she said. "You say you ended their lives to keep them from suffering, but in many cases you made them suffer more."

Continuing, she briefly traced her father's life from his birth to Moravian missionaries in Nicaragua, through his marriage, devotion to his family, and his religious devotion. "I asked my mother, who is almost eighty-three years old, if she wanted me to say something for her," Toth read.

"She told me to tell you that 'what's done is done.' She wants me to tell you that she feels sorry for you, and especially sorry for your children." It may have been the reference to his children, but for the only time in the hearing, Cullen raised his eyebrows, blinked his eyes, and appeared to be showing a flicker of emotion. Moments later he was his old, coldly detached self.

Kristina Toth continued to speak calmly and audibly as she neared the conclusion of the two-page handwritten statement. "I hope you live a long life in confinement and I hope that you are haunted every day by what you have done," she said. "I think justice has been served in this life—and most certainly will be served in the next."

With the message delivered, the woman's brittle control of her emotions snapped and she broke into tears while returning to the seat in the gallery beside her husband and mother. Cullen was also clearly rattled and unnerved by the time the dramatic three-minute statement was concluded.

Judge Baratta then took over and asked the confessed killer if he administered the drug with an intent to kill.

"Yes, Your Honor," Cullen responded, nodding his rapidly graying head, up and down, in assent.

The judge then asked if he wished to explain why he picked the retired steelworker and family man as a victim. "At this time I'd prefer not to make a comment," Cullen replied.

Kristina Toth's heartrending courtroom statement was made possible by a bit of legal legerdemain on the part of Morganelli. Cullen's defense lawyers had made it clear that his client planned to skip his sentencing—a move permitted by Pennsylvania criminal statutes—so the Northampton County DA asked her to make her statement during the plea hearing. The matter wasn't ended with the dramatic afternoon courtroom appearance, and surprising repercussions from the bitterly emotional confrontation would soon emerge to play a significant role in the case.

Six days after the guilty plea in the Schramm death, District Attorney Martin and Pennsylvania state police investigators from Troop M at the Bethlehem Barracks huddled in an early-evening meeting with families of nine patients who died or nearly died on Cullen's watch at hospitals in Lehigh County. Counselors from the Lehigh Valley Crime Victims Council and victim's advocates from the DA's office were also present, while the families were brought up to date on the exhaustive investigation. Months earlier most of the families had provided to detectives photos of their relatives who died at the area hospitals.

State police captain Scott Snyder told reporters immediately prior to the meeting that his biggest concerns were dealing with the frustration of families who would be learning for the first time that their loved ones were among Cullen's victims, and explaining why they had to wait so long for information. It was very important for police to get through the complicated investigation first, he explained.

The ten months that elapsed between the time of Cullen's arrest was a sore point with many families who suspected that their relatives may have been attacked by the critical-care nurse in their hospital beds, and some were still talking bitterly about the absence of information from authorities when they arrived at the state police barracks. Seongchun Park, whose father, William M. Park, died at St. Luke's, told a reporter he was so frustrated about his inability to obtain answers to questions from investigators that even if he was told at the meeting that his father was a victim, he wouldn't believe it.

A few days earlier Pennsylvania state senator Lisa Boscola hosted a forum, where family members complained that they weren't being kept up to date by police and prosecutors on the progress of the investigation. Not knowing what was going on was making them miserable.

After the meeting at the state police barracks, Captain Snyder told reporters that new charges would be filed against Cullen in the Lehigh County courts the next day, Thursday, October 14, 2004. About fifty other families who were worried their relatives may have been victimized by the critical-care nurse had also contacted authorities, but the suspicions weren't yet confirmed by investigators. Snyder said they would be contacted soon. Police spokesmen and Martin promised more information Thursday afternoon at a press conference in Allentown.

Several people left in tears after the meeting broke up, and some brushed off reporters who tried to collar them for information with brusque "No comments." Others, like Carolyn Henne and her husband, Walter Henne, the daughter and son-in-law of Irene Krapf, talked briefly about their relatives and the critical-care nurse who poisoned them with unauthorized medications when they were at their most vulnerable. Cullen did "dishonor" to his victims, Walter Henne said, adding that the news about his mother-in-law was disheartening and difficult to accept.

John Gallagher's volunteer caregiver, Julie Sanders, said her "heart broke" when a state trooper called her to the meeting and she learned that Cullen would be charged with attempting to murder the elderly man.

Thursday, as expected, Martin filed six new charges of murder and three counts of attempted murder against Cullen with district justice Anthony Rapp in the Allentown suburb of Salisbury Township. The new charges stemmed from ten meetings with Cullen by investigators and the accumulation of forensic and other evidence. Cullen spent hours over the summer with investigators examining huge stacks of files of more than seventy patients who died in critical-care units at Lehigh Valley Hospital and at St. Luke's during his tenure as a night-shift nurse. He pulled seven files from St. Luke's of patients he recalled killing or attempting to kill, and pinpointed two files from among those of nineteen patients who died in the Lehigh Valley burn unit while he was assigned as a nurse there.

Six of the criminal complaints accused him of the murder of Matthew Mattern at the Lehigh Valley Hospital, and of five patients at St. Luke's: Irene Krapf, Daniel George, William M. Park, Samuel Spangler, and Edward O'Toole.

The attempted murder charges were filed for attacks on Gallagher, for twice administering unprescribed medications to retired radio personality Paul Galgon at St. Luke's, and for twice administering digoxin to Stella Danielczyk at Lehigh Valley. Cullen admitted to the attacks on Gallagher, Galgon, and Danielczyk, but investigators were unable to accumulate other evidence to prove that the drug overdoses were the cause of death. Exercising reasoning that may have looked to some observers like judicial dancing on the head of a pin, investigators explained that the two men and the woman were given potential lethal injections of medication, but they didn't die until after the effects of the drug wore off.

Cullen also admitted the attempt to murder Francis Henry with insulin at the Liberty nursing home, and detectives dug up enough forensic evidence to support a conviction. Unfortunately, Pennsylvania's five-year limitation for filing attempted-murder charges ran out about seven months before Cullen's arrest, and he couldn't be called to account for the 1998 assault. There is no statute of limitations on murder.

The announcement and filing of charges provided some degree of satisfaction to the nine families most directly affected. Others—perhaps most—of the sixty-five to seventy-five other families that had notified state police of suspicions their relatives were murdered by the treacherous RN were left to deal with emotions ranging from disappointment to outrage. They complained to anyone who was willing to listen that they were left in a frustrating limbo and would never know if their kinfolk were murdered in their hospital beds or died natural deaths. State police officers began telephoning and knocking on doors to advise individual families left out in the cold when charges were filed that Cullen was not responsible for the deaths of their relatives.

Spokesmen at St. Luke's, Lehigh Valley Hospital, and the Liberty Nursing and Rehabilitation Center quickly released statements sympathizing with families of patients who died at their facilities, or expressing outrage over Cullen's betrayal of his profession and of the patients whose health and welfare was entrusted to him.

Susan Schantz, a spokesman for St. Luke's, issued a written statement to the media pointing out that Cullen was immediately confronted when he was caught attempting to discard medications, was forced to resign, and was reported to the Pennsylvania State Board of Nursing. "We are outraged that one individual could act in a manner so opposed to what health care and the profession of nursing represents," she wrote.

Dressed in a pair of loose orange jail scrubs and manacled with his hands in front of him, Cullen was led into the Lehigh County Court of Common Pleas on November 17 by two tall Pennsylvania state troopers to appear before President Judge William H. Platt.

Pennsylvania state police detectives Andrew Ashmar and Robert Egan testified at the proceeding in Allentown about the methods and medications Cullen used in the murderous attacks on patients at the two Lehigh Valley area hospitals, and about his confessions to the crimes during ten interrogation sessions at the jail in Somerville.

When Judge Platt asked the defendant, whose head was bowed toward the floor in front of him, if the testimony was correct, he replied: "Yes, Your Honor." Flanked by Asteak and Mask, he replied to all of the judge's questions with his usual two- or three-word responses.

As he did at previous hearings, Cullen studiously avoided the eyes of relatives and friends of his victims gathered in the courtroom. Also, like at previous hearings, he didn't offer any apologies or make any attempts to explain his diabolic acts.

At the conclusion of the approximately forty-five-minute hearing, he pleaded guilty to the six slayings, and to the charges of attempted murder. The pleas brought the rogue nurse's official two-state death toll to twenty-three, including seven in Pennsylvania and sixteen in New Jersey. He had admitted attempting to murder a total of six other patients: four in Pennsylvania and two in New Jersey.

Paul Galgon's daughter Connie Keeler was among a crush of family members who attended the plea hearing. She told reporters she remembered Cullen as one of the nurses who was caring for her father. She was uneasy when he was around, and one time when a beeper sounded in her father's room, she was afraid to approach the strange nurse because he was "so creepy," she said.

Shanagher was also in the gallery, after driving from his home in Bridgewater for another look at his father's killer. He was outraged by a remark from Cullen's court-appointed Pennsylvania attorney, Asteak, defending his client's wish to skip sentencing hearings and avoid confrontations with families reading victim impact statements. Noting that his client had accepted responsibility and was paying for his behavior with his life, Asteak suggested: "Perhaps a pound of flesh is that which is sought?" Shanagher responded to the insensitive remark by firing off a stream of angry letters to local newspapers.

Cullen's ghastly reign of terror was also bringing on a blizzard of lawsuits in the two-state area, and by the time he entered his plea in the Lehigh County Court, nineteen families had filed civil actions against St. Luke's. The hospital issued a news release claiming that no relatives of the families filing the civil actions were victims of the rogue nurse. None of the families whose relatives were listed among the victims had yet filed civil actions. Cullen preyed only on patients in his unit, and there was no evidence to show that he roamed the halls looking for victims, Martin told the press.

Residents of the two-state area were already bundling up in their winter clothes and shopping for Christmas presents on December 16 when Cullen appeared before state superior court judge Donald Volkert Jr. in Newark and pleaded guilty to the murder of his first-known victim—Judge Yengo. The latest plea, entered and accepted in a rapid, no-frills fifteen-minute hearing at the Newark Courthouse, boosted the official two-state death toll to twenty-four, along with five attempted murders.

For a brief time it appeared that Cullen might be sentenced early in the new year for some of the atrocious crimes he committed in Lehigh County hospitals, but those hopes were quickly extinguished when hearings

were postponed indefinitely. Court proceedings scheduled for Friday, January 7, 2005, before Judge Stephen
Baratta in Northampton County, and Judge William Platt
in Lehigh County, couldn't be held because Cullen hadn't
yet been sentenced for his crimes in New Jersey. According to the plea agreement worked out months earlier by
court and law enforcement authorities from both states, he
had to be sentenced first in New Jersey because prison
terms ordered by the Pennsylvania courts were to run
consecutive to those in the Garden State. Judges in Pennsylvania couldn't order prison terms served consecutive to
sentences in another state that hadn't yet been imposed.

Another unexpected monkey wrench was thrown into
the proceedings when Cullen's pauper attorneys in New
Jersey and Pennsylvania challenged efforts by relatives of
their client's victims to compel him to attend sentencing
hearings while they read victim impact statements. The disgraced RN who coldly snuffed out the lives of thirty to forty
men and women didn't have the guts to face their survivors.
He was so unnerved and rattled by Kristina Toth's scathing
statement that he had decided to waive his constitutional
right to appear at his sentencing hearings in order to
avoid further confrontations.

Mask had announced in December that his client didn't
plan to attend his sentencing hearings, and contended that
relatives of Cullen's victims had no legal right to compel
him to appear and listen to their statements.

"There is no provision that mandates the presence of defendant," he wrote in a letter to Judge Armstrong. "Such
a requirement would serve to deny defendant's constitutional rights." Mask contended that New Jersey's Crime Victims Bill of Rights permitted relatives only to deliver "an
in-person statement directly to the sentencing court concerning the impact of the crime."

Mask contended in later remarks the constitutions of
New Jersey and of Pennsylvania gave relatives of crime
victims the right to speak at sentencing—but neither state

required defendants to attend sentencing hearings. If a defendant wanted to waive his constitutional right to attend his sentencing hearing, it was up to him.

A request by Gary Asteak, Cullen's Pennsylvania lawyer, to excuse the confessed serial killer from attending scheduled sentencing proceedings was rejected by Judge Platt. Asteak appealed the decision to the Pennsylvania Superior Court, and prosecutors and defense attorneys around the state began speculating that it would become a test case.

Family members of victims in the Garden State acquired strong allies in their struggle to force Cullen to appear for sentencing and listen to impact statements when the New Jersey Victims of Crime Compensation Board (VCCB) and the New Jersey Crime Victims' Law Center intervened in the case.

Led by Chairman Richard D. Pompelio, an aggressive, longtime victim's rights lawyer, the VCCB filed a motion asking Armstrong to force Cullen to attend his sentencing "and be present when the victims deliver their oral victim impact statement to the court." The motion was supported by four relatives of Cullen's victims, who provided statements that were part of a fifty-page brief submitted to the court.

Jean Haff, Edward Zizik's daughter, wrote: "Like a thief in the night, he stole away my dad's life. He took from us this most precious man before God was ready to call him. Now, Cullen seeks to minimize the importance of my father's life by arrogantly refusing to face me and the other victims at the time he is sentenced."

Shanagher expressed similar sentiments. "I am sure he does not want to face me and the many other murder victims he created through his evil acts," the schoolteacher wrote. "I respectfully state that such a decision should not be within his discretion. He should not be able to control these proceedings."

Pompelio declared that Cullen should be present at

the sentencing to "hear the voices and see the faces of the victims he has created through his criminal acts."

The nonprofit victim's law center, which Pompelio founded and operated out of his office in Sparta before moving to work full-time with the state agency, filed a motion supporting the VCCB's move. Both the public and the private victim's rights agencies said they were acting on behalf of the eighteen families of patients Cullen had already admitted murdering at three New Jersey hospitals.

Mask countered that the board had no authority to make the request. "In this instance, applicants clearly seek to raise and argue issues not pending before the court," he wrote in his response to the motion. "Any statements made by counsel or any other hearsay are inadmissible and cannot be considered by the court."

Pompelio told reporters that the judge had the power to order Cullen to attend his hearing, and said everything was coming down to a matter of weighing the rights of defendants against the rights of the victims. The rights of the victims should prevail, he insisted.

The VCCB's intervention in the increasingly convoluted Cullen matter and recent moves to step into other criminal cases on the side of prosecutors by filing amicus curiae, or "friends of the court," motions were red-letter events. The actions marked the first time in New Jersey and in the United States that a state agency established to compensate victims of violent crimes for their financial losses was actively opposing defense lawyers in felony cases.

The VCCB was established by the state legislature in the Criminal Injuries Compensation Act of 1971 as a victim's rights agency, and during its early years piled up a backlog of more than three thousand compensation claims by crime victims. When Pompelio was installed as the new board chairman in February 2003—just about the time Cullen was beginning to murder patients at Somerset Medical Center—he quickly eliminated the claims backlog and started looking for new realms to conquer. The VCCB began to assume a new dual role as a criminal justice agency.

Pompelio was a determined, forceful crusader, whose passion for victim's rights stemmed from the 1990 murder of his seventeen-year-old son, Tony. As soon as Pompelio was settled solidly in the role of VCCB chairman, he began redefining it as a victim-centered agency focusing on direct personal assistance and advocacy, as well as compensation for victims of violent crime.

Although the VCCB is headquartered with the Department of Law and Public Safety, the five-member gubernatorial-appointed board operates independently. A sister agency, the Office of Victim-Witness Advocacy, is part of the New Jersey State Attorney General's Division of Criminal Justice and provides services and grants—but does not involve itself in the courtroom jousting between the prosecution and defense in criminal cases.

The Office of Victim-Witness Advocacy didn't have the manpower or other resources to go to court, Pompelio said. So he began doing the job to enforce victim's rights. As part of that mission, he instituted a new program that led to training of 110 lawyers in 2004 to represent crime victims, and devised a plan to pay them $125 per hour for their work, up to a maximum of $1,000 per case. The VCCB had already interceded in other high-profile and in lesser-known cases around the state, in addition to Cullen's. One of the most closely watched was the Jayson Williams case, which drew the VCCB in on the side of the Hunterdon County Prosecutor's Office to challenge defense efforts to ban references to the slain chauffeur as the "victim" during the second trial.

The VCCB and the scrappy attorney at its head were potential nightmares for defense lawyers, but they were just what the doctor ordered for relatives of Cullen's victims who were determined not to be cheated out of their day in court. Pompelio was a skilled and determined combat veteran of

New Jersey's legal system and he knew all about the games of loopholes and technicalities that lawyers play.

Asteak stumbled over one of those technicalities when he filed his appeal with the court in Philadelphia on December 20, thirty-three days after Judge Platt ruled against Cullen's effort to sidestep his sentencing hearing so he could avoid a confrontation with relatives of his victims. Pennsylvania state statutes provided only thirty days for filing the appeal, and Asteak was three days late. Lehigh County DA Martin filed a motion in the superior court to have the tardy appeal tossed out.

Suddenly the would-be test case that Cullen's New Jersey lawyer, Mask, had said he hoped would help clarify the law and set a precedent solidifying the rights of defendants was wiped off Pennsylvania's high-court dockets. It wouldn't even be heard—because of a technicality.

Although Cullen's legal representatives seemed to have muffed an opportunity to block relatives from successfully mandating his presence during reading of victim impact statements in Pennsylvania, there was still plenty of fighting room for his New Jersey lawyer. While preparing for a hearing on the motions by the VCCB and the New Jersey Crime Victims' Law Center to enter the fray as friends of the court, Mask notified Judge Armstrong that Cullen wouldn't be attending the proceeding. The lawyer submitted a written waiver from his client.

Several relatives of patients killed by Cullen made it clear they would be present at the courthouse in Somerville for the fireworks when the motions by the victim's advocacy agencies were argued.

On February 9, the day of the hearing, state superior court judge Armstrong, presiding in Somerville, ordered Cullen brought to the courtroom from the jail. Manacled at hands and feet and flanked by guards, Cullen shuffled inside a few minutes later and was helped into a seat at the defense table barely ten feet from the first row of spectators.

Mask pushed his chair back from the defense table, stood up, and walked out! The agonized relatives gathered for the hearing were given a sudden, unanticipated glimpse of the criminal justice system at its most trivial—and most of them were shocked and outraged by the callous disregard for their feelings. Zach Martin and Emily Stoecker, Thomas and Mary Strenko, John Michael Shanagher and Janece Strickland, daughter of James R. Strickland, were among about a dozen relatives gathered in the courthouse for the proceeding.

When Armstrong was notified that the defense attorney had gone over the hill and was seen crossing Main Street, the judge ordered sheriff's deputies to chase him down and bring him back. "Tell him that the court directs him to return," Armstrong demanded.

With the judge in his chambers and Mask AWOL from the courtroom, wandering around somewhere in downtown Somerville, spectators reacted to the slap in the face by taking out their frustrations on his client. Deserted by his protector, Cullen was left alone to face the scorn and calumny of the people whose lives he forever blighted by the murder of their loved ones. It was his worst nightmare.

While the confessed serial killer slumped miserably alone at the defense table in his jailhouse orange uniform, with his face averted and his shoulders hunched, they showered him with a barrage of vocal abuse. If the defense lawyer's puerile theatrics were designed to somehow spare his client's delicate sensitivities by leaving him alone with the angry relatives, they backfired.

Emily Stoecker was in the front row and her frustrations and anger boiled over. Sliding forward in her seat and leaning over the railing, she taunted, "You look good in neon orange. It's your color! How does it feel to be alone, Charlie? How does it feel to be alone and vulnerable now?"

Cullen's head, with hair that was cropped so close it looked like a skull with bristles, sank even lower between his bony shoulders. He stared at the table while Emily continued to yell: "You don't deserve your kids! You don't deserve to see your children again." A man sitting nearby was shouting, "Rot in Hell, Cullen!"

A lawyer finally approached Emily and a few others, who were among the maverick nurse's most persistent tormentors, and asked them to stop. He cautioned that they might be kicked out of the courtroom or held in contempt if they continued the abuse. Emily didn't know the lawyer by name, but later described him as one of the victim's rights attorneys. "It was someone from our side," she said.

Cullen was helped to his feet a short time later and was escorted out by two uniform officers. He hobbled outside the courtroom to wait until his absent lawyer was run down and returned to take his place at the defense table. The prisoner kept his head down and averted from the gallery until he was clear of the courtroom and the door closed behind him.

Mask and his client were back in their places, and the turmoil had quieted when Judge Armstrong swept into the courtroom from his chambers accompanied by all the judicial solemnity and authority of the black robe. In accordance with courtroom custom everyone stood up. One of Cullen's husky guards reached over, grabbed his metal shackles, unceremoniously hoisted him from the chair, and propped him up and onto his feet.

Judge Armstrong sternly demanded that Mask explain his peevish behavior. "Why is it," the jurist asked, "that you unilaterally decided to leave this hearing?"

Mask replied that his client signed a waiver, giving up his right to appear, and said he had anticipated being allowed to "place something on the record without Mr. Cullen here." He claimed the business before the court was an "extraneous matter brought by outsiders," and didn't require the presence of his client.

"Who gets to make that decision?" the judge demanded.

If spectators expected Mask to concede that the judge
was the decision maker, they were in for a surprise.

"Mr. Cullen," the lawyer replied.

Patiently, and seemingly choosing his words carefully, the
judge explained that it was his responsibility to make certain that Cullen's decision to waive his rights and skip the
hearing was "knowing, intelligent, and voluntary." The
only way to do that was to have Cullen brought into the
court and questioned, he said.

Armstrong ordered the fractious attorney to produce a
written explanation of his behavior and an apology for the
court. "In thirty-two years at the bar, including five years on
the bench, I've never seen a counsel elect to leave an important motion like this," the judge lectured. The tense
face-off between Armstrong and Mask sounded to some of
the spectators, who were parents, like the stern jurist was
reprimanding a naughty child.

When Cullen was questioned by the judge, he said he
wished to waive his right to appear at all future court proceedings, including the sentencing hearing. Minutes
later, after conferring with Mask, he took the advice of his
attorney and retracted his remarks about skipping the sentencing. Families were puzzled by the defendant's abrupt
change of mind, but his motivations and those of his
lawyer would become clear later on in the lengthy proceeding.

Armstrong granted the waiver of Cullen's right to attend
the current proceeding, and the defendant was again
helped to his feet, then shuffled awkwardly out of the
courtroom to be transported back across the street to his
cell at the Somerset County Jail.

Court officers at last turned to the main purposes of the
hearing: efforts by the two victim's advocacy agencies to
file friend-of-the-court briefs on behalf of the prosecution
and relatives of patients murdered by Cullen, and their requests that the court force Cullen to attend his sentencing hearing and listen to victim impact statements from

families. Assistant Somerset County prosecutor Timothy Van Hise was present, but didn't take an active role in the contest between the deputy public defender and the victim's rights advocates.

Mask attacked the victim's rights groups in his arguments against the friend-of-the-court motion by branding them as "self-serving, self-aggrandizing publicity seekers."

"We are not here for self-aggrandizement," Clifford Weininger, Pompelio's successor as head of the Crime Victims' Law Center, responded in defense of the motions. "We are here because these people have a legitimate pain and a right to confront Cullen. They are a party to this action. You can't use a slur to avoid that right."

Pompelio demonstrated his own exotic command of the language by responding that Mask's client was responsible for "a river of grief that will flow and flow and flow. . . ." It was up to the court to do the honorable thing and do whatever it could to make the lives of the survivors easier, he said.

Armstrong granted the petitions by the victim's rights groups, citing precedent-setting rulings by higher tribunals, including the U.S. Supreme Court, that encouraged filing amicus curiae briefs on issues that are important to the public. "It is preferable to err on the side of caution in granting leave to petition," he noted.

The victim's rights agencies had won the right to file briefs and to present arguments in the increasingly complicated and labyrinthine case, while logging a judicial milestone. The decision marked the first time that a judge permitted the VCCB to enter a criminal case over the objections of the defense. Another judge allowed the board into a case in Ocean City the previous year, but no one objected.

Mask claimed the issue shouldn't even be before the court because Cullen hadn't yet decided if he wanted to waive his appearance at sentencing. He said he couldn't respond because his client hadn't yet made a decision.

"Well, he almost did today," the judge replied. Armstrong was referring to Cullen's flip-flop when he said he wished to waive his right to appear at all future hearings, then—after conferring with his lawyer—retracted the part about skipping the sentencing.

Almost wasn't good enough, and Armstrong avoided a decision on the other request seeking to compel Cullen to attend his sentencing. A decision on the request would be premature because the defendant hadn't formally waived his right to appear, he explained. Cullen's puzzling about-face a few minutes earlier made sense suddenly to spectators who weren't lawyers and who weren't skilled in the sometimes puzzling courtroom maneuverings of people who were.

The victim's rights advocates had contended in their arguments that impact statements were meaningless unless the defendant was present to hear them. Even though the judge's decision made the argument a moot point for the present, granting friend-of-the-court status to the victim's rights groups left the door open for future consideration. That would occur only if Cullen filed a formal waiver request to skip his sentencing, but it seemed clear that Armstrong would eventually have to settle the issue of conflicting rights. Mask indicated he would appeal the ruling on friends of the court.

When the little band of family members gathered outside the courtroom to talk with each other and with the press after the proceeding was adjourned, they were clearly exhausted and emotionally drained by the nearly six-hour ordeal. The purported majesty of the legal system had just lost some of its luster, and the proceeding witnessed by the relatives seemed to have created as much pain and anguish as it healed. Some were still seething over the shoddy disregard for their feelings and the defense antics that played such a visible role in extending the lengthy hearing from the early afternoon to early evening.

Emily described Cullen as a "psycho," although he was

"still cognizant of what he did." She insisted that he should be forced to face the people he hurt so terribly.

Mary Strenko called the man who murdered her son "a coward" and said he had no right to avoid facing the families. The distraught woman, whose father died of cancer about a year before her son was murdered, talked of her agony at not being able to vent by reading a victim statement during a face-to-face confrontation with his killer. Mary Strenko said she had trouble sleeping and lost her job as a customer-service representative because her supervisor couldn't continue dealing with her fragile emotions. The family was devastated by the tragedy.

Shanagher didn't talk about it to the press, but he was already mulling over in his mind just what he hoped someday to say in a victim impact statement during a face-to-face courtroom confrontation with Cullen. He shared his thoughts with Zach Martin.

"I want to tell Cullen that he may have had some difficulty in his life, but who didn't?" he asked. "We all make choices in life, and your choice was to give yourself a sense of power, and a sense of value in the world by taking away people that we love.

"I want you to know that you have disrupted my mother's life. These are her later years. She should be sitting here enjoying her time with her grandchildren, doing what she wants to do. Instead, she's sitting here reading newspapers, her husband constantly being referred to as 'murder victim, John Shanagher.'"

Jack Shanagher was much more than a murder victim, and to allow the tragedy that ended his life to overshadow the sense of comfort, security, joy, and good humor that he brought to the lives of his family unfairly soiled his memory. "The most important things in my father's life," John said, "were my mother, his children, his grandchildren—and beer. He was an Irishman!"

After learning the truth about the elder Shanagher's death, it was hard even for the family to tell the old stories they used to recount about loving experiences they shared with him, or the funny things he said. Instead, the talk turned inevitably to the manner of his death, and public descriptions of him as a murder victim. "That's inexcusable, and there is no reason for it," his son declared. "And I'm going to resent it until the day I die." It wasn't right, or fair, and the schoolteacher refused to give up hope that he would have an opportunity someday to get things off his chest in a confrontation with his father's executioner.

"When this is all over," he said, "I'm hopefully going to be allowed to make my victim statement. Then I'm going to walk out of that court, and I'm going to go somewhere with my kids and my wife, and my mom and my sisters, and we're gonna go on with our lives. And he's gonna go where he belongs. Forever!"

Chapter 15

Good from Evil

We watched her murder on Feb. 12, 2003, and didn't even know it. That has hurt our family more than anyone can imagine.
> —Emily Stoecker, from a letter to the
> *Bergen Record*, Bergen County, New Jersey

The slaughter of innocents in hospitals in two states was a ghoulish wake-up call that alarmed citizens, regulatory agencies, health-care professionals, police, and legislators.

In response to the horror, public officials began taking the first faltering steps toward reform and tightening of security measures to protect the ill and the infirm from health-care professionals who turn predator.

New Jersey attorney general Harvey began investigating means of tailoring antiterror procedures developed after the 9/11 World Trade Center attacks to identifying and catching nursing and other health-care workers who turn on their patients.

The state's leading prosecutor was also looking into

developing a system for reporting trouble with nurses that was similar to rules already in effect for doctors. Health-care facilities were required to notify the state when a doctor was fired or resigned, and whether or not the facility was considering a review of his or her conduct. Rules governing the behavior of nurses should be at least equal to those that governed the deportment of doctors, Harvey concluded.

Early in 2004, New Jersey legislators passed a new Patient Safety Act, which was signed into law by Governor James E. McGreevey, who has since resigned. The new law required doctors, hospitals, and nursing homes to report medical errors, and to create individual review boards to examine medical mistakes and reduce errors. The reporting proviso required the facilities to notify state officials of all adverse events or negative outcomes of patient care that resulted in death, disability, loss of a body part or body functions. Employees would be encouraged to anonymously snitch to authorities about less serious blunders.

Importantly, the new state code also shielded hospitals and nursing homes that alerted authorities about medical blunders and so-called near-miss mishaps from being sued or prosecuted for making the reports.

The newly enacted statute required every medical hospital, psychiatric hospital, and nursing home in the state to develop patient-safety plans, and to establish individual review boards to investigate medical errors and develop solutions to reduce or eliminate similar mistakes in the future. In a stipulation that Lucille Gall must have been pleased to see included in the new law, the state health commissioner was required to notify patients or their relatives when a medical error occurred.

After the state senate approved the measure by a vote of thirty-six to zero, legislators said they were hopeful the Patient Safety Act would restore faith in the health-care profession, which was badly damaged by the scandalous Cullen case. Joseph F. Vitale, a Middlesex state senator and a cosponsor of the legislation, suggested that patient safety wouldn't be the only benefit of the new code. He said he believed the statute would also lower costs of medical malpractice insurance by trimming the number of lawsuits.

New Jersey legislators also began working on a new state code that would permit medical facilities to share information about professional misconduct, improper patient care, and disciplinary actions with sister institutions in the health-care business. The Healthcare Professional Responsibility and Reporting Enhancement Act was designed to help weed out incompetent, negligent, or otherwise dangerous employees. Approximately 120,000 health-care workers in New Jersey would be covered by the proposed new law.

After McGreevey left office, in the midst of a political and sexual scandal, Acting Governor Richard J. Codey nominated an executive with the St. Barnabas Health System in West Orange to replace Dr. Clifton R. Lacy, who was resigning as commissioner of the Department of Health and Senior Services. The new chief, Dr. Fred M. Jacobs, a medical doctor and an attorney, was instructed by Codey to examine means of improving hospital patient safety.

Legislators in Pennsylvania ran into a temporary snag with a bill designed to permanently ban some convicted felons from ever working in hospitals in the state, and stipulating a ten-year wait after release for some others sent to prison for certain lesser crimes. Anyone convicted of homicide, kidnapping, rape, stalking, sexual abuse of children, or various other especially repugnant crimes would never be allowed to work in a Pennsylvania hospital, according to the proposed legislation.

Ten-year bans would be put into effect for people convicted of witness intimidation, retaliation against a witness, prostitution, indecent exposure, concealing the death of a child, use of a controlled substance, forgery, and offenses linked to obscene sexual materials or performances and corruption of minors, among other offenses.

The proposed statute was designed to apply to hospital workers whose jobs brought them into direct contact with patients or unsupervised access to patient rooms. Nurses, nurse's aides, interns, students, X-ray technicians, and people applying for any of those jobs would be covered by the law. Job applicants would be required to submit to criminal background checks conducted by the state police if they were schooled or had been working in Pennsylvania. The FBI would be expected to conduct the checks for prospective employees moving in from outside the state. People already working at a Pennsylvania hospital would have one year to complete a criminal background check, or leave their job.

The legislation breezed through the Pennsylvania House in 2004, but died in the Pennsylvania Senate without being voted on. Early in 2005, newly elected state senator Pat Vance, the Cumberland County Republican who earlier sponsored the bill in the House, reintroduced the legislation in the Senate. Some of the approximately two hundred hospitals in the Keystone State already required similar criminal background checks for their employees and prospective new hires. The newly proposed law would extend the same kind of strict and meticulous screening to every hospital in the state.

Also in Pennsylvania, Lisa Boscola, a state senator, introduced a bill to make it mandatory for hospitals to do background checks of employment history before hiring nurses.

Members of professional health-care organizations were also alarmed by the latest scandal to shake up the industry, and joined in the scramble to devise improved methods for ensuring patient safety.

Most medical facilities followed quality assurance guidelines recommended by the Joint Commission on the Accreditation of Healthcare organizations, which already provided accreditation services for about sixteen thousand hospitals and other patient-care facilities in the

United States. But when it came to reviewing suspicious patient deaths, the job was usually left to the chief of a department to conduct investigations, which could be a painfully slow process. Leading health authorities began pushing for a streamlined approach to the job, with hospitals adopting tracking programs, preferably calling on techniques routinely used in epidemiology research for sniffing out the spread of infection. Using those methods would help investigators learn quickly if a cluster of deaths had a pattern that might point to an employee, equipment, or drugs.

Similar recommendations were made after the exposure of other especially notorious health-care killers, and failure to follow up and act or to cover all the bases was fatal to patients like Daniel George, Samuel Spangler, Edward Zizik, and Eleanor Stoecker. It was long past the time for senior health officials to act.

The American Hospital Association announced formation of a task force to examine the phenomena of health-care professionals who murder their patients. Beatrice Crofts Yorker, director of the School of Nursing at San Francisco State University and a task force member, disclosed that she had discovered seventy-six medical murderers in the United States and other countries who were caught since 1974. Many others, she said, went undetected and unpunished. Curiously, although men compose only a small fraction of people in the nursing profession, somewhere between 5 and 7 percent, 38 percent of the killers were male.

Senator Corzine and fellow U.S. senator Frank R. Lautenberg, of New Jersey, called for improved utilization of an existing National Practitioner Data Bank created nearly twenty years ago to document hospital errors. The New Jersey solons urged the federal Health Resources and Services Administration to integrate disciplinary measures ordered against nurses and other health-care providers into the national database. If the proposal was successfully followed up, it would go a long way toward plugging a hole that Cullen exploited by moving back and forth across state lines. Even if he had gotten into trouble with a licensing board in one state, he still had another license permitting him to work in the neighboring state. More vigilant federal monitoring could change that.

Efforts to extract good from evil weren't restricted to new legislation or tightening of security and other measures to protect patients at hospitals. The plea agreement was already paying off in ways unrelated to helping identify victims, and hospital and law enforcement authorities were gathering valuable information from interviews with the Death Angel about how he was able to thwart security systems established to safeguard the medication-dispensing system, how he was able to obtain records of patients not assigned to his care, and other means he used to cover up his assaults on gravely ill patients.

Months before investigators seeking out new victims were through with Cullen, New Jersey attorney general Harvey was looking forward to his turn at bat and an opportunity to meet with the serial killer and dig out more of the dark secrets locked in his chaotic mind. Cullen knew a lot about glitches, vulnerabilities, and weak spots in the health-care system and could provide information to help make it more difficult for the next Death Angel to operate.

Individual hospitals in both states were also reviewing drug-dispensing operations and taking steps to institute other safety measures for the protection of patients. When the Somerset Medical Center first became aware of the problems surrounding their rogue nurse, the pharmacy was instructed to begin handling the nonnarcotic heart drug digoxin as if it were a controlled dangerous substance. The supplies of digoxin were locked up with narcotics. After Cullen's arrest digoxin was also removed from the hospital's Pyxis system.

Before Cullen's arrest and the shocking disclosure that a medical serial killer had been roaming critical-care wards in New Jersey and Pennsylvania, the Muhlenberg Regional Medical Center initiated a double safety-check system for dispensing narcotics and other high-risk drugs, including insulin and digoxin. Signatures of two registered nurses were required before the carefully secured medication was provided. The double safety-check system also mandated the presence of two nurses when insulin was administered: one RN to check the dosage, while the other drew the medication into a syringe. Both nurses were required to sign verification forms.

Some who were touched by the tragedy also took other approaches.

On a bright, sunlit Sunday, just eight days short of the first anniversary of Father Gall's untimely death, approximately one hundred parishioners gathered on the lawn outside Our Lady of Lourdes Roman Catholic Church to attend an outdoor benefit concert in memory of the quiet priest, whom some remembered as "the Music Man."

The reserved, undemonstrative man of the cloth would probably have been embarrassed but secretly pleased by all the fuss. And even though he would certainly have preferred classical or church music as his own personal choices, he couldn't have helped but feel good while members of his flock lounged on blankets and chairs listening to the classic rock and other tunes belted out by eleven members of the music ministry. It was a day for memories and music as the musicians belted out pieces by the Beatles and John Denver and other popular tunes of the present and recent past.

Members of the Our Lady of Lourdes Knights of Columbus chapter prepared food for the event, which was the kickoff of a fund-raising drive to establish a memorial scholarship fund in Father Gall's name. The scholarship was designed for high-school seniors from the parish and other parishioners who planned to further their education in the study of music and liturgy. The church pledged $500 to $1,000 annually to support the fund.

On June 28, the anniversary of Father Gall's death, his memory was honored again when the church's Community House was rededicated as the Very Reverend Florian J. Gall Community House. The building included classrooms, a meeting room, and offices. The dedication was immediately preceded by a 7:30 P.M. memorial mass.

In Pennsylvania, former radio-talk-show host Paul Galgon's son, Patrick Galgon, was taking a practical hands-on approach to improve patient protection at hospitals by launching a one-man campaign promoting more widespread use of the Pyxis MedStation and similar computerized drug-dispensing machines, like the device at the Somerset Medical Center that helped pinpoint Cullen as the renegade nurse who was killing the gravely ill on his wards.

In an interview with reporter Ann Wlazelek, of the *Morning Call*, the fifty-year-old self-employed broadcast engineer said three years after his father died that he was still living with guilt for persuading his father to have pacemaker surgery at a time a rogue nurse was preying on critical-care patients at Lehigh Valley Hospital. Other family members were also suffering from emotional fallout from the tragedy, and Galgon spent hours the previous October calming the fears of his wife, Andrea, before she was finally admitted to a hospital for treatment of a severe asthma attack.

Politicians were promising to fix the health-care system while Cullen was "running around" for sixteen years, Galgon said, and he figured that if citizens didn't step up on their own and get involved, it wasn't going to happen. "I will do anything I can to make sure we get more machines like this in more and more hospitals," he told the reporter.

Galgon showed his sincerity by going directly to the leading manufacturer of the drug-dispensing machine, Cardinal Health, in San Diego. The company was so impressed with Galgon's grass-roots activist approach to spreading the technology that Cardinal Health personnel flew in from California to provide a personal demonstration and explanation for Galgon at Sacred Heart Hospital in Allentown. Karen Nishi, the company's director of regulatory affairs, offered to help him produce a video and assist him in other ways.

Nishi estimated that more than half the hospitals across the country with three hundred beds or more have Pyxis MedStations or similar technology produced by other companies. By early 2005, when Galgon's crusade was picking up steam, all four hospitals in the Lehigh Valley, where Cullen worked had installed Pyxis or similar computerized drug-dispensing apparatuses in operation. Some were already using the devices before his arrest, although they weren't in use in every inpatient unit.

Galgon said he didn't want the image of the victims to be tainted forever as "a negative" by Cullen's acts. He wanted "something positive" to come from it, and for those who lost relatives to be recognized as heroes for their efforts to save others.

At their home in Oradell, Zach Martin and his wife, Emily, were busy organizing Ellie's Angels in his mother's memory. Planned as a nonprofit agency, Ellie's Angels was being designed to put food on the table for poor children from rural areas and to provide financial assistance for their education.

In June 2004, a letter from Emily Stoecker was printed in the *Asbury Park Press* thanking Governor McGreevey for signing legislation requiring medical facilities to report medical errors to the state. Emily also encouraged lawmakers to support more comprehensive background checks of health-care workers, and more stringent security measures at medical and other care facilities. A more intense system to monitor the access by nurses to patient charts, rooms, and medications needed to be adopted in order to weed out the minority of health-care workers like Cullen so that "the potential dangerous behavior can be prevented," she declared.

Her mother-in-law was murdered by Cullen, who was not assigned as her caregiver, but who entered "her room without reason or authorization to inject her IV with the digoxin," the writer pointed out.

Cullen's spotty career at other hospitals and his history of "misusing medications," reports of problems with patients under his care, and his treatment at mental-health centers were also briefly traced. His murder spree could have been shut off earlier if the danger from "his past and patterns" had been recognized and acted on.

"My mother-in-law loved life and enjoyed her family and friends," Emily wrote. "She was only 60 years old when Cullen robbed her grandchildren of the gift of being with her, gaining her wisdom and feeling her unconditional love."

Chapter 16

Bitter Medicine

If medical-care facilities where Cullen carried out his cruel vendetta against the old, the sick, and the infirm were really motivated by fear of slander suits when they failed to share negative information with their sister institutions while passing him along to avoid dealing with a nasty situation, it was seriously faulty reasoning.

After Cullen's arrest and confession to murdering thirty to forty patients over a decade-and-a-half, the hospitals where he worked were snowed under by an avalanche of civil lawsuits filed by families whose relatives were known or suspected of having been murdered by the darkly venal Death Angel.

The rogue nurse avoided the death penalty, but he left hospitals where he carried out his abysmal crimes on the hot seat, facing the music from relatives of the men and women he murdered in their beds. The reputations of hospitals and health-care professionals in the two-state area were the first to be seriously battered, and they paid a stiff price among government and private agencies involved with the health-care community and the general public for their failings. The serious assault shaping up on their pocketbooks had all the earmarks of litigation that could be stretched out for years.

It was bitter medicine.

Issuing statements in press releases and during interviews with the print and electronic media—sympathizing with the families and promising to do better—fell far short of satisfying survivors and adequately dealing with the loss, grief, guilt, and feelings of colossal betrayal left in the killer's wake. Letters of condolences that some hospitals sent to survivors were sometimes awkwardly handled, or hospital staff did a poor job of handling follow-up calls.

Jack Shanagher's son was so upset when a condolence letter was addressed to him instead of to his mother that he grabbed the phone and dialed the Somerset Medical Center to let them know about the blunder. "My name is John Shanagher," he announced. "I received your letter regarding my father's murder by Charles Cullen."

The stunned silence at the other end of the line was so frozen it was almost audible. He explained that although he was named as the person to contact in case of problems when his father was admitted to the hospital, the letter should have been sent to his father's widow. When he demanded that another copy of the letter be sent to his mother, where it should have gone in the first place, the flustered hospital employee immediately agreed. She sounded like she could hardly wait for the call to end, so she could get off the phone.

It was obvious that no one at the hospital deliberately intended to rub already raw emotions the wrong way, but that's how it worked out. The entire matter, including the way the telephone call was handled, could have been better executed. The medical center should have been better prepared to deal with the badly frayed emotions of relatives who felt they were betrayed by the very institution they had trusted the care and lives of family members to—only to have them murdered in their beds by a nurse.

Employees could have been better trained to deal with what had become a local tragedy of epic proportions.

The bitterness directed toward hospitals where patients died at Cullen's hands wasn't restricted to Somerset, and there was plenty of blame to go around on both sides of the New Jersey–Pennsylvania state line.

Cullen's arrest was barely announced in the media before families were lining up at the offices of trial lawyers and vowing to make hospitals pay through the nose for lapses of judgment and security failures that permitted the health-care serial killer to continue his bloody work for so long. To some of the relatives, filing civil negligence and unlawful death lawsuits was seen as the most effective way to satisfy their desire for justice and get the message through that shallow promises or after-the-fact patchwork fixes weren't acceptable. It was time for hospitals and nursing homes to initiate fail-safe security measures and make the protection of patients their number one priority.

Zach Martin didn't go looking for a lawyer until he became fed up with what he considered to be shabby treatment from the hospital, then decided on civil litigation. Jack Shanagher's family didn't decide to contact a lawyer until a couple of weeks after Cullen admitted at the plea hearing to his father's murder and that of twelve other men and women at the Somerset Medical Center. A major story in the *New York Times* that traced the twisted RN's murderous career while he moved freely from hospital to hospital played a big part in their decision to sue. He was the hands-on killer, but the news article seemed to make it plain that there was plenty of additional culpability to go around.

The attorney representing the family of Edward Zizik, who was believed to have been Cullen's last victim at Somerset Medical Center, described the case to reporters as especially "egregious." Zizik's case was different from others, Leonard Weitzman said, because it occurred after the hospital contacted the prosecutor and investigators there identified Cullen to Somerset authorities as a suspect in patient deaths. The hospital already knew that a potential killer was roaming the ICU, they knew who the suspect was, and yet Cullen was permitted to continue working and wasn't fired until ten-days after Zizik died.

Somerset was also accused in the lawsuit with negligently inflicting emotional distress on Zizik's widow, Helen, because she was the one who decided to admit her husband to the medical center. The hospital had a duty to be honest and forthright with her about problems on the critical-care unit before she allowed her husband to be admitted, it was claimed. The Bedminister lawyer also represented the family of Melvin Simcoe.

In February, attorneys for Lucille Gall filed a lawsuit in Middlesex County Superior Court in New Brunswick against Cullen and the medical center seeking damages for the wrongful death of her brother. Like similar lawsuits filed by the relatives of other patients believed to have died or who were suspected of dying at Cullen's hands, the civil action accused the hospital of failure to investigate his credentials properly before hiring him. Somerset Medical Center was also accused in the filing of concealing the true nature of Reverend Gall's death.

Cullen was pinpointed as a defendant in most of the lawsuits, but since he had no appreciable assets and was expected to spend the rest of his life in prison, hardly anyone—if anyone at all—expected to collect any damages from him personally. There also seemed to be little chance of collecting for any damages assessed against Cullen from insurance carried by hospitals since the policies typically covered employees only against claims of negligence that occurred while they were carrying out their normal duties. Stealing medication and deliberately using it to poison patients wasn't part of Cullen's normal duties. And the acts weren't negligence, they were criminal.

Payoffs in lawsuits against hospitals, their insurers, and other elements of the health-care industry can be enormous, and that's a big reason there are so many medical malpractice lawyers. Backed by insurers covering compensatory claims, hospitals are seen by trial lawyers around the country as having invitingly deep pockets. Many hospitals, however, aren't covered for punitive damages, which would require proof of wanton and reckless disregard of the lives of patients. Punitive damages can offer the biggest paychecks when all the courtroom finagling and legal jousting are over, but while Cullen cooled his heels in the county jail, that appeared to be a long time in the future.

One law firm in Easton represented almost sixty families who believed that relatives were among Cullen's victims. Various other law firms or individual lawyers in Pennsylvania and New Jersey gathered as many as twenty to a half-dozen or fewer separate clients who were suing or planned to sue over the deaths of family members in hospital units while Cullen was on the nursing staff. Some families filed more than one suit.

Many of the civil suits were filed on behalf of patients who died in ICUs where Cullen was working at the time, but who were not yet singled out by him as victims of his murder rampage. Some survivors of patients who were not named as victims were unwilling to accept the judgment of law enforcement investigators or Cullen's truthfulness or memory. The word of a known serial killer, especially when it didn't mesh with what you already believed or feared, didn't carry much credibility.

Lawsuits over deaths not yet officially attributed to the killer by law enforcement authorities were permitted because the burden of proof was different in civil and criminal cases. Prosecutors in criminal cases are required to show they had proof beyond reasonable doubt, while lawyers in civil cases had the opportunity of convincing judges or juries by a preponderance of the evidence that hospitals were negligent by employing the Death Angel.

Even the Hunterdon Medical Center, where Cullen

claimed to have taken a rare vacation from murder, and Morristown Memorial Hospital, where no slayings were known to have occurred, were sued. Plaintiffs blamed various hospitals for negligence in permitting their patients to be murdered, for failing to properly investigate Cullen's work history before hiring him, and for passing on a known malcontent without warning other employers of scrapes he got into over his misbehavior.

A few suits or notices of intention to file were withdrawn by the plaintiffs, dismissed by the courts within a few days or weeks of filing, or were simply dropped and not followed up. The lawyer who notified the court of an intention to sue for a Pennsylvania man who suspected Cullen may have been responsible for his becoming blind said later in a document that the civil action wouldn't be filed.

The civil litigation wasn't all one-sided, and after Cullen admitted the murder of Ottomar Schramm at Easton, the hospital filed a lawsuit in the Northampton County Court of Common Pleas against the Harrisburg-based staffing agency that arranged for the RN to obtain periodic work there and paid his salary.

Operating as Healthforce when Cullen was placed at the hospital, by the time the lawsuit was filed, the agency was known as the Gula Staffing Services. The hospital had a contract with the agency that indemnified it for Cullen's acts because he was an employee of the staffing firm, Easton claimed. The agency was accused in the action of negligence in failing to screen nurses sent to the hospital, by failing to perform a criminal background check, and failing to administer a psychological test or mental-health evaluation. The service was also negligent in failing to provide only appropriately qualified nurses, and that was a shortcoming that left Cullen "in a position where he could cause harm resulting in the untimely death of patients such as Ottomar Schramm," it was claimed.

Experienced lawyers figured that was just the beginning, and that cross-claims and legal jousting would flourish between hospitals, staffing agencies, and insurance companies.

In New Jersey, Attorney General Harvey did his best to put a happy face on the flutter of litigation at a news conference a few months after the arrest. He suggested that as the cases moved through the courts, they would probably help answer questions about what went wrong in the hiring and supervision of the virulently dangerous nurse, while providing clues about how to avoid similar problems in the future.

"We have to be just a little bit sensitive," the Garden State's top prosecutor said. "And that's why we want to use this as an opportunity not just to say, 'This guy's involved, that guy's involved, and this place should have done it better.' That is, believe me, going to be examined very closely by civil-practice lawyers."

Public documents filed in the criminal cases against Cullen were available to the private trial lawyers, just as they were to anyone else. But for anything else, the lawyers and private investigators working for them would have to do their own digging. There was nothing in the plea agreement that bound Cullen to work with the private attorneys in the wrongful death or negligence suits they filed on behalf of clients.

The Death Angel was barely back at the county jail after his stay at the psychiatric hospital in West Trenton before civil lawyers were complaining that they couldn't get to him to take sworn statements they hoped to use as part of their lawsuits. Obtaining forensic evidence on their own was also a daunting task for civil lawyers, since few if any families could bear the prodigious expense of exhuming bodies, hiring pathologists to conduct autopsies, then paying for costly toxicology tests on tissues.

Private attorneys claimed they were willing to share information they assembled with law enforcement authorities, but weren't getting much cooperation in return. A spokesman for the New Jersey Division of Criminal Justice summed up what may have been the prevailing attitude when he observed that local law enforcement authorities didn't need any help from private attorneys. Thanks to Cullen's cooperation and the work of investigators for law enforcement agencies, prosecutors already knew who the victims and suspected victims were. And they either already had or were in the process of acquiring the backup forensic evidence to confirm the killer's claims.

By the early fall of 2004, so many civil practice lawyers had "examined" the case that the New Jersey Supreme Court ordered the naming of a single Middlesex County judge to handle all pretrial matters in all civil suits filed throughout the state on behalf of Cullen's victims. The court acted at the request of Peter Korn, of McDonough, Korn & Eichhorn in Springfield, New Jersey who was defense attorney for the Somerset Medical Center. The order was seen as a necessary move to prevent lawyers from shopping around for jurisdictions known for favoring plaintiffs with large awards, and to hold down the number of appeals.

Superior court judge Bryan Garruto was assigned to the job. The jurist appeared to be a good choice, because he had a glowing reputation for the ability to handle convoluted litigation deftly. Prior to his appointment to the superior court bench in 1998, he was a private practice trial lawyer who represented workers exposed to asbestos as part of their jobs, and women who suffered injury from breast implants. The supreme court ruling gave Garruto the option of personally presiding at trial over any of the cases.

Judge Garruto was expected to confer frequently with his peers in Pennsylvania, but more than eighteen months after Cullen's arrest and shocking confession, no similar consolidation of pretrial matters was ordered for civil actions filed in the Keystone State. Pennsylvania courts had, however, begun to deal with the matter of shopping for friendly jurisdictions by civil lawyers.

Several suits filed against Cullen, medical facilities where he worked, and, in some cases, other defendants in Pennsylvania were ordered transferred from Northampton County Court of Common Pleas to the courts in Lehigh County, where the toxic RN was employed by St. Luke's Hospital when patients named in the civil actions were killed. Some lawyers believed that plaintiffs tended to be better treated in Northampton County courts than in those of the neighboring county. None of the first five lawsuits affected by the rulings involved patients whom Cullen had admitted murdering or attempting to kill. Two suits filed by relatives of Ottomar Schramm, who died at Easton Hospital, remained where they were originally filed—in Northampton County.

Citing a new medical malpractice statute in Pennsylvania, Northampton County president judge Robert A. Freedberg issued two opinions ruling that jurisdictions for hearing cases should be based on where it was alleged by families that their relatives were drugged by the renegade nurse and where the medical facilities failed to "provide adequate medical services."

Pennsylvania and New Jersey each had statutes on the books establishing two-year limitations from the time of a patient's death to the filing of civil suits. Many of the deaths Cullen admitted responsibility for and others he was still suspected of playing a role in occurred more than two years before he was arrested near the end of 2003 and identified as a health-care serial killer. That included all the murders committed at St. Barnabas, Warren Hospital, Easton Hospital, the Lehigh Valley Hospital, and more than half of those at St. Luke's.

Impelled by the two-year deadlines, many of the civil attorneys filed paperwork advising the courts of their intent to sue in order to reserve the rights of their clients to seek redress. Lawyers for hospitals responded by asking the courts to order the plaintiffs to file formal complaints, which required more supporting information. The move seeking to make plaintiffs show their hole cards was all part of the games that lawyers play.

Citing the logical argument that an unlawful death suit couldn't be filed until it was learned that a crime had occurred, civil law attorneys in both states moved in the meantime to challenge the statutes or to win an exception to the time limit for filing. A similar statute prevented authorities from filing criminal charges in the attempted murder of Francis Henry, but wisely no such limitation existed in cases of homicide.

While bracing themselves against legal assaults that had the potential of costing them millions of dollars, medical facilities and their insurers in both states fought back with their own lawyers. Any losses in hard cash would be added to the damage to reputations that would continue piling up while the civil suits limped slowly through the courts.

Despite pleas that Somerset should be acknowledged for helping bring the rogue RN's ghastly sixteen-year tear to an end, the medical center was the focus for much of the anger and resentment directed at the health-care industry in the wake of Cullen's arrest. Additional disputes, frustrations, and disappointments that continued through most of the fiscal year from July 2003 to July 2004, and apparently had nothing to do with Cullen, added to the woes.

Hopes by the award-winning hospital of becoming a regional cardiac surgery center were dashed in February when the state health department ruled that Somerset Medical Center hadn't documented a need. Even if it had shown a demand for the center, the state said, it wouldn't have been approved because the hospital improperly closed its thirty-bed psychiatric unit. Huge fines were assessed over the closing before an agreement was reached to reopen the psychiatric unit and reduce the amount of the penalties.

Somerset Medical Center also had to deal with tumultuous labor problems, and an election aimed at forming a nurse's union that the hospital won by a two-to-one margin was overturned by the National Labor Relations Board (NLRB). The NLRB ruled that the hospital unfairly restricted distribution of pro-union literature during organizing efforts.

Amidst all the other turmoil, the medical center's fifty-four-year-old chief, Dennis C. Miller, was hospitalized four times. The good news for Somerset Medical Center was that amidst all the agitation and hubbub, admissions, elective surgery, and emergency-room visits increased. Miller may have been right when he told a reporter that the community didn't blame the hospital for the criminal acts of its former employee.

There may not have been enough good news, because late in July 2004, only two weeks after the Somerset Medical Center's Board of Trustees gave Miller a vote of confidence, the trouble-plagued executive stepped down as the hospital's president and CEO. The hospital issued a news release after a morning meeting of the trustee board, announcing that their chief had "taken a leave of absence for personal reasons and will not be returning." Questions from the press about the surprise move were answered with excuses that respect for the former CEO's privacy prevented sharing more information about his reasons for leaving two years before expiration of his contract.

Miller had achieved great accomplishments since taking over at Somerset Medical Center in 1999 after it marked up a $7 million loss, quickly wiping out the deficit and turning the hospital into a profit-making operation. A $100 million expansion of facilities was launched, and a $20 million fund-raising campaign was opened to pay the bills. But it was a rocky ride at the helm, especially the last eighteen-months or so after the turbulent Cullen case whipped up the waters.

On February 22, 2005, the man who was responsible for so much pain and misery in the two-state area spent his second straight birthday behind bars at the Somerset County Jail. There was no cake.

Four days before Cullen's subdued forty-fifth birthday observance, investigators with the Hunterdon County Prosecutor's Office met with him during a grueling three-hour interview and poured over records of patients who died at the HMC during the last year he worked there. The meeting in the Somerset County Prosecutor's Office across the street from the jail, marked the first time Hunterdon county investigators had sat down with the former RN since his arrest more than a year earlier. The team of sleuths included Raritan Township Detective Scott Lessig; Detective Michael Falcone, who joined the Hunterdon County Prosecutor's Office as an investigator after retiring from the FBI; and Renee Raffino, a forensic nurse. They had been busy snooping into Cullen's activities at the Hunterdon Medical Center.

Despite Cullen's earlier claims during his initial interrogation by Somerset county detectives Braun and Baldwin that the HMC "was a place where nothing, I believe, occurred," authorities weren't ready to accept the word of a confessed serial killer. For more than a year, the Hunterdon county investigators tediously poured over stacks of medical records, conducted interviews and collected other information. The February meeting with Cullen was the first of several, and he eventually inspected the records of about 20 patients who died in the ICU and CCU during his last year at the hospital. The files included patient records that were traps, deliberately assembled to test his honesty. It had already been determined he had nothing to do with the deaths.

Several weeks after the first of the skull sessions, Cullen had confirmed the sleuths' worst suspicions. He belatedly recalled that he had killed at the HMC after all. Clearing up the crimes after so many years was satisfying for the hard-working sherlocks, but troubling questions about possible earlier slayings at the HMC by the Death Angel were left unanswered. Medical records for 1994 when he first began working there, and for 1995, his next full year at the hospital, had already been discarded. The New Jersey Department of Health and Senior Services Records Retention and Disposition Schedule required that medical files be kept for only seven years, and the investigation was initiated barely in time to save the documents from 1996. No files were destroyed after hospital authorities learned about the criminal investigation.

On June 27, 2005, Cullen appeared before state Superior Court Judge Roger A. Mahon at the Hunterdon County Courthouse in Flemington, and pleaded guilty to five counts of first-degree murder for slayings at the HMC. About a dozen survivors of the recently identified victims watched from the gallery as the subdued little man in the yellow-orange jailhouse uniform awkwardly placed his shackled left hand on a Bible to be sworn in. The prisoner's spindly ankles were also shackled.

As he did in earlier court appearances, Cullen stood silently and stared at the defense counsel's desk or at his feet during most of the brief early Monday morning courtroom appearance. A series of questions from Judge Mahon brought barely audible responses of "Yes, Your Honor," and "No, Your Honor."

Cullen listened and watched silently as First Assistant Hunterdon County Prosecutor Stephen C. Lember named the five HMC patients identified as victims. "I used a non-prescribed injection, digoxin, to cause his death," Cullen admitted when he was asked about the death of Leroy G. Sinn. "And it was my intent to cause his death." Similar responses were given when he was asked about the deaths of Earl A. Young, Catherine Dext, Frank Mazzacco and Jesse W. Eichlin. Like most of Cullen's victims in the two-state area, they were all killed with overdoses of digoxin.

Limited by the plea agreement, which ruled out the death penalty, Judge Mahon declared that Cullen would be required to serve life in prison, with a 30-year parole eligibility stipulation for each of the slayings. Seventeen-minutes after the court was convened, the hearing ended and Cullen was returned to the Somerset County Jail.

There was also no early end in sight for the complex and arduous tangle of criminal and civil proceedings making their way so tediously through the courts. Families were still frustrated in their desire to confront the killer of their relatives with victim impact statements, and some even kept a faint hope alive that Cullen would make an effort of some sort to apologize for his ghastly crimes. Mask told reporters several months after his client's arrest that Cullen would like someday to explain his actions to relatives of his victims. They weren't holding their breath.

Chapter 17

Message for a Killer

Zach Martin had hoped to meet with his mother's murderer either in the jail or later after he was sentenced and transported to prison, but that wasn't about to happen while the case was still limping through the courts. Like other survivors, he had been mulling over things that he would like to say to his mother's killer in a victim impact statement. He was disturbed at Cullen's claim that the murders were acts of mercy, and wanted to tell the killer face-to-face that mercy had nothing to do with his mother's death.

"I'm sure Mom had a horrible, painful death because she probably felt her heart rate go up, but she couldn't say anything. She couldn't do anything," Zach confided to a colleague. "Cullen says it was a clean death. I think it was a brutal death."

As a survivor, Zach had a legal right to confront the Death Angel, but even if someday in the distant future they finally faced each other on opposite sides of a bulletproof glass in a prison visitor's room, it didn't mean that Cullen could be forced to utter so much as a single word. So Zach did the next best thing available to him in the meantime. He composed a letter and gave it to Cullen's New Jersey attorney, Johnnie Mask. Mask said he would deliver it to his client.

Addressing his mother's killer as "Charles," Zach introduced himself as the son of Eleanor Stoecker, victim of the first murder of those the former RN pleaded guilty to during the April 2004 hearing in Somerset County State Superior Court. "I have no hatred toward you, and have forgiven you for what you did," he wrote. It wasn't easy, he said, but he learned how hatred for others could destroy one's inner soul.

"I guess we all have demons that we must deal with at one time or another," he continued. "I hope that you will also find peace in your heart. I hope that you will be able to make something positive come out of this horrible situation."

The father of a four-year-old daughter, Zach wrote that he often thought of Cullen's children and hoped they could grow up to become happy adults free of harassment. "In a way, I guess, we both share some of the same memories, tragedies, triumphs and failures," he said. "So in essence, I believe we might have more in common than most might think."

Without getting into specific queries, he advised the prisoner that he was working on a book about the hospital murders and would like to follow up in another letter with questions for him.

"If you are not willing to participate, that's okay too. If you find that you need someone to write, someone to pray with, someone to perhaps become a friend to, I am willing to try," the former seminary student wrote. "Circumstances have linked us forever, and I do not wish to see any more suffering."

Months later, Zach Martin was still waiting for a reply.

Afterword

Charles Cullen was no master criminal like fabled safe-cracker Willie Sutton or international swindler, Victor Lustig, who twice sold the Eiffel Tower to scrap dealers, then topped off his career by audaciously bamboozling Chicago crime boss Al Capone out of $5,000. He wasn't even a brilliant archfiend like the fictional Professor Moriarty, who was locked in epic battles of wits with supersleuth Sherlock Holmes.

He was a pathetic, mentally addled, lifelong loser who was in and out of psychiatric hospitals and mental-health clinics, couldn't commit suicide despite more than twenty attempts, couldn't pay his bills—although he earned a better annual salary than most middle-class Americans, couldn't keep his marriage together, and committed so many glaring blunders during his lethal career as a health-care killer that he might just as well have signed his name in blood on the bodies of his victims.

Yet, while sprinkling a trail of evidence as clear as Hansel and Gretel's bread crumbs (before they were gobbled up by birds), he managed to maintain a killing career that spanned nearly sixteen years and claimed a still-unknown number of lives before he was stopped and brought to justice. Cullen was probably truthful when he told Detective

Baldwin two days after his arrest that he thought he wanted to be caught.

He knew when he was the only nurse on duty on a particular ward and stole medications or poisoned patients on his shift, and when he used his nurse's ID number to tap repeatedly into the Pyxis device to obtain unauthorized medications, that he was leaving glaring "catch me" signals in his trail. "I knew—I knew that they kept permanent records, and I knew that even if I entered it, that they would see those entries," he said of the Pyxis thefts during his lengthy interview with Braun and Baldwin.

Cullen was also aware he was leaving his fingerprints behind when he stole, then tossed away large amounts of medications at St. Luke's. He didn't bother to use rubber gloves while helping himself, even though he knew that his fingerprints were on file with law enforcement authorities as a result of his arrest and conviction in the stalking incident way back in 1993. "They had my fingerprints. I didn't try and disguise my fingerprints," he said.

He was suspected of underhanded behavior by authorities at three or four hospitals, he told the sleuths, and "they didn't do anything."

A confessed serial killer with a record of psychiatric breakdowns and suicide attempts may not be the most credible commentator about such things, but law enforcement agencies accumulated sufficient additional evidence to back up his observation. They showed that in all too many cases lax security measures, glaring lapses of judgment, and professional cowardice contributed to the tragedy. When he was finally fired, forced to quit, or anything else was done to protect patients and stop the slaughter, it was usually too little or too late.

A prosecutor told reporters there was "no evidence" that accomplices assisted or joined in with the malignant nurse during the extended murder spree, but that doesn't mean there isn't an excess of blame to go around. Trial lawyers, teamed up with survivors of known and suspected victims, are already working on that aspect of the case. But inflicting collateral financial damage on institutions that may or may not be found to have been legally negligent for contributing to the dreadful carnage won't bring the dead back to life or prevent another Death Angel from following in Cullen's bloody footsteps. Somewhere in the United States a homicidal nurse is probably killing hospital or nursing-home patients today.

ICU nurses play a unique frontline role in caregiving, and they must make decisions that people in few other professions are expected to make. There are times when terminally ill patients enduring intense agony can be helped only by being given pain-relieving medications that may include side effects that could hasten death. Nurses, not doctors, are the individuals who spend the most time with patients and are the closest witnesses to suffering. Providing adequate pain relief permitted by the treatment plan worked out by physicians is one of the main roles of critical-care nurses. But in their efforts to alleviate suffering, they must exercise great care not to violate stringent rules of conduct set in place to protect the lives of patients.

Sometimes, unfortunately, like the nurses in the Pennsylvania University study who admitted hastening the deaths of some patients, they stray over the line and make decisions they have no legal or ethical right to make. At the time of Cullen's arrest there were about 2.7 million nurses in the United States, but it takes only a few renegades who abuse their position of trust to sully the reputation of an entire profession. It only took one to claim the lives of Eleanor Stoecker, Father Gall, Ottomar Schramm, Helen Dean, and more than twenty other patients.

Critical-care nurses working with the most seriously ill patients sometimes burn out, but when they burn out, they should get out. Was burnout from the emotional pressures and high-level responsibilities of accepting an assignment to a burn unit on Cullen's very first job as a nurse to blame for his horrendous behavior? Who knows?

He already had tried suicide at least twice, was ushered out of the navy—probably with a medical or less than honorable discharge—and his tenuous hold on sanity was frayed and fried long before he ever enrolled in nursing school.

Considering the fragile state of Cullen's mental health, he was not the best candidate for handling the enormous responsibilities of being a critical-care nurse that he experienced throughout his sixteen-year career as an RN. It is difficult for families who lost relatives to Cullen's murderous rampage, and for just about anyone else who is paying attention, to understand how employers could close their eyes to psychotic episodes and suicide attempts by the troubled RN and permit him to continue working with critically ill patients.

When he attempted suicide after stalking his fellow RN, he was treated by colleagues in the emergency room at the same hospital he worked in, before being sent off for treatment at a mental-health clinic and a psychiatric hospital. Two months later he was back working at Warren, presumably because the hospital didn't dare discriminate against someone with mental problems. Would one of his employers intervene finally if he was caught naked and howling at the moon? survivors might have asked.

Cullen should have been recognized for what he was years before he ever worked his first night shift at the Somerset Medical Center. He didn't just emerge out of the blue as a bizarre new kind of serial predator when he murdered his first patient at St. Barnabas, or slaughtered whole strings of patients at St. Luke's and at Somerset Medical Center. Hospital homicides are not isolated aberrations, and Cullen's kind of self-appointed "executioners in white" have been with us for a long time. Donald Harvey, Orville Lynn Majors, Richard Diaz and baby-killer Genene Jones provided grim proof of that long before Cullen publicly emerged on the scene. Employed in south Texas during the early 1980s, Nurse Jones over-

dosed babies with medications and basked in the attention she attracted while working over the tiny forms
during code-blue emergencies. Everyone in a position of
authority in the health-care business, hospital workers and
nursing-home administrators and supervisors, directors
of regulatory agencies, professional nursing associations,
and others knew about health-care killers—or they should
have known.

People with expertise in the field were already advocat-
ing routine psychological screening for nurses and calling
on hospitals to promote the practice. Firefighters submit
to psychological screening, and Andrea Aughenbaugh,
chief executive officer of the New Jersey State Nurses Association, recommended similar safeguards to ensure that
nurses were also mentally and physically sound, according
to the Associated Press.

If Cullen's late father, Edmond, was hired as a bus driver
today, he would be embarking on a profession that in
most areas of the country requires rigorous and regular
competence reviews. The same holds true for airline pilots.
The requirement is good and proper because when a bus
driver takes the wheel he may have the lives of sixty or more
passengers in his hands. An airline pilot flying a loaded 727
or a 757 may be responsible for the lives of hundreds of
people. Passengers shouldn't be expected to take a chance
of entrusting their safety to a bus driver or an airline pilot
who is incompetent, fighting depression, hears disembod-
ied voices, or is experiencing a drug-or alcohol-induced
high.

But if the competence, mental health, and possible destructive habits of firemen, bus drivers, and pilots are important enough to justify close supervision and oversight,
then it's time that similar safeguards are put in place for
men and women in the health-care professions—designed
with sufficient care so that they actually work. At most of
the facilities where Cullen worked, whatever screening
methods that were in place for new-hire nurses to weed out

drug and alcohol abusers, brutal sexual predators, the dangerously mentally ill and unstable, or simply burned-out professionals failed miserably in the intent to protect patients.

Much of the fault for the security breakdown was human. Prehiring and regular competence reviews, including criminal background checks, should be mandatory throughout the country for medical professionals. There is no question that more effective screening methods are necessary to pinpoint and remove potentially dangerous individuals from jobs in the medical field. That is especially true for hospital nurses, doctors, and other health-care professionals who work closely with patients or residents of medical facilities and nursing homes.

Importantly, steps must also be taken to ensure that known misfits with appalling work records are identified and the information accompanies them when they apply for new jobs at other facilities. That is all vitally necessary, and a much-needed remedy to protect helpless patients in hospitals and nursing homes in the future.

In too many instances hospital authorities, who overlooked obvious violations of protocol for handling medication and caring for patients, or fired or forced out the bad actor without reporting him to prosecutors, police or the state nursing board, appeared to have established self-perpetuation as their number one priority. The number one priority should have been patient safety, and people died because of the mix-up.

On May 3, 2005, New Jersey acting Governor Codey signed legislation designed to prevent health-care workers with suspicious or poor work histories from being allowed to skip from job to job because prospective new employers were unaware of their backgrounds. The law beefed up existing reporting requirements, made truthful job references obligatory and shielded employers from lawsuits for complying with the statute. Like the Patient Safety Act signed by McGreevey in 2004, the new statute was an important step in the right direction.

Importantly, the bill signed by Codey at St. Joseph's Senior Home in Woodbridge, where he and state Senator Joseph Vitale of Middlesex county, and Assemblywoman Loretta Weinberg of Bergen county, met with relatives of some of Cullen's victims, closed the job reference loophole left by the earlier legislation. Vitale, who sponsored the bill in the New Jersey senate, said input from Cullen was an important factor in shoring up weak spots in the reporting system. The former RN provided a blueprint of his actions, during questioning by investigators, the legislator said.

Approximately six-weeks later, on June 15, 2005, Pennsylvania Governor Edward G. Rendell signed legislation providing legal immunity to employers in the Keystone State who provide honest job evaluations and work histories to prospective new employers. Authored by state Senator Patricia H. Vance of Cumberland county, the new statute permitted employees who dispute the information to sue for damages if they prove in court that the employer failed to act in good faith.

Hospitals, of all places, should not be refuges for mediocrities or cowards who refuse to see wrong until it is too late. Tough-minded leaders with the energy, imagination, and intestinal fortitude to tackle unpleasant problems, and let the ax fall where it will, should be at the helm of the hospitals and of the state and federal agencies that oversee their operation.

The primary question on the minds of many of the relatives of patients who were attacked and murdered in the New Jersey and Pennsylvania hospitals is focused on the punishment meted out to the killer. Is life in prison proper punishment for a man who is responsible for such widespread misery and who committed the atrocious crimes that Cullen confessed and pleaded guilty to?

If the death penalty is used as the yardstick, it seems that there is no bag limit for some of the most fearsome and dangerous of all serial killers—Death Angels. John Wayne Gacy, Jr. Ted "the Troller" Bundy, "Nightstalker" Richard Ramirez, Aileen Wuornos, and other masters of horror and torture have almost routinely been sentenced to death for their monstrous crimes—some have even been executed— but somehow medical serial killers consistently elude capital punishment.

Regardless of how many victims are claimed—and no matter if they are the frail, elderly, and gravely ill, or innocent infants with the bad luck to be born in the wrong hospital—somehow the crimes of ruthless health-care killers, like Cullen, Jones, Harvey, Diaz, and Majors, never seem to be bad enough to justify capital punishment.

Even Harold Shipman, the drug-addicted physician who pleaded guilty to the murder of fifteen patients and was later found to have killed two hundred more before his bloody twenty-three-year rampage was ended, never had to worry about dying in the gas chamber, the electric chair, or by lethal injection. England abolished capital punishment years ago, and Dr. Death never faced the possibility of execution, but was sentenced to spend the rest of his life behind bars. He died at the end of a hangman's noose of his own making when he attached bedsheets to window bars in his cell at Wakefield Prison in northern England and committed suicide. His death occurred on January 13, 2004, one day before his fifty-eighth birthday.

If the death penalty is ever to be carried out in order to protect the innocent and send an unmistakable message to criminals that some crimes are so odious and chillingly frightful that execution is society's only responsible answer, special accommodations should be reserved in death chambers and electric chairs for medical serial killers.

Anti-death-penalty activists and other apologists for the criminal class are unlikely to agree with that, but long ago the arguments on both sides of the Cullen case were made mute by acceptance of the plea agreement. Whether or not it is right and proper that Cullen die in the unused gas chamber in New Jersey or in the rarely used death chamber in Pennsylvania, as Emily Stoecker hoped, it isn't going to happen. The death penalty for the Death Angel is permanently off the table.

That's disturbing because rogue nurses and other health-care workers are the most uniquely bloodcurdling of all serial killers. Studies show that at any given time, one in three Americans is either hospitalized or has relatives or close friends who are being treated by health-care professionals. Everyone at some period of their lives is almost certain to spend time in a hospital or nursing home. And at some time in their lives, almost everyone will have someone they love in a hospital or nursing home, who is potential prey for a psychologically twisted and lethally malevolent nurse or a doctor, like Cullen, Jones, and Shipman.

A preponderance of victims of serial killers put themselves at special risk by their behavior. Prostitutes of both sexes, drug abusers, runaways, hitchhikers, and people who pick up hitchhikers are classic victims. They don't deserve to die for their errors or errant ways, but their bad choices helped to place them in the crosshairs of serial killers.

Becoming a patient in a hospital or nursing home isn't a choice, and society and the administrators of medical facilities can do a far better job than is being done now of protecting patients while they're there. There have been other calls for changes in the system after previous outbreaks of health-care murders or the exposure of a series of especially heinous hospital slayings; then things slid back into the old routine after the uproar died down. Frail, infirm, and helpless patients continued to die mysteriously in hospitals and nursing and retirement homes.

It is long past the time for public officials and hospital administrators to stop talking and begin doing if they are really sincere about addressing safety concerns and restoring public confidence in the health-care system. Legislators, public servants, and everyone else who cares about

their personal safety—and the safety of those they love—
should see that they do.

It is already too late for all those who died at the hands
of the puny little weirdo who betrayed their trust and his
profession by turning on them with such deadly savagery
in New Jersey and Pennsylvania health-care centers. It is also
too late for the people who loved them to avoid the agony
and regret over lives cut short by a cowardly medical serial
killer. All they can do is wait and hope that public servants
finally replace talk with action and do their job—and
hope for justice in the still-developing saga of Charles
Cullen, the Death Angel.

Time Line

February 22, 1960—Charles Cullen is born in West Orange, New Jersey, to Edmond Cullen, a bus driver, and Florence Cullen, a homemaker.

September 1960—Charles is not yet seven months old when his father dies.

1969—Charles is nine years old when he swallows a mixture of chemicals from his chemistry set in an attempt to kill himself. It is the first of numerous suicide attempts he will make throughout his life.

December 6, 1977—He is a seventeen-year-old high-school junior in West Orange when his mother is killed in a traffic accident.

April 1978—Cullen joins the navy after dropping out of high school.

June 1979—He is assigned to Submarine Group Six.

July 30, 1979—Cullen joins the crew of the nuclear-powered *Woodrow Wilson* (SSBN-624).

October 30, 1981—He is assigned to the USS *Canopus* (AS-34), a submarine tender.

March 30, 1984—Cullen is discharged from the navy, possibly after a suicide attempt and treatment at a psychiatric hospital.

1984—Cullen enrolls in the Mountainside Hospital School of Nursing in Montclair, New Jersey.

May 1987—Cullen graduates from Mountainside as a registered nurse (RN).

June 7, 1987—Cullen marries Adrienne Taub in West Orange.

June 1987—Cullen begins working at St. Barnabas Medical Center in Livingston, New Jersey.

June 11, 1988—Former Jersey City municipal judge John W. Yengo Sr. is injected with a toxic dose of lidocaine and dies at St. Barnabas, after being admitted with an allergic reaction to a blood-thinning drug.

January 1992—Cullen is fired from St. Barnabas after an investigation by hospital authorities to determine who has been tampering with stored IV bags. Police are not advised of the probe.

February 1992—Cullen begins working in the coronary-care unit (CCU) at Warren Hospital in Phillipsburg, New Jersey.

January 15, 1993—Adrienne files for divorce.

January 22, 1993—Cullen is served with divorce papers at work.

March 9, 1993—Lucy Mugavero, ninety, Phillipsburg, New Jersey, is given a fatal injection by Cullen and dies at Warren Hospital.

March 23, 1993—Cullen is arrested for breaking into the home of a female nurse and colleague at Warren Hospital he has become infatuated with.

April 16, 1993—Adrienne files a domestic violence complaint and applies for a restraining order. Cullen is admitted to the Carrier Clinic in Belle Mead, New Jersey and a few weeks later he is treated at the Greystone Park Psychiatric Hospital in Parsippany, New Jersey. The restraining order is later granted.

June 11, 1993—Cullen begins representing himself in court.

June 30, 1993—The second restraining order is

granted to Cullen's wife, barring him from visits with his children.

July 12, 1993—Cullen's request for a public defender in the trespassing case is denied.

July 23, 1993—Mary Natoli, eighty-five, Phillipsburg, New Jersey, dies at Warren Hospital.

August 10, 1993—Cullen pleads guilty to defiant trespass and harassment for breaking into the home of his colleague.

August 11, 1993—Another suicide attempt by Cullen fails.

September 1, 1993—Helen C. Dean, ninety-one, of Lopatcong Township, New Jersey, dies soon after leaving Warren Hospital and having been admitted to a nursing home.

December 1, 1993—Cullen quits his job at Warren Hospital, two months after he and other nurses are questioned in Helen Dean's death.

April 1994—Cullen begins working at Hunterdon Medical Center in Flemington, New Jersey.

June 1994—Cullen is issued a nursing license by the Commonwealth of Pennsylvania.

December 7, 1994—The divorce becomes final. Adrienne retains custody of the girls.

January 21, 1996—Leroy G. Sinn, seventy-one, of Tewksbury Township, Hunterdon County, dies of a lethal dose of digoxin at the Hunterdon Medical Center (HMC).

May 31, 1996—Earl A. Young, seventy-five, of Flemington, dies of a lethal dose of digoxin at the HMC.

June 9, 1996—Catherine Dext, forty-nine, of Hampton, dies at the HMC of a lethal dose of digoxin.

June 24, 1996—Frank J. Mazzacco, Jr., sixty-six, of Lambertville, dies at the HMC of an overdose of digoxin.

July 10, 1996—Jesse W. Eichlin, eighty, of Franklin

Township, Hunterdon County, dies at the HMC of a lethal dose of digoxin.

October 1996—Cullen resigns from his job at Hunterdon Medical Center.

November 1996—Cullen begins working at Morristown Memorial Hospital in Morristown, New Jersey.

August 1997—Cullen leaves his job at Morristown Memorial. Hospital authorities later say he was fired for poor performance.

October 30, 1997—Cullen is treated in the emergency room at Warren Hospital for depression, then admitted to Greystone Park Psychiatric Hospital in Parsippany, New Jersey.

February 1998—Cullen is hired by the Liberty Nursing and Rehabilitation Center in Allentown, Pennsylvania. It is his first job in Pennsylvania, and his first job in a nursing home.

May 7, 1998—Francis J. Henry Jr., eighty-three, of Richland Township, who was admitted to Liberty after a traffic accident, is rushed to Lehigh Valley Hospital with insulin poisoning. After treatment he is returned to Liberty.

May 13, 1998—Cullen declares bankruptcy.

May 19, 1998—Henry dies, and the traffic accident is listed as the cause of death. Laboratory tests later suggest that insulin poisoning may have been a factor.

October 1, 1998—Cullen is fired from Liberty after an elderly resident's arm is broken during a scuffle with him. He is accused of failure to follow proper procedures for administering drugs.

November 1998—Cullen obtains periodic work through a temporary agency and begins filling in as a night nurse at Easton Hospital in Wilson, Pennsylvania. He is assigned to the intensive-care unit (ICU).

December 1998—Still working for the agency, Cullen also begins filling in as a night nurse in the burn unit at the Lehigh Valley Hospital in Salisbury Township, in suburban Allentown.

December 30, 1998—Laboratory tests on the blood of Ottomar A. Schramm, a cancer patient in Easton Hospital's intensive care, disclose a high level of digoxin. The powerful heart medicine was not prescribed for him.

December 31, 1998—Schramm, seventy-eight, of Nazareth, Pennsylvania, dies, and Easton Hospital authorities notify Northampton County coroner Zachary Lysek of the suspicious death.

March 1999—Cullen leaves Easton Hospital.

August 1999—Lysek meets with Easton Hospital authorities to review the autopsy results in Schramm's death. He recommends an inquiry, which will continue for eight months.

August 31, 1999—Matthew L. Mattern, twenty-two, of Shamokin, dies while under treatment in Lehigh Valley Hospital's burn unit.

1999—Late in the year, Kimberly Pepe, a registered nurse who blames Cullen for being forced out of her job at the Liberty nursing home, files a wrongful firing lawsuit against her former employer. She points to Cullen in the suit as a suspect in Henry's insulin poisoning.

January 3, 2000—Cullen is treated at the Warren County Crisis Center after a suicide attempt in his basement apartment in Phillipsburg.

February 26, 2000—Stella Danielczyk, seventy-three, of Larksville, dies in the Lehigh Valley Hospital's burn unit.

April 2000—Cullen leaves his job at Lehigh Valley Hospital.

June 2000—Cullen begins working in the CCU at St. Luke's Hospital in the Allentown-Bethlehem suburb of Fountain Hill.

February 11, 2001—John P. Gallagher, ninety, is a

patient at St. Luke's after fracturing a hip in a fall when he dies in the CCU.

March 2001—Cullen's brother Edmond dies, leaving him as the last surviving male in the family.

June 22, 2001—Irene Krapf, seventy-nine, of Tamaqua, dies in the CCU at St. Luke's less than an hour after arrival at the hospital for pacemaker surgery.

November 8, 2001—William M. Park, seventy-two, of Franklin Township, is being treated for a heart attack when he dies in St. Luke's CCU.

December 29, 2001—Paul Galgon, seventy-two, of Bethlehem, is recovering from routine pacemaker surgery when he survives a life-threatening overdose of digoxin at St. Luke's. He succumbs nine hours later to what are later said to be unrelated causes.

January 9, 2002—Samuel Spangler, eighty, of East Allen Township, is a cancer patient admitted to St. Luke's for a blood transfusion when he dies in the CCU of a heart attack.

May 5, 2002—Daniel George, eighty-two, Bethlehem, Pennsylvania, dies at St. Luke's after undergoing heart surgery.

June 2, 2002—Edward O'Toole, seventy-six, of Fountain Hill, dies at St. Luke's. A cache of arrhythmia and blood pressure medications are discovered stashed in a needle-disposal bin in the hospital's CCU.

June 3, 2002—Stolen medications are again found stashed in the needle-disposal bin.

June 4, 2002—Cullen is questioned about the stolen drugs and barred from contact with patients.

June 2002—St. Luke's notifies the Pennsylvania State Board of Nursing of suspicions that Cullen was wrongly diverting drugs. He is interviewed by an investigator and denies doing anything wrong.

June 7, 2002—Cullen resigns under pressure from St. Luke's after being accused of diverting medications.

June 2002—A nurse who worked with Cullen tips off

Northampton County coroner Zachary Lysek that Cullen was investigated by St. Luke's for stealing medication and may have been harming patients. A colleague passes on similar information to the Pennsylvania state police.

July 8, 2002—Cullen is hired by Sacred Heart Hospital in Allentown.

July 24, 2002—Cullen is still in orientation when other nurses issue an ultimatum to the Sacred Heart human resources director declaring that either he goes or they go. He is fired for what his employers describe as "interpersonal problems."

July 26, 2002—A report is completed by St. Luke's pinpointing Cullen as the person responsible for hiding medications.

August 29, 2002—At a meeting arranged by Lysek, he and the tipster nurse sit down with Lehigh County coroner Scott Grim and DA James B. Martin to discuss Cullen's activities at St. Luke's. Martin opens an investigation.

September 3, 2002—While continuing its own inquiry into the deaths of sixty-seven patients, St. Luke's writes the Pennsylvania Nursing Board, notifying the agency of Cullen's unprofessional conduct, and calling for an investigation.

September 6, 2002—At Martin's request, Pennsylvania state police launch an inquiry into the problems with Cullen and stolen medications at St. Luke's.

September 9, 2002—Cullen begins working at the Somerset Medical Center in Somerville, New Jersey.

September 26, 2002—The Pennsylvania State Nursing Board begins an investigation of Cullen's activities at St. Luke's.

January 2, 2003—St. Luke's authorities learn that Cullen is under investigation by the Lehigh County DA.

January 6, 2003—The Pennsylvania State Nursing

Board probe is completed, and the report is shared with state police investigators.

February 12, 2003—Eleanor Stoecker, sixty, of Bedminster, New Jersey, dies in the Somerset Medical Center's ICU after she is injected with digoxin.

February 23, 2003—Joyce E. Mangini, seventy-four, of Raritan, New Jersey, dies in the Somerset CCU after she is injected with Pavulon.

February 23, 2003—Giacomino J. Toto, eighty-nine, of Bridgewater, New Jersey, dies in the Somerset critical-care unit after being injected with Pavulon.

February 27, 2003—A forensic pathologist is retained by Lehigh County to review death records at St. Luke's.

March 10, 2003—A cardiologist from the University of Pennsylvania is contracted by St. Luke's to look for "inexplicable" clinical events in 69 sets of patient files.

March 11, 2003—John J. Shanagher, eighty-three, of Bridgewater, New Jersey, dies in the Somerset CCU after he is injected with norepinephrine.

April 6, 2003—Dorothea K. Hoagland, eighty, of Middlesex, New Jersey, dies in the ICU after an injection of norepinephrine.

May 5, 2003—Melvin T. Simcoe, sixty-six, of Green Brook, New Jersey, dies in the ICU after he is injected with sodium nitroprusside.

May 15, 2003—Michael T. Strenko, twenty-one, of Manville, New Jersey, dies in the ICU after he is injected with norepinephrine.

May 28, 2003—Lehigh County DA James Martin writes to St. Luke's, advising hospital authorities he has closed his investigation and has no plans to file for prosecution. He reserves the right to reopen the probe.

June 16, 2003—Cancer patient Jin Kyung Han, forty, of Basking Ridge, New Jersey, is injected with a potentially lethal dose of digoxin, at the Somerset intensive-care unit, but recovers when an antidote is administered. Mrs. Han was released from the hospital, then readmitted on September 5, and died of causes unrelated to the digoxin injection several weeks earlier.

June 26, 2003—Somerset Medical Center sends a sample of herbal tea to the New Jersey poison control center, requesting an analysis by toxicologists to determine if it could be responsible for the elevated levels of digoxin found in the system of Jin Kyung Han. She is identified as "Patient 3."

June 28, 2003—The Very Reverend Florian J. Gall, sixty-eight, of Whitehouse Station, New Jersey, dies at Somerset after he is injected with digoxin.

July 9, 2003—Dr. Steven M. Marcus, executive director of the New Jersey Poison Information and Education System (PIES), warns the Somerset Medical Center that the drug overdose of Mrs. Jin Kyung Han may have resulted from "a malicious act."

July 13, 2003—Pasquale M. Napolitano, eighty, of Peapack and Gladstone, New Jersey, dies in Somerset's CCU after an injection with dobutamine.

July 22, 2003—Dr. Marcus reports after an investigation that Somerset Medical patient number 3 was given a deliberate overdose of digoxin. The woman recovered from the overdose but dies later of other causes.

August 11, 2003—Christopher B. Hardgrove, thirty-eight, of Somerville, New Jersey, dies in the CCU after he is injected with norepinephrine.

August 27, 2003—Frances Agoada, eighty-three, of Franklin Township, New Jersey, survives after she is given an injection of unprescribed medication.

September 20, 2003—Krishnakant Upadhyay, seventy, of Bridgewater, New Jersey, dies at Somerset after an injection of digoxin.

September 23, 2003—James R. Strickland, eighty-three, of Bowie, Maryland, dies in the medical center after an injection of digoxin.

October 3, 2003—Somerset Medical Center reports "a number of potentially suspicious deaths" to the Somerset County Prosecutor's Office. Prosecutor Wayne J. Forrest opens an investigation.

October 21, 2003—Edward P. Zizik, seventy-three, of Three Bridges, New Jersey, dies after he is injected with digoxin.

October 2003—Late in the month Father Gall's body is exhumed from a church cemetery in Woodbridge, and an autopsy is conducted.

October 31, 2003—Cullen is fired from Somerset Medical Center. It is more than three months after Dr. Marcus's warning that one of Cullen's patients could have been killed by a deliberate overdose.

October 31, 2003—New Jersey police contact St. Luke's Hospital in Fountain Hill, Pennsylvania, and request Cullen's employment records.

December 11, 2003—Somerset County prosecutor Wayne J. Forrest confirms that his office is investigating the death of Father Gall at the medical center.

December 12, 2003—Police arrest Cullen shortly after he drives away from the Office restaurant in Bridgewater, New Jersey, where he and a girlfriend ordered an early dinner. He is held on a single charge of murder in Father Gall's death and another charge of attempted murder for the efforts to kill Mrs. Han.

December 14, 2003—Cullen tells homicide investigators during a seven-hour interrogation that he administered lethal drug injections to thirty to forty patients in New Jersey and Pennsylvania during a sixteen-year murder binge.

December 15, 2003—Cullen is charged in Somerset County with Father Gall's slaying and the attempt on Mrs. Han's life.

December 16, 2003—Law enforcement authorities are banned from further questioning of Cullen by Somerset County deputy public defender Johnnie

Mask, who was assigned to represent the murder suspect. Gary N. Asteak, a private practice attorney with offices in Easton and Nazareth, was named to represent Cullen in Pennsylvania.

December 16, 2003—Warren County prosecutor Thomas S. Ferguson reopens the decade-old investigation into the death of Helen C. Dean.

December 17, 2003—After spending most of the day in a padded cell at the Somerset County Jail, Cullen is transferred to the Anne Klein Forensic Center at the maximum-security Trenton State Psychiatric Hospital for psychiatric evaluation.

December 17, 2003—Cullen's New Jersey nursing license is voluntarily surrendered.

December 18, 2003—Mask announces that his client will not help in the rapidly expanding investigation unless authorities agree not to seek the death penalty. The New Jersey Department of Health and Senior Services issued a disciplinary notice to the Somerset Medical Center for failure to tell the family of the Reverend Florian J. Gall that he died of an overdose of digoxin.

December 2003—In Pennsylvania, Northampton County DA John Morganelli names Cullen as a suspect in the death of Ottomar Schramm at Easton Hospital.

December 2003—The Pennsylvania State Board of Nursing temporarily suspends Cullen's license.

January 2004—Helen Dean's body is exhumed for an autopsy.

January 6, 2004—Cullen is returned to the Somerset County Jail from the Anne Klein Forensic Center in suburban Trenton.

January 7, 2004—Prosecutors and DAs from seven counties in New Jersey and Pennsylvania meet with other law enforcement authorities in the offices of Somerset County prosecutor Forrest to coordinate their investigations, and to discuss the demand for immunity from the death penalty for Cullen in return for his cooperation.

February 22, 2004—Cullen observes his first birthday behind bars when he turns forty-four in the Somerset County Jail.

April 29, 2004—At a hearing in state superior court in Somerville, Cullen pleads guilty to the murder of thirteen patients and the attempted murder of two others at Somerset Medical Center. The appearance seals the plea agreement with prosecutors in two states, and binds him to a promise to help authorities identify other victims he killed or attempted to kill during his sixteen-year nursing career in New Jersey and Pennsylvania.

May 19, 2004—Cullen pleads guilty to the murder of three elderly patients at Warren Hospital, bringing his total of known homicide victims in New Jersey to sixteen. The plea marks him as the most prolific killer in the state's history, surpassing the 1949 outburst of violence by WWII veteran Howard Unruh, who shot and killed thirteen people in a single day.

October 7, 2004—Appearing in Northampton County Court in Easton, Cullen pleads guilty to first-degree murder in the death of Ottomar Schramm in Easton Hospital.

October 14, 2004—Six new murder charges are filed against Cullen by Lehigh County DA James B. Martin.

November 17, 2004—Cullen pleads guilty in Lehigh County Court of Common Pleas in Allentown to the murder of five patients at St. Luke's Hospital and one patient at Lehigh Valley Hospital. He also pleaded guilty to the attempted murder of three other patients at Lehigh Valley. The pleas bring the official two-state death toll to twenty-three.

December 16, 2004—Cullen pleads guilty in state superior court in Newark to the 1988 slaying of former Jersey City municipal judge John W. Yengo Sr. The court appearance brings the Death Angel's known two-state death toll to twenty-four, in addition to five admitted murder attempts.

January 7, 2005—Sentencing hearings for the murder of patients in hospitals in Lehigh and Northampton County hospitals in Pennsylvania are postponed indefinitely because Cullen hadn't yet been sentenced for his crimes in New Jersey, as required by the plea agreement.

February 9, 2005—Petitions by the New Jersey Victims of Crime Compensation Board and the New Jersey Crime Victims' Law Center are granted, allowing them to enter the Cullen case as "friends of the court." The approval by Judge Paul Armstrong opens the door for the victim's advocacy agencies to file briefs and present arguments in support of the prosecution and on behalf of families.

February 22, 2005—Cullen observes his second consecutive birthday behind bars at the Somerset County Jail, when he turns forty-five.

February 26, 2005—Investigators with the Hunterdon County Prosecutor's Office meet for the first time with Cullen since his arrest. It is the first of several skull sessions, during which they provide him with medical records and other information that leads him to recall five murders committed while he worked at the Hunterdon Medical Center.

March 2005—U.S. government authorities disclose that federal agents have opened an investigation of hospitals in Pennsylvania and New Jersey to determine if federal laws were broken by failure to act more promptly against Cullen.

May 3, 2005—New Jersey acting Governor Richard Codey signs legislation designed to shield hospitals from lawsuits for providing truthful job references, and initiate other reforms to prevent problem health-care workers from floating from job to job as Cullen did.

June 15, 2005—Pennsylvania Governor Edward G. Rendell signs legislation providing legal immunity to employers who provide honest job evaluations and work histories to prospective new employers.

June 27, 2005—Cullen pleads guilty to five counts of first-degree murder for slayings committed at the Hunterdon Medical Center. Accepted by State Superior Court Judge Roger Mahon at the Hunterdon County Courthouse in Flemington, the guilty pleas bring the total number of murders in two states admitted by Cullen to 29, in addition to five attempted slayings.

Plea Agreement

PLEA AGREEMENT between Charles Cullen and prosecutors in New Jersey and Pennsylvania:

PARTIES

This is an Agreement between the New Jersey Office of the Attorney General, by and through the Division of Criminal Justice; the County Prosecutor's offices of Somerset, Essex, Hunterdon, Morris and Warren within the State of New Jersey, (collectively referred to as "the New Jersey Counties"); the District Attorneys of Lehigh and Northampton Counties, (collectively referred to as "the Pennsylvania Counties"); and Charles Cullen ("the Defendant") by and through his attorneys, the State of New Jersey office of the Public Defender.

PURPOSE

The purpose of this Agreement is to set forth the terms of a global plea agreement between the New Jersey Counties and the Pennsylvania Counties with the Defendant for the murders and attempted murders for which he claims responsibility, and that occurred between the time period of 1984 through 2003 while Defendant was employed as a nurse in the New Jersey and Pennsylvania Counties. In ex-

change, these law enforcement agencies agree not to seek
the death penalty, but will recommend sentences of life im-
prisonment as set forth herein in the prosecution of these
crimes, provided Defendant fully cooperates according to
the terms and conditions of this Agreement. It is the intention of the parties that this Agreement shall be incorporated
by reference in any other plea agreements entered into by
the Defendant for the crimes covered by this Agreement.

TERMS AND CONDITIONS

l. Representation of Defendant

For purpose of this Agreement, the Defendant agrees to
be represented by the State of New Jersey Office of the
Public Defender, not only for murder committed in the
New Jersey Counties, but also for murders that are or shall
be attributable to him that occurred in the Pennsylvania
Counties. The State of New Jersey Office of the Public Defender also agrees to represent the Defendant in the State
of New Jersey and the Commonwealth of Pennsylvania for
the cases contained and contemplated in this Agreement.

2. Waiver of Pennsylvania Attorney

Defendant waives any right to have a Pennsylvania attorney
appointed for him to negotiate the terms of this Agreement,
and in doing so, acknowledges that the terms of this Agreement are binding upon the Defendant in the event of subsequent prosecution(s) in the Pennsylvania Counties.

3. Pro Hac Vice Admission of Johnnie Mask, Esq.

Defendant's New Jersey Public Defender, Johnnie Mask,
Esq. attests that he will apply to be admitted pro hac vice in
the Commonwealth of Pennsylvania and will comply with any
other rules of the Commonwealth of Pennsylvania courts for
purposes of representing the Defendant in connection with

this Agreement and for any subsequent charges filed by the Pennsylvania Counties under the terms of this Agreement.

4. Scope of the Agreement

All parties acknowledge that the scope of this Agreement is strictly limited to the specific jurisdictions where the Defendant was employed as a nursing student and later as a licensed nurse in various hospital and medical facilities within the New Jersey counties of Somerset, Essex, Hunterdon, Morris and Warren within the State of New Jersey and/or the counties of Northampton and Lehigh within the Commonwealth of Pennsylvania from 1984 through 2003.

5. Agreement Intended as Part of Formal Plea Agreements

Defendant acknowledges that this Agreement shall be incorporated by reference into any subsequent written plea agreements entered in the courts of the State of New Jersey and/or the Commonwealth of Pennsylvania.

6. Previous Admission of Defendant

Defendant acknowledges that he has previously admitted to causing or attempting to cause the deaths of patients during his nursing career in New Jersey and Pennsylvania between 1984 and 2003. These admissions include: causing or attempting to cause at least two murders while employed as a nurse in Somerset Medical Center, Somerville, New Jersey; a number of murders or attempted murders while employed as a nurse in the counties of Essex, Warren and possibly Morris in New Jersey; and a number of murders or attempted murders in medical facilities in Lehigh County and Northampton County, Pennsylvania.

7. Benefit to Defendant

Defendant expressly acknowledges that in exchange for his truthful, full and complete cooperation with the New

Jersey Counties and the Pennsylvania Counties, he will not be subject to the death penalty for the murders he committed, discloses and pleads guilty to, pursuant to the terms of this Agreement.

8. Sentencing of Defendant to Life Imprisonment in New Jersey

Defendant acknowledges that he has been advised by his attorney that entering guilty pleas to the charges of at least two murders filed by the Somerset County Prosecutor (outlined below) will result in recommendations by the Somerset County Prosecutor of at least two consecutive life sentences which, if imposed by the court, will cause the Defendant to be sentenced to two life sentences with a period of eighty-five percent or approximately one-hundred twenty-seven (127) years of parole ineligibility under the No Early Release Act, NJ. S. A. 2C 43-7.2. Defendant acknowledges that it is the intent of the New Jersey Counties to keep him imprisoned for the rest of his life and that they will make sentencing recommendations accordingly. Nothing in this agreement should be construed to limit the New Jersey Counties from seeking additional consecutive life sentences for the murders outlined in Paragraph 11 or for any additional charges filed and resolved pursuant to this Agreement.

9. Sentencing of Defendant to Life Imprisonment in Pennsylvania

Defendant acknowledges that he has been advised by his attorney that a life sentence in Pennsylvania means life without the possibility of parole. Defendant also acknowledges that any admissions he makes regarding murder or attempted murder pursuant to the terms of this Agreement may result in the Defendant being charged with additional crimes. The Pennsylvania Counties agree that they will not seek the death penalty for the murders, but that

Defendant shall serve a life sentence for each murder for the first degree to which he pleads guilty. Any sentence imposed in the Commonwealth of Pennsylvania shall run consecutively to the sentence(s) imposed in the State of New Jersey; however if the Defendant pleads guilty to more than one murder he committed in the Pennsylvania Counties, then his life sentences in Pennsylvania shall run concurrently with each other. Similarly, Defendant acknowledges that if he pleads guilty to one or more attempted murders either alone, or in addition to a murder he committed in the Pennsylvania Counties, then his sentences in Pennsylvania shall run concurrently with each other, but consecutively to any sentence(s) previously imposed by the courts of the State of New Jersey.

10. Acknowledgment of Guilt

Defendant shall accept criminal responsibility for causing and attempting to cause the deaths of patients whom he has already identified, and whom he will identify through his truthful, full and complete cooperation in connection with future investigations.

11. Entry of Pleas as Initial Step

Defendant agrees to enter guilty pleas as an initial step in his cooperation for the murders in Somerset County, New Jersey of:

FLORIAN J. GALL
ELEANOR STOECKER
JOYCE E. MANGINI
GIACOMINO J. TOTO
JOHN J. SHANAGHER
DOROTHEA K. HOAGLAND
MELVIN T. SIMCOE
MICHAEL T. STRENKO
PASQUALE M. NAPOLITANO

CHRISTOPHER B. HARDGROVE
KRISHNAKANT UPADHYAY
JAMES R. STRICKLAND
EDWARD P. ZIZIK

Defendant also agrees to enter pleas to the attempted murders in Somerset County of:

JIN KYUNG HAN
FRANCES AGOADA

Defendant further agrees to enter a guilty plea for the murder of the first degree in Northampton County, Pennsylvania of:

OTTOMAR SCHRAMM

12. Waiver of Certain Criminal Proceedings

In any murder or attempted murder case set forth or contemplated by this Agreement, the Defendant knowingly and voluntarily waives his rights and if necessary, will execute all documents required by the New Jersey Counties, the Pennsylvania Counties, and their respective courts to: (1) waive indictment by grand jury; (2) waive trial by jury; (3) waive extradition and any rights under the Uniform Extradition Act; (4) waive preliminary hearings including probable cause hearings; (5) waive any pre-trial motions, specifically including, but not limited to, motions for change of venue, change of venire, and motion to suppress statements; (6) waive any speedy trial rights under the United States, New Jersey and Pennsylvania Constitutions, or under the United States, New Jersey or Pennsylvania Rules of Criminal Procedure; (7) waive any right to withdraw any guilty plea entered pursuant to this agreement; (8) waive any and all rights under the Interstate Agreement on Detainers; (9) waive any right to be present in court at the time of sentencing and agree to be sentenced (in absentia) if necessary; (10) waive any post-sentencing motions or Post Conviction Relief Act motions attacking his guilty pleas or sentences in the New Jersey, Pennsylvania and/or Federal Courts.

Defendant acknowledges that if he does not waive any of his rights as outlined above, or withdraws or appeals any guilty plea entered pursuant to this agreement, the New Jersey Counties and Pennsylvania Counties may at their discretion declare the Agreement void and be returned to the same legal position they enjoyed prior to entering into this Agreement with the defendant.

13. Cooperation

Defendant agrees, when requested, to provide truthful, full and complete cooperation to the New Jersey Counties and the Pennsylvania Counties throughout the course of their investigations and to help them identify as many of his victims as possible whose death he caused or attempted to cause.

a. The New Jersey Counties and the Pennsylvania Counties agree to evaluate Defendant's cooperation under a reasonableness standard. Defendant shall cooperate fully and completely with investigators and shall answer all questions truthfully and candidly and shall not withhold, conceal, or misrepresent any facts or information. Defendant also promises to give a full, complete, and truthful account of all his activities and conduct to the best of his ability.

b. To the extent possible, the New Jersey Counties and the Pennsylvania Counties may provide the Defendant with sufficient information regarding the identity and medical records of possible victims to refresh his recollection and to provide him with a reasonable opportunity to confess if he committed the crimes. The information and records that will assist investigators in evaluating Defendant's culpability will include any and all information discoverable under the criminal court rules or laws of the State of New Jersey or the Commonwealth of Pennsylvania.

c. Defendant agrees, when requested, to meet with representatives of the New Jersey Counties and the Pennsylvania Counties in the presence of counsel to satisfy his obligations under the terms of this Agreement. Defense counsel will accommodate such requests expeditiously and within a reasonable time period.

d. Defendant further agrees to completely and thoroughly review and explain any documents and records provided to him by the New Jersey Counties and the Pennsylvania Counties for his review and examination in connection with their investigations.

e. The New Jersey Counties and the Pennsylvania Counties agree to prepare and execute, and Defendant agrees to execute, any documents necessary to transport the Defendant between the two jurisdictions to accomplish the purposes of this Agreement.

f. Defendant shall voluntarily appear before any investigating grand jury impaneled in the State of New Jersey and/or the Commonwealth of Pennsylvania and waive any right against self-incrimination and testify fully, truthfully and completely in such proceedings.

14. Sequence of Pleas and Sentencing

Defendant shall plead as soon as practicable to the charges identified and set forth in Paragraph 11 of this Agreement: first to the charges in the New Jersey Counties and second to the charges in the Pennsylvania Counties. The sentencing for the crimes set forth in Paragraph 11 will be held in abeyance until the Defendant has had the opportunity to fully cooperate in the investigations conducted by the New Jersey Counties and the Pennsylvania Counties. After the Defendant's cooperation is exhausted and the guilty pleas are entered for the crimes set forth in Paragraph 11, as well as any additional crimes pursuant to this Agreement, Defendant will first be sentenced for all the crimes to which he has pleaded guilty in New Jersey Counties. Defendant will then be moved to Pennsylvania and sentenced for all the crimes he committed in the Pennsylvania Counties. After Defendant has been sentenced in Pennsylvania he will be returned to New Jersey to serve the sentences imposed by the courts of the State of New Jersey and the Commonwealth of Pennsylvania. The New Jersey Counties and the Pennsylvania Counties agree to work with their respective Governor's Offices to permit Defendant to be moved to the Commonwealth of Pennsylvania for purposes of entering guilty pleas and sentencing. If the movement of the Defendant to Pennsylvania for sentencing purposes cannot be accomplished, then Defendant agrees to remain in New Jersey, and then permit the Commonwealth of Pennsylvania courts to sentence him in absentia, thereby waiving his right to be present during the Pennsylvania sentencing proceedings.

15. Testimony at Regulatory Hearings

The Defendant agrees to cooperate with and answer questions of any regulatory agency of the State of New Jersey and appear before said agencies if requested to do so by the regulatory agencies and with the approval of the New Jersey Attorney General. The Defendant also agrees to cooperate with, answer questions and appear before regulatory agencies of the Commonwealth of Pennsylvania. However, this cooperation will not be required until all criminal investigations and prosecutions are completed. The District Attorneys of the Pennsylvania Counties will use their good offices to make good faith efforts to ensure that

such requests by Pennsylvania regulatory agencies to interview the Defendant are held in abeyance until the completion of all criminal investigations and prosecutions.

16. Voiding Agreement

In the event that the Defendant knowingly provides false,
untruthful, or misleading information, or is not in all respects candid and truthful, the New Jersey Counties and/or
the Pennsylvania Counties may void this Agreement and
move to sentence the Defendant according to the terms
of this Agreement for those cases in which he has already
entered a plea of guilty.

If the New Jersey Counties and/or the Pennsylvania Counties declare this Agreement void because of the Defendant's
lack of cooperation or truthfulness, the New Jersey Counties and/or the Pennsylvania Counties reserve the right to
prosecute the Defendant and to seek the death penalty for
cases to which he has not pleaded guilty. Notwithstanding
the foregoing, no individual New Jersey County that is
party to this Agreement can declare this Agreement void
or seek the death penalty without the express written approval of the New Jersey Attorney General.

Defendant acknowledges that if the New Jersey Counties
and/or the Pennsylvania Counties declare this Agreement
void because of the Defendant's untruthfulness or lack of
cooperation, such declaration shall void any previously
entered guilty plea or accompanying sentence(s).

17. Waiver of Right to Withdraw Plea and
   Specific Right to Use Statements

Defendant knowingly and voluntarily waives his right to
withdraw any guilty plea entered pursuant to this Agreement and agrees that any withdrawal will constitute prejudice to the New Jersey Counties and/or the Pennsylvania

Counties. In the event a New Jersey or Pennsylvania court should permit the withdrawal of a guilty plea in the New Jersey Counties and/or Pennsylvania Counties may be returned to the same legal positions they enjoyed prior to the entry of the Agreement and as permitted by law, will have the right to use any admissions and statements made by the Defendant about the investigation and deaths to which a guilty plea was entered, in a subsequent prosecution for that death.

18. No Promises of Assistance to Defendant for Crimes in Other Jurisdictions

In the event that the Defendant committed any murder(s) or lesser crimes outside of the specific counties that are signatories to this Agreement, there are no promises, express or implied, made by the New Jersey Counties or Pennsylvania Counties to assist the Defendant or dissuade any other prosecuting authority from seeking the death penalty or pursue any other prosecution for any lesser criminal charges against the Defendant for acts committed within their jurisdiction.

19. Publicity of Agreement

Defendant acknowledges that upon entry of a guilty plea in New Jersey, this Agreement shall become part of the public record and agrees that the District Attorneys of Lehigh and Northampton Counties, Pennsylvania, may comment upon the terms of such agreement as it affects their jurisdictions without regard to any prejudice that might result to Defendant, and that they may do so in the absence of his yet having been charged with criminal offenses in the Pennsylvania Counties. Therefore, Defendant waives any claim of prejudice resulting from publicity generated by the entering of his guilty pleas pursuant to this Agreement.

20. No Threats or Coercion

Defendant acknowledges that he has not been threatened or coerced to enter into this Agreement. Defendant acknowledges that this Agreement is entered into knowingly and voluntarily with the advice of counsel. Defendant further agrees that he is satisfied with the services of his attorney and that his attorney has answered all of these questions to Defendant's satisfaction.

21. Entire Agreement

The parties acknowledge that this is their entire Agreement, no other promises or inducements have been made to the Defendant other than what are contained in this Agreement and this Agreement can only be modified or amended in writing and signed by all the parties.

The Agreement, dated April 29, 2004, bears the signatures of Yvonne Smith Segars, Public Defender, New Jersey; Charles Cullen; Johnnie Mask, Deputy Public Defender; Peter C. Harvey, Attorney General of New Jersey; Vaughn L. McKoy, Director, Division of Criminal Justice; Wayne J. Forrest, Somerset County Prosecutor; Michael M. Rubbinaccio, Morris County Prosecutor; Steven Lember, Hunterdon County First Assistant Prosecutor; Thomas S. Ferguson, Warren County Prosecutor; Paula T. Dow, Essex County Acting Prosecutor; James B. Martin, Lehigh County District Attorney; and John M. Morganelli, Northampton County District Attorney.

(This agreement has appeared as it was written—with minimal editing by the authors to facilitate understanding for readers outside the legal profession.)

GREAT BOOKS, GREAT SAVINGS!

When You Visit Our Website:
www.kensingtonbooks.com
You Can Save 30% Off The Retail Price
Of Any Book You Purchase

- • All Your Favorite Kensington Authors
- • New Releases & Timeless Classics
- • Overnight Shipping Available
- • All Major Credit Cards Accepted

Visit Us Today To Start Saving!
www.kensingtonbooks.com